Praise for *Now Bea*

A *New York Times Book Review* Notable Book of the Year

"Acute, intimate and exceedingly fair . . . This is the story of a son who is trying to dissect and understand the love that remains—and sometimes emerges—after death. We may have a greater cultural appetite for eulogies, but an autopsy, in looking directly at the cold corpse of a family in all its gruesomeness and mystery, can be just as profound, and in the hands of a writer as restrained and humane as Sorrentino, just as beautiful."
        —Eleanor Henderson, *The New York Times Book Review*

"For fans of Vivian Gornick's memoirs that bring back a New York that's pretty much vanished at this point . . . It's a very clear-headed look at a family and what it means to come from strange people, which we all do, by definition."
        —John Williams, *The New York Times Book Review* podcast

"Mothers and sons have rarely been captured with such dark intimacy as in *Now Beacon, Now Sea*, an open wound of grief and regret."
        —*Esquire*

"With excoriating candor, with empathy enough to give you gooseflesh, [Sorrentino] gleans exciting new clues in that never-ending mystery, the lives of the artists."   —John Domini,
        Los Angeles Review of Books

"*Now Beacon, Now Sea* is an ambitious balancing act of summary and scene that painstakingly reveals an unsettled mind doing the work of reconfiguring its understanding of the past."
—Richard Scott Larson, *Chicago Review of Books*

"Sagacious and heartbreaking . . . Christopher Sorrentino has written a stunning, gutting memoir about his life as the son of a chronically depressed mother and a celebrated writer father."
—Nell Beram, *Shelf Awareness*

"An unvarnished portrait of a family . . . A sharp, sad tale of bitterness and regret."   —*Kirkus Reviews*

"[A] raw and intimate memoir . . . Even at its darkest, this rich narrative shines."   —*Publishers Weekly*

"Christopher Sorrentino's memoir is an incredibly moving masterpiece. *Now Beacon, Now Sea* is a coming of age story set in a place whose time was coming to an end as told through the comforting, confounding, and crushing story of Sorrentino's relationship with his mother. I had to reach back to Nabokov's *Speak, Memory* to find another memoir as powerful and poignant as this one and to find one that as profoundly explores the art of memory."   —David Treuer, author of
The Heartbeat of Wounded Knee

"Few, if any, are the memoirs of mothers and sons that are as excoriating and unforgettable as Christopher Sorrentino's *Now Beacon, Now Sea*. Written equally in wrath and powerfully and patiently illuminated love, Sorrentino's account of filial anguish will linger long in memory. What an imperative contribution to the memoir form and to our literature generally. I could not admire this book more." —Rick Moody, author of *The Ice Storm* and *The Long Accomplishment*

"The mother at the heart of Sorrentino's absolutely compelling memoir represents a generation of women whose lives were based on mystery and chance, on reinvention and the fierce reach for survival. But it's the sharpest shards of detail in her existence that make this so readable—this son's talent for capturing the secret life of a woman once his unreachable light, the beacon, and then the diffuse memory of the sea." —Susan Straight, author of *In The Country of Women*

"Every genre, every form, has its strengths and weaknesses; the memoir, especially the contemporary American memoir, can fall into a default mode of progress narrative. One of the many accomplishments of Christopher Sorrentino's extraordinary new book is the way in which it refuses to sentimentalize, even slightly, its brutal material. *Now Beacon, Now Sea* is impressively astringent art." —David Shields, author of *The Thing About Life Is That One Day You'll Be Dead* and *The Trouble with Men*

"As irresistible as it is unflinching, *Now Beacon, Now Sea* is a family memoir, a literary memoir, an American memoir, a memoir about the nature of identity in our time—and if that means only Christopher Sorrentino could have written it, for all its singularity it does what riveting memoirs do: reveals not only its own secrets but ours as well." —Steve Erickson, author of *Shadowbahn*

"In memoirs by great novelists any distance between those arts shrinks, imagination and testimony lending prose the clarity of an engraving. Put Christopher Sorrentino's accomplishment in *Now Beacon, Now Sea* with Roth's *Patrimony*, Schwartz's *Leaving Brooklyn*, Gornick's *Fierce Attachments*, Conroy's *Stop-Time*, books in which the necessity of commanding trauma onto the page has galvanized the language from within."
—Jonathan Lethem, author of
Motherless Brooklyn and *The Arrest*

Praise for *The Fugitives*

"Elegantly constructed . . . Satisfying. Given that big novels often seem to warrant attention just for their size, it is its own kind of daring for an author to aim for the understated, the concise and the perfectly joined." —Viet Thanh Nguyen,
The New York Times Book Review

"*The Fugitives*, rife with Sorrentino's dark wit and acute cultural observations, does not disappoint." —Dana Spiotta, *BOMB*

"An entirely new kind of novel with exceptional interior monologues animated by deception, double-dealing and a doomed affair that lends an air of existential dread to the story."
—Jim Ruland, *Los Angeles Times*

"A dynamic and enigmatic tapestry of cross-pollinated genres populated by some terrifically drawn and profoundly unreliable narrators . . . Sorrentino brings a pristine beauty to every multiple subterfuge, while delivering scene after scene with near surgical precision. His pacing is immediate, deliberate, and simultaneously sidereal. *The Fugitives* is effortlessly expansive, finely crafted, and an absolute pleasure to read."   —Donald Breckenridge,
Los Angeles Review of Books

"Smart and mordant . . . Brilliantly cranky."
—James Camp, *Bookforum*

"The language of *The Fugitives* is at once remarkable, startling, and invisible. I was completely sucked into the worlds of these characters. It takes a master to make me forget I'm holding a book. Well, I forgot that for more than 300 pages. Brilliant."
—Percival Everett, author of *The Trees*

"A powerful and fiercely unsentimental novel that blazes past all the well-worn pieties about love and loss and leaves them in ashes."   —Jenny Offill, author of *Dept. of Speculation*

Praise for *Trance*

National Book Award Finalist for Fiction
International IMPAC Dublin Award Finalist
A *Los Angeles Times Book Review* Favorite Book of the Year
A *Publishers Weekly* Top Ten Novel of the Year

"Sorrentino has something of Don DeLillo's ear for American white noise—for the hiss and crackle that fills the country's derelict spaces."
                                        —Tom Shone, *The New York Times Book Review*

"Sorrentino's vision here is kaleidoscopic, eliding fluidly from individual to individual, taking on a wide array of points of view."
                                        —David L. Ulin, *Newsday*

"This sprawling work is so ambitious and irreverent that it doesn't fit easily into any genre . . . Full of descriptions sublime in their precision . . . *Trance* is a pleasure to read—delightful and often funny."
                                        —Carmela Ciuraru, *Los Angeles Times*

"*Trance* doggedly dismantles the pedestal of celebrity and myth."
                                        —Theo Schell-Lambert, *The Village Voice*

"*Trance* is a work of startling insight, marvelously and masterfully evoking the grim stuff of true American nightmares."
                                        —Colson Whitehead, author of *Harlem Shuffle*

"Playful, scathing, gripping, and profound, this book is a meditation and a provocation, full of humor and menace. Sorrentino has broken new ground at the border of fiction and history."
                                        —Sam Lipsyte, author of *Hark*

"An ambitious, intelligent, and kaleidoscopically opulent book, remarkably evocative of the textures and tones of the seventies.

Sorrentino has a talent for creating authentic, microscopic moments that capture the spirit of the era."

—Lydia Millet, author of *A Children's Bible*

Praise for *Sound on Sound*

"Writers like Christopher Sorrentino bring us back to the pleasures of reading."
—Alexander Laurence,
American Book Review

"Flawlessly executed . . . Sheer virtuosity . . . Funny, perceptive and dead-on the satirical mark."
—*Publishers Weekly*

"A funny, funny novel . . . What drives *Sound on Sound* is its judgment as to what constitutes a real novel as well as its expressed awareness of the link between the novel and its culture. Its politics lie in the death grin in a celebrity's celestial teeth."
—Steve Tomasula, author of *The Book of Portraiture*

Now Beacon, Now Sea

ALSO BY CHRISTOPHER SORRENTINO

Sound on Sound

Trance

American Tempura

Death Wish

The Fugitives

Now Beacon,

Now Sea

A SON'S MEMOIR

Christopher Sorrentino

Catapult  New York

Copyright © 2021 by Christopher Sorrentino

Hardcover ISBN: 978-1-64622-042-7
Paperback ISBN: 978-1-64622-156-1

Cover design by Nicole Caputo
Book design by Wah-Ming Chang

Library of Congress Control Number: 2020949981

Catapult
New York, NY
books.catapult.co

Printed in the United States of America
1   3   5   7   9   10   8   6   4   2

The title of this work owes a debt of gratitude to
Molloy by Samuel Beckett.

Now Beacon, Now Sea

1

I spoke to my mother for the last time on May 27, 2017. Sometime within the next few days, she died. I found her on June 15. The sight of a decaying corpse is horrifying, but it's also a wondrous thing. My mother's body lay on its back on her bed, one leg crooked at the knee, identical to the position in which I usually fall asleep. One small, blackened hand lay across the abdomen. The face was a nightmare, although her hair was still lustrous, the corpse wearing it down in a way I hadn't seen my mother wear it in years. It framed her skull on the pillow. The body seemed simultaneously collapsed and inflated. Maggots were busy at work. Her expensive mattress was ruined. The oxygen machine was still grinding away. The smell was overpowering; I felt that I deserved it. But abruptly, without thinking about it, I cut off my examination. I closed the bedroom door on her; I closed it as if trying to shut out something that threatened to engulf me. That was the last time I saw her.

I have seen both of my parents dead, but watched neither of them die. Eleven years earlier, when my father died, the sight was a reassurance I had demanded—the first thing I'd said, when my mother had called to give me the news, was "Don't let them take him away." There he was, silent, wasted, flat on his back in a hospital room filled with the morning light of a beautiful spring day. It was the end of an ordeal. In my mother's case, her corpse took the form of a rebuke. My mother's final message to me felt like: You are a bad son. My negligence had killed her. Nothing could have emphasized her loneliness, boredom, infirmity, frustration more than her poor remains, her having finally become one of those neglected elderly the neighbors recall only once they begin to stink.

But even the neighbors had let her down. No one investigated when the newspapers began piling up outside the door to her apartment, a dozen or more copies of the *Times*, each in its shiny blue plastic bag. None of the porters or the other staff of the nice building in which she lived questioned how likely it was that the elderly widow who tipped them generously, who chatted with them as if they were human, who never went anywhere, who never left a thing out of place, would have left on a trip without mentioning it or without stopping her mail, which accumulated to such an extent that the postman bundled it up with rubber bands and gave it to the doorman to hold for her return. So I was not spared the gruesome discovery. But clearly I was at fault, clearly I was the one who had been responsible for her, so I was also responsible for her final journey through the freshly papered and carpeted corridors of her nice building, her arrival at the morgue, in the deplorable condition in which I'd found her. Over the next hours and weeks, I expected everyone I spoke to in connection with her death—the 911 dispatcher, the EMTs who responded, the police who followed them, the personnel from the medical examiner's office who followed the police, the funeral director, her doctors, her doormen, my relatives, her accountant, the manager of her co-op building, the lawyer I hired to probate her estate—to ask, "Where were you? Why didn't you call more often? What kind of son are you?"

2

She was born Vivian Dora Ortiz at Bellevue Hospital on July 2, 1937, the day Amelia Earhart vanished. Under the designation for color or race, her birth certificate categorically identifies her: BLACK. And then her parents: BLACK, BLACK. Like many other aspects of her origins, this was something my mother disregarded for her entire life. When I first discovered her birth certificate as a child and questioned her about this intriguing vital fact, she said only, "Do not ever mention it to your grandmother. It is the shame of her life."

Going through census records, passenger lists, and the like, I have discovered that my grandparents' race mutates depending on the circumstances, the place, the authority charged with making the designation. Here black, here white, here mulatto, here West Indian. It seems to have been something over which they had no control, which perhaps is unsurprising. The results of a DNA analysis I obtained a few years ago from a testing service indicate that a substantial portion of my genetic material is not European in origin. Neither of these things adds

up to a heritage, much less an identity. Still, the birth certificate was a strange revelation, thrilling but also somehow self-
alienating, as if my own body, the face I saw each day in the
mirror, had been keeping a central and defining secret from
me. In what sounded a lot like an assurance, my mother told
me that I was not black, that none of us was black. But what
were we? At the time of my discovery, I'd already begun to dis-
cern that my mother, as well as my grandparents, uncles, cousins, great-grandmother, great-aunts and -uncles, and the rest of
the extended family that I visited in the Bronx on holidays and
other occasions, was not quite white. I still *felt* white. I spoke
no Spanish. My mother frequently told me that I wasn't really
Puerto Rican. Unlike her assurance that I wasn't black, this
could sound like censure, as if I had betrayed values and traditions that my mother had never made the slightest effort to
pass on, and had instead taken pains to distance herself from.
Even the name she used—Victoria—was an invention. Vivian,
invariably pronounced by my grandparents as "Veev-yon," had
struck her as ethnic, in the way that certain Anglo names given
to children of immigrants mark the child's otherness indelibly
(I remember many Puerto Rican men of my mother's generation
with names like Hector, Nelson, and Edwin, anomalous names
that satisfy the mouth's yearning to form certain shapes, for
the tongue to strike a certain way against the palate). Or so she
thought. In retrospect, *Victoria* sounds like what it was—the
choice of a fourteen-year-old reaching for sophistication—as
does her preferred spelling of her nickname, "Vicki." And yet,
when my mother told me that I was not Puerto Rican, I never

felt as if she was protecting some status she'd fought for, but that she was dividing me from her.

My mother's parents, Octavio and Dora, met in New York in the early 1930s, both having recently emigrated from Puerto Rico. Dora was from San Juan, the daughter of a shopkeeper's widow who I would come to know as my ancient abuelita Doña Ana. Doña Ana was a mestiza whose own mother had, while working as a domestic, gotten pregnant by her employer's son. Apparently a fierce woman well into late middle age, a matriarch who unsparingly wielded her authority over her children and grandchildren, by the time I knew her she had mellowed considerably, to the extent that I found her, if anything, embarrassingly affectionate. She had married Carmelo Bravo as a teenager and, my mother's story goes, was cheated out of his estate and business by his family after he died in 1922, leaving her with five children to raise. Unable to support them all, she kept her sons by her side and placed the girls, my grandmother and her older sister, Rosalina, in a Catholic orphanage for several years, where they were trained to be costureras, or seamstresses. In January 1930, she and Dora traveled aboard the SS *Coamo* to the mainland, where they went to work as servants to a family named Berry living in Margate City, on the Jersey shore. This apparently didn't last long, and when Rosalina joined them early in 1931 it was at an address on East 107th Street in Manhattan.

Octavio's family were fairly affluent rural landholders in the vicinity of Villalba, where he was born. According to my mother, my grandfather disavowed my great-grandfather for remarrying "too soon" after my great-grandmother's death, and left Puerto Rico for New York, also aboard the *Coamo*,* in 1928. Octavio's siblings remained on the island and grew up to be privileged people, professionals and academics. Although the rift evidently was healed—the only time my mother ever left the U.S. mainland was when Octavio took her to visit his father, and for many years she would on occasion receive small checks drawn on a Puerto Rican bank, apparently her share of the proceeds from a trust account that had been set up after the sale of his land—my grandfather remained in New York and spent his life working menial jobs. The occupation listed for him on my mother's birth certificate is Busboy. He was thirty-one at the time.

My grandparents met in the city in the early 1930s. My mother told me that Octavio apparently provoked the ridicule of the self-styled cosmopolite Doña Ana when he turned up courting Dora wearing a billiard-green suit. Forever after, mother and daughter referred to the natty suitor as a "jíbaro," a Puerto Rican term roughly corresponding to *hillbilly*. Nevertheless, as my mother always gleefully related, my grandmother and great-grandmother were intimidated by my grandfather's refined and educated relatives, when they visited. I recall one of them, a great-aunt who came to see us at our apartment when I was little. She was elegantly dressed and wore her hair in a tight, neat coif.

---

* In 1942 the *Coamo*, while serving as a U.S. Army transport ship, was torpedoed and sunk by a German U-Boat while en route from Gibraltar to New York City. All 186 souls on board were lost.

Her Spanish was similarly elegant, with none of the loanwords and street cadences most of the rest of my family used.

Whatever Dora's feelings for Octavio, the two of them married in December 1932. In the surviving wedding photograph, a badly damaged proof copy that I found among my mother's things after she died, my grandfather looks trim, happy, almost smug. My grandmother looks imploringly at the camera. She wears the expression of someone trapped. My uncle Jim was born the next November.

Before my mother's birth, Dora and Octavio had another son, who died in infancy. I don't know his name. The family lived in Spanish Harlem for a few years before settling in the Bronx, on Charlotte Street near Boston Road, an intersection that would become the symbolic epicenter of the South Bronx's destruction after Jimmy Carter toured its ruins in 1977. I can't recall my mother's description of the apartment there. I can see, though, the narrow corridor that probably ran nearly the length of the place, the misshapen kitchen, crowded with table and chairs, overlooking yards and alleys and the flapping banners of drying laundry. The bathroom with its two basin taps, one always dripping, the recessed wall hamper that didn't quite close, the greenish stain around the tub drain, the cracked tile underfoot, black and white hexagons. These tenements looked old twenty years after they'd been built. I grew up in one, too. The small rooms, the poor furniture, the molding black with grime in its crevices. The badly plastered ceiling, the splintering parquet, the radiators leprous with rust under flaking paint. They played in the streets, on the rooftops, in nearby Crotona Park. They had a dog, Scottie, that was not a Scottish terrier. Family was close by, but the South Bronx was not yet a Puerto Rican neighborhood. My mother's friends were mostly Jewish kids. I remember her demonstrating for me certain traits of local speech that she had adopted—adding a brief, explosive *s* after an initial *t*, for example, so that *talk* became something like *tsalk*—her first attempt to alter her accent. Altering your accent, it became clear to me much later, was a way of altering the trajectory of your life. My mother had very few photographs from this time, and did not retail the sort of heroic anecdotes of the Old Neighborhood that my father delighted in telling. I assumed that her experience had been less rich than his, even if his was rich mainly in disorder and early sorrow. After she died, I was surprised to find among her things a number of books about Bronx childhoods.

My mother told me about her childhood in two separate phases. The first was while my grandfather was still alive, and my mother would speak generally, generically even, of growing up, and it was from this phase that I get the sense of the streets, the candy stores, the movie house, the church, the live poultry market where Dora would select a chicken from among those running around in a filthy enclosure and it would be killed and dressed for her on the spot (Doña Ana preferred to bring hers home alive and kill them herself, grasping them by the head and whipping them over her shoulder to break their necks). Then my grandfather died, the summer I was thirteen, and my mother decided to tell me the truth—granted, her truth—about my grandmother. All at once, my mother's portrayal of life at home darkened, made it sound oppressive. She adored my grandfather, but he worked long hours at the Brooklyn Navy Yard throughout the war, and

Dora, who worked in the Garment District, apparently favored my uncle. From an early age, my mother was assigned the bulk of the household chores, including cleaning, shopping, and starting supper. When she was old enough, she was expected to get a job and contribute part of her wages to the household, while also continuing to do the housework. Dora would arrive home exhausted and irritable from her sweatshop job, and if she was looking for trouble she generally could locate its source in my mother. My mother told me stories of being hit, slapped, pushed, whipped, restrained, berated, embarrassed, ignored, and, on one occasion, struck on the head with a cast-iron skillet by my grandmother. Concerning the last, when I asked her what had happened afterward, she said, "I burst into song," and I could see her relishing the triumph, thirty years later.

I allied myself with my mother, which wasn't entirely fair. My grandmother had always been loving, if slightly hysterical, toward me. But my mother dug deep, telling me stories whose villain completely displaced the old woman I knew, and in any case disloyalty to my mother was not an option.

One reason I was sold on these stories was that my grandmother was not permitted to refute them—her presence diminished sharply after that summer of my grandfather's death. She'd moved from the apartment on Marion Avenue where she and my grandfather had lived during my childhood into a place up in Co-op City, where all my relatives had moved. It was harder to get to, but not that much harder. Regular contact with the family, though, all but stopped after my grandfather died.

My mother's stories also were compelling because it was

obvious to me that these were things she'd wanted to say for a while—not necessarily to me, but to anyone who might listen receptively. The mid-'70s were full of explosive stories from the last generation of American children whose routine abuse had gone mostly unremarked. I was the vessel into which my mother now poured her scalding rage at her own mother. It must have been satisfying, since I'd loved my grandmother, and my mother managed effectively to kill my love.

My mother had loved her father, but apparently he was unable to protect her, or unwilling to further alienate his wife. She told me now that her parents had separated on at least one occasion when she was a child. When I became an adult, my mother further told me that Dora had regularly cuckolded my grandfather and that, even as she was going into the hospital for a double mastectomy in the 1960s, my grandfather had come across passionate correspondence from her current lover. "He should have left her," she said to me, just as she would frequently say about my father, after he died, "I should have left him."

Clearly, something got screwed up. My mother had wanted to leave my father, but had succeeded only in leaving my grandmother, and only after her father, for whom she had preserved her relationship with her mother, got cancer and left everyone. Maybe that was enough leaving for my mother. She hunkered in her situation with my father, refusing to leave, or having no means to leave, or having no energy, or being afraid, or being ashamed of failure, or not wanting to argue over who got what, pots and pans—whatever motivated her to remain. She tried instead to win a contest for household dominance in which my father—who met conflict by cutting through it cleanly, serenely, his nose in the air like the prow of a ship turning the waves it breasted into rolling cylinders that met astern to form a wake bearing his impress, echoing his will—was constitutionally destined to prevail. My mother's anger was the latent condition of our household, awaiting its moment to jet, boiling, from the place where she kept it ready. Then she would fall into silence, a silence that could last for days. So I grew up feeling not only that I was victimized (which was perhaps justified) but that my father was victimized too, forced into patience with an unreasonable person. Only much later would I realize that my father's patience was a false patience. Only much later would I realize how my mother's disruptive rage was provoked by my father's secret and unquestioning belief that we were the waves through which he had to sail, course and obstacle at once.

3

My mother grew up. She enrolled at the High School of Performing Arts, on West Forty-sixth Street, but left after a year. She was vague about her departure. What she told me amounted to something like she "just didn't like it," which I have no choice but to accept, although my mother remembered the names of her classmates and teachers for the rest of her life, and kept photos from that time. She had a beautiful singing voice, and apparently played the piano well, although I never once heard her play. She loved the theater and was much more familiar with modern drama than my father was. She once amused me by listing the Broadway plays and musicals she'd seen only the second half of, mingling with the crowds on the sidewalk at intermission and then entering the auditorium at the bell to take a vacant seat. She told me how she'd sneaked into a theater where José Ferrer was directing the rehearsal of a new show and, feeling pleased with herself for having remained undetected, was surprised when Ferrer concluded his directions to his actors in one scene by adding, in that famous voice, "And if the young lady sitting in the back of the house will please remove herself..." Nevertheless, for her remaining three years of high school she attended the Rhodes Preparatory School, a now-defunct institution located on West Fifty-fourth Street, directly across from the sculpture garden of the Museum of Modern Art. I'm not sure how my grandparents paid for it; whether it was a scholarship opportunity they felt they couldn't turn down or if they believed that Performing Arts constituted a bad influence to be avoided even at grievous cost.

Manhattan in the 1950s would have been a bad influence in either case. Perhaps anyplace other than the Bronx parochial schools attended by "nice girls" would have been. Is this when my mother decided to become white, or American, or polished, or however she may have conceived it? Is this when Veev-yon became the regal Victoria, or, alternatively, the modern Vicki? Unlike my father, who never completely lost his accent and was perfectly happy to sound as if he'd never set foot outside of Brooklyn when he felt the occasion called for it, my mother, in the years I knew her, left no trace of her background in her speech or her carriage.

She started smoking. She discovered music. Bud Powell. Thelonious Monk. Sarah Vaughan. Jimmy Rushing. Billie. She started going to clubs and bars. Underage drinking was easy to manage in New York well into the 1980s. She ran away at fifteen, but was found and brought back by her parents. Sexually, I have no idea, although she once told me, with a mixture of pride and self-amusement, that she had been "a good girl." Many of her friends then, she said, were gay men, explaining that she felt safe with them—they were male company that she didn't have to fend off at the end of the evening. These friends, whoever they were, had disappeared from her life by the time I was born. She met George Bradt while still in high school or immediately after graduating. He was eight years older than she was. They moved in together, marrying in May 1958, when my mother was twenty. Vivian Ortiz had become Vicki Bradt, which strikes me as a less than felicitous swap.

My mother always referred to her first husband as "poor George Bradt" or "poor old George Bradt," but toward the end of her life, when she spoke of him, she talked about how much fun they'd had, how generous he was, how spontaneous, how he loved to surprise her with tickets to shows, dinners out, stylish gifts. They lived for a while on Garden Place, one of the more beautiful blocks in Brooklyn Heights, for a while on Central Park West. But poor George Bradt, an electrical engineer who evidently was quite well paid and well regarded, was an early casualty of the postwar desire of Americans with little artistic talent to express themselves creatively. He was unhappy in his work, my mother told me, and yearned for more. "He was one of those people," my mother said, "who thought life wasn't worth living if you weren't an artist." My mother, who would spend years with my artist father surrounded by other artists, couldn't have been clearer: none of that nonsense had rubbed off on her. Or, maybe: I've seen what their lives are like; the booze and the poverty and the envy and the spite, the triumphs and the disappointments that, petty or large, never are anything but defeat. Anyway, apparently poor George Bradt dabbled, and apparently he mingled, and his mingling and dabbling, my mother told me, had brought him into the orbit of Alexander Trocchi—"that fucking Alex," she called him—and under Trocchi's tutelage his artistic dabbling became drug dabbling, which became addiction, and after a couple of years my mother left him and moved to the Lower East Side. What this cost her, I don't know; whether what had passed from her life was the fun and spontaneity she would longingly recall as an old woman, or if that was simply nostalgia; but one token of loss from that time was in the auction of her belongings, the bill for their storage left unpaid by poor old George Bradt. "I had a beautiful spinet. Sheet music. All my seventy-eights. Books. A trunk full of photographs." I imagine that for my mother, for whom control was the principal means of ordering reality, this was nothing less than an unforgivable sin. In any event, after leaving him she began a rather unsettled period, a period of financial instability, a nomadic period, that lasted about two years. My mother made allusions to boyfriends, lovers; jobs she had, lost, quit; apartments she'd moved into and out of. Bathtubs in the kitchen, overhead light fixtures, the radio left murmuring to deceive burglars. Matchbooks under the legs of the table to keep it from wobbling on the visibly slanted floors. For a while she lived at the Broadway Central Hotel, later a welfare hotel infamous for its wretched conditions (one of my second-grade classmates died in an elevator accident there; in 1973 the place would partially collapse, killing four residents). She hung out at the Cedar, at Dillon's, at the San Remo. Went to openings on Tenth Street, shows at the Five Spot. She lived the life that Fred McDarrah photographed. She told me that she'd gone on a date with Steve McQueen but that he was a jerk. She told me that her criterion for going to bed with a man was that he had to have something to say, while my mind reeled at the thought of my mother preparing to go to bed with somebody. Twenty-three, twenty-four; friends and lovers in the midcentury Manhattan demimonde, rubbing elbows with Great Men. It was something. However disappointed she'd been with poor George Bradt, with the hidden face that freedom had turned to her after she'd arranged her escape from Morrisania, she must have felt that she'd arrived somewhere, that life was larger than it was for her cousin Alba, exactly the same age, who'd already married Ralph, a bellhop at a midtown hotel, who'd already had two daughters, who still lived within yelling distance of her mother, my great-aunt Rosalina; larger than it was for all the girls she'd left behind whose goal, as her fellow Morrisanian Vivian Gornick wrote, was to get "from the working-class part of the Bronx to the middle-class part of the Bronx"; and larger than it was for Uncle Jim, who'd joined the Air Force as soon as he'd graduated from Aviation High School. Even what was harrowing—all that moving, for example, compressed into the space of a couple of years, from one bad place to one worse—must have been met with the clean spirit of hope, despite her probably having been badly scared a lot of the time. For years, she kept a mysterious, ugly club, heavy and misshapen, its solid core wrapped in brown paper and tape, which she told me had been made for her by a friend, to protect herself from a psychotic neighbor in some tenement where the water closet was located in the common hallway. The fact that she bore this fearsome souvenir with her throughout her life, eventually into suburban Palo Alto, seemed to bestow it with protective properties more talismanic than physical: perhaps it was her defense against the present.

Dora and Octavio seem far away at this time. Whatever they thought of her marriage, I assume that they considered my mother to be her husband's business. What little she revealed to them of her life after her separation from poor George Bradt was probably sufficient to keep them at arm's length. And then she met my father.

For years George Bradt was a complete cipher to me, the man who'd been married to my mother before my father, the man who'd lost her things, the man who'd become a junkie, the man who'd died uselessly and young in an accident. Later, when my mother began speaking about him expansively, almost elegiacally, I realized that she saw him in a different light entirely: as the man whose failure to right himself had driven her, inadvertently, into my father's clutches.

4

My mother and father first encountered each other in the fall of 1961 at the Cedar Tavern, although they did not quite meet. As my mother told it, after sending her a drink via the bartender, my father then inexplicably avoided speaking to her. He then repeated this performance nights later. They finally spoke some weeks afterward, when—again, as she told it—my mother approached him at a party and said, "If you're not going to say something, I figured I'd better." I asked what happened next. "I took him home with me," she deadpanned.

Apparently my father faced a hurdle in the form of at least two other men my mother was seeing at the time. My mother spoke matter-of-factly about the process of selecting my father over these other men, if "selection" accurately characterizes what occurred, or her sense of what had occurred. Certainly the others did not quickly fall away like the insubstantial beaux a child might hope to hear of in the story of his parents' mythic romance: the prologue to the story of himself. They lingered, they pressed their suits; there was suspense to this story, even though I knew how it turned out.

My mother was steadfastly unromantic about my parents' courtship. I never heard her say that she had been madly in love with him, blinded by love, smitten, head over heels, crazy about him, unable to think of anything but him; that he'd hung the moon, that he was the one she'd been waiting for, that she knew they were meant for each other, that she'd seen him across a crowded room (as, literally, she must have) and instantly felt a zing in her heartstrings. She always made it sound more like a complication that had arisen in the course of things. Until the month I was born, my parents lived separately, my father on Avenue A and St. Marks Place and my mother on East Ninth Street between B and C. Sometimes, my mother told me, they would argue late at night and, if they were at my father's apartment, my mother would leave, crossing Tompkins Square Park to get home. My father, my mother said, would stand at an open window overlooking Avenue A and the park, and yell after her: "Vicki! Come back! Come on!" She told me that he frequently embarrassed her by drinking too much, the spectacularly emblematic story here being the time my father managed, during a party at Dawn Powell's home, to fall through a skylight. She told me that he drove her crazy by rising no later than nine o'clock no matter what hour they'd gone to sleep, and then expected her to get up as well. She told me that he was critical of her library, her reading habits. When I was a kid, she would tell these stories in a good humor—they curdled and became dark only much later, when she'd been a widow for some years; in fact, by then they had ceased to be stories at all, retaining only the complaint, the aggrieved feeling, that had been their kernel all along—but even then they struck me as unusual courtship stories. I believe my mother—having married her first husband to escape home and the Bronx, having separated to escape his self-destruction, having spent a couple of years, at an age when the years run long, starting again without regressing to the Bronx, without the spinet and the sheet music and the 78s and the books and the photos she had prized, without the dinners and the shows and the gifts—I believe my mother felt as if she'd passed through something, come out whole and free. The last thing on my mother's mind was the thing we are told is always on the minds of young single women. While I don't know what it meant to my father, for my mother I'm sure that to accept a drink from a stranger was hardly to bargain for a lifelong entanglement.

But that was what she got. In the summer of 1962, less than a year after meeting my father, she became pregnant with me. At the time, she was still legally married to poor George Bradt. My father was still legally married to his first wife, Elsene, and had two young children. As my mother described it to me in the casual, offhand manner she often used to disabuse me of my childish notions, the pregnancy was unplanned. My parents had arrived at the shack they'd rented on the Long Island shore to discover that there was a puncture in my mother's diaphragm. "I thought about having an abortion," my mother said, "but I'd already had a couple and I was afraid I wouldn't be able to have children *when I wanted them.*" Emphasis added. I was about ten when she told me this.

It's very likely that my mother felt trapped by her condition. I can't blame her. Things had just gotten started for her, and now there was this *role* she was going to have to assume, side by side with a man who day by day was revealing his human deficiencies to her, as humans do. She kept the apartment on East Ninth. How much time she spent there, I don't know, but theoretically it was the escape pod to which she could retreat. Finally, on the first of May 1963, she gave in to the inevitable. My parents settled together in the place where I would live until I was seven, a two-bedroom apartment on the top floor of a six-story walkup at 541 East Thirteenth Street.

She told me, "Your father swore up and down that we'd sleep in one bedroom and you'd sleep in the other. He said he'd put his desk in the dining room." This was a small alcove just off the kitchen, probably about eight feet square. "But no. He begins to move his stuff into the bedroom straight off. Looks at me like I'm crazy. How'm I supposed to work out here, with the baby, with the noise? So we ended up sleeping in the dining room, do you remember?"

"Sure I remember. And then you got the fold-out couch."

"Oh, that damned couch. I nearly broke my back on that couch. And of course I'm the one who had to make it up and put everything back in place every morning."

This was the sort of turn our conversation inevitably took every time I saw my mother during the last four or so years of her life. We would assume our accustomed places across from each other at my mother's small dining table and she would fill me in on how it really was. I would reassure her that my father, whom I had loved to distraction, had earned her rage and the useless recriminations she was voicing years after his death. He probably had earned those things, the rage and recriminations, at least from her. Toward me, my father almost unfailingly had been attentive, reciprocating my utter fascination with him and basking in my immediate and unquestioning acceptance of nearly every opinion he held, ranging from the inferiority of the Yankee teams of the 1940s and '50s that had routinely defeated his Brooklyn Dodgers in the World Series, to, say, the questionable merits of Robert Frost's poetry. In retrospect, I surmise that even as a toddler I must have realized that the way to capture my father's attention was to engage it on his terms. I was his son, I was his student, and I was, I now realize, something very much like his fan. If my mother could be stern, even forbidding, my father was patient, charismatic, and outrageously funny, the life of the party that began for me as soon as he disengaged himself from his work each day. My disagreements with him always felt like painful ruptures, while the disagreements I had with my mother were routine irritants, too common to worry about beyond feeling apprehensive about the punishment she might mete out.

To agree with my mother now did my father no harm, it made her feel better, and it brought me closer to her. Besides, I never doubted my mother's emotional honesty. Her candor was one of the most constant things about her. I questioned the accuracy of the details. I understood that she was presenting herself in the best possible light. I recalled earlier variations on these sorts of stories, told when my father was still alive, that were, what? Fonder, softer, more forgiving.

They moved in together. My father got one bedroom, just off the living room, in which he put his desk, his chair, his file cabinet, his bookcases. I got the other bedroom. My mother got to sleep in the eight-by-eight alcove off the kitchen.

But wait—this can't be right: there are photos of me at about a year old standing in my crib, which obviously is placed in the eight-by-eight alcove. And I remember having being told about what had occasioned those photos: my parents slept in the bedroom that later became mine, just beyond the alcove, and they'd put the crib there so that I'd be nearby. I was in the habit of waking early and, standing and gripping the rail, I would rock back and forth so that the crib traveled jerkily across the floor, just far enough to allow me to peer through the open door into the bedroom, my parents' bedroom. This amused them, and one morning my mother had grabbed her Instamatic and taken pictures of me doing it. So whatever territorial battle ultimately erupted, it's clear that my parents moved in, allocated the bedrooms according to their immediate needs—one, off the living room, to my father for his study; the other, off the alcove, to my parents for sleeping—and then later changed things.

Again, though, my mother's sincerity in telling the story about the revoked bedroom pledge is beyond question. Her sense of my father's *encroaching* upon her was not merely a constant theme of her stories about their lives together, but a consistent aspect of my childhood memories. He took and took, and she defended and retreated. I saw both the defense, which I mistook for aggression, and the retreat, which I mistook for pique. As we sat across from each other at that small dining table, a plain, dark-stained oak table that she bought almost immediately after my father's death to replace the one he'd selected nearly twenty-five years earlier, which she hated; as we sat there reviling and making fun of him, I felt guilt for profaning his memory, but I felt more guilt and remorse toward the diminished woman sitting opposite me: guilt and remorse for having blatantly preferred him, for having absorbed and recapitulated whatever tacit attitudes about her insignificance he may have taught me.

My mother may have felt some guilt and remorse as well. She had reason to. She soothed herself by controlling with iron rigidity the things that fell within her sphere. Most of these things—the placement of objects, the stacking of magazines, the clockwork enactment of certain household rituals—offered little or no resistance. I was different, being a person, although for several years I was happy to acquiesce to her idea of the normal. Eventually, though, contamination set in, as I became more observant about how other households operated, how the people in them conducted themselves. And that was when our troubles began in earnest.

5

At first, though, we were each other's constant companion. My memories of her are continuous and clear, even if I have no idea which remembered event preceded another, or what else was happening in our lives. Nothing else was happening, is the answer. I lived the life of an animal, a domestic animal with a blissful routine. We set our own schedule; my father, who became an assistant editor at Grove Press in 1965, was out of the house all day. He was important and consequential, but hardly material to the household she and I ran together. She did the housework, I played. Then we hit the street: Errands. The park. The library. Up and down Avenue B, Tenth Street, Avenue A, St. Marks Place, Eighth Street, University Place, Fourteenth Street, First Avenue, Second Avenue. Years later, when I began hanging around on the Lower East Side as a teenager, the tininess of our range impressed me. But what did we need? The drugstore, the Pioneer supermarket, the greengrocer's, the candy store, the bakery, the fishmonger's, the post office, the Chemical branch, the five-and-ten, the laundromat, the dry cleaner's, Tompkins

Square, the library, the Charles, the Academy of Music, Mays and S. Klein.

It was an entire world, as was the world of our apartment. I look at the old photos now and the poverty, or maybe the shabby austerity, is unsettling, needling forward through the decades to pierce the IKEA Age. Found items. Secondhand items. Mismatched items. Scratched, scarred, torn, cracked. For a couple of years we watched TV on a set my parents had acquired for next to nothing, which had a chunk of glass missing at the upper right corner of the picture tube. We sat around the table on three different chairs, like the three bears. My mother's was a thinly padded stool she'd covered with Con-Tact paper. Later she covered it with Con-Tact paper of a different color and used it as a side table. My mother was good at painting and refinishing things, repairing things, basic carpentry, rewiring lamps and appliances. She could mat and frame a picture, caulk a tub, fix a leak, lay new linoleum on the kitchen floor. For the rest of her life, after my parents had passed into something like the middle class, my mother had nothing but contempt for people who deliberately cultivated the careless look of bohemia, the studied disarray, the unmatched tableware, the shabby chic of scuffed and scarred furniture. For her, these things were emblems of the privation she'd endured, their voluntary use an insult to her experience.

Tompkins Square Park was at the center of everything. It was where I made my friends, and it was where my mother made hers. The playground on the Avenue B side was where we went, where my mother sat on the benches and watched me as I played with my friends, while she talked with their mothers. These were the last friends my mother would enjoy in her lifetime, all of them met, lived with, and, for the most part, done with by the time she was thirty-three, when we left the neighborhood. After that came various facsimiles of friendship, and then, for her final thirty-five years, my mother was alone.

All the bohemian mothers gravitated toward one another, some having met before becoming parents, others arriving at the park with their children and instinctively determining which group they belonged with. They were writers and poets and textile artists and activists and musicians and dancers and painters, or they were married to writers and poets, etc., and they more or less froze out, or were frozen out by, the neighborhood natives, the Ukrainians and Puerto Ricans. The only time I recall my mother speaking a word of Spanish in the park was once when she sharply rebuked a group of older boys who were up to some mischief. They stared at her in naked astonishment, so thoroughly had she turned herself, by then, into a white person.

Nowadays this sort of self-segregation would presage a neighborhood's gentrification; the beauty salons, shoe repair shops, hardware stores, junk stores, newsstands, coffee shops, pizzerias, bodegas, and even the churches would gradually and then abruptly disappear, to be replaced by more suitably up-scale alternatives, and sure enough this did begin to happen on the Lower East Side in the early 1980s, sooner on strips like St. Marks Place. But in the 1960s it was a place where people lived because they could afford nothing better. Although the various groups of women stationed on the benches throughout the park dressed differently, often spoke different languages, raised their children differently, they all floated in a state of economic equipoise. Their marginal household incomes were served by marginal enterprises that everyone shared: the cheap neighborhood movie theater, the cheap neighborhood restaurant, the cheap neighborhood grocery, the cheap neighborhood clothing store, the cheap neighborhood laundromat, and, as a cornerstone, the cheap neighborhood housing. One made do: with a lack of heat and hot water, with splintered floors and crumbling walls, with shady neighborhood characters and sudden victimhood. For my mother and her friends, poverty was the imperative their decisions had imposed upon them; it was not an ideal state but these were not people who confused bohemianism with entrepreneurialism, art with fashion, education and culture with a means to financial gain; they did not expect the benefits of capitalism in return for living their outré lives. And, likewise, capitalism did not mistakenly attribute to them an affluence that wasn't there. If one lived there, one was poor, QED. Amenities meant schlepping across town.

But again, what did we need? You became, if you weren't already, an expert at frugality, at making food from scraps, from butcher's bones. The hippies—whose presence in the neighborhood began rapidly increasing around 1967—simply mystified my parents with their institutionalized incapacity to tend to even the most basic aspects of self-care. Going hungry, being dirty, getting lice, allowing the electricity to be shut off, persistent sniffles and coughs, torn and soiled clothing, unsanitary homes, blowing money on things you couldn't afford—to my mother, that was for stupid people, people insensible to the requirements of life. She recognized their behavior for what it was: a middle-class gesture, an empty performance of nonconformity, a performance that engulfed them when they began to take heroin.

We were burglarized fairly often. They came in off the fire escapes, through the bedroom windows. Once, it was through the window off the alcove, which overlooked the roof of the neighboring building across a narrow air shaft that descended six stories to the alley below. The policeman who came to take the report theorized that the burglars had held a child suspended over the chasm, enabling him to break the window, enter the apartment, and admit them through the front door. One time, my father became enraged—not by the theft of our TV or blender, but because the burglars had evidently taken a break from their labors to sit at our table and drink a glass of his whiskey and eat a bag of his Chuckles. On another occasion, the theft of my father's heavy coat went unnoticed until winter had arrived and he'd gone into the closet to get it. They stole a new black-and-white television days after we'd bought it. They stole my father's Smith Corona typewriter. They stole my stroller. They stole a second-hand toaster my mother had bought at a junk shop on Avenue B. They stole the change I'd saved in a Seneca apple sauce jar. They stole blank checks, a can opener, a transistor radio, an electric alarm clock, a Kodak camera, a portable record player. All of it disappeared into their arms; we saw them nodding in doorways, on benches, in the middle of the sidewalk. Then they would awake to their insatiable need. They took shit that wasn't worth anything, they ignored things of value. They didn't think, they needed. One evening, after my parents and I had returned from supper at Ya-Ya's, a coffee shop around the corner, to discover that we'd been burglarized again, I snuck into the bathroom while my parents went through the routine of surveying the ransacking and I pulled the fuzzy cover off the toilet seat, then called them in to point out that the burglars had looked there, too. It was in keeping with the burglars' odd and random way of searching for things, which I'd learned. For years, I felt guilty about having done that, as if I'd somehow tainted the evidence. One afternoon, my mother and I came home from wherever we'd been and walked slowly up the six flights. When we reached the sixth-floor landing, my mother froze outside the door of our apartment, listening. Without a word, she turned me around and in silence—I knew not to speak—we walked back downstairs, where my mother knocked on the door of Mrs. Hanlon's first-floor apartment. Mrs. Hanlon, or rather her son, Anthony, was the building super. She took us into her dim apartment, gave me a Coke or something, and let my mother call the police. I sat on the couch staring at a large, luridly colored painting of a matador that hung on the living room wall, marveling at the mystery of other people's lives.

One day, when I was four or so, I saw my mother standing at the kitchen window, looking out, talking on the telephone to the police. "Are you calling about Con Ed, Mommy?" My parents sometimes looked out that window and complained about the smoke pouring from the stacks at Con Ed's power plant on Fourteenth and C; in my innocence I imagined that my mother had finally gotten fed up and was going to *do something about it.* "Hush," she told me, "there's someone on the roof across the way"—that same roof from which they'd held that kid, their accomplice, suspended—"and I think he's thinking about breaking in."

We went into the living room and sat on the couch together. I climbed into her lap and tried to bury myself in her. My face was pressed between her breasts. She held me close. The terror was excruciating. *Would they come now?* Around that time, Con Ed was running this commercial on television. Against a black screen you could hear the creak of a door opening. A woman's voice hissed: *"Harry! What's that noise?"* Then, the creaking again. *"Harry! There's someone in the house!"* Suddenly, the screen was flooded with light, and a stern male voice announced, "It takes a light to stop a thief." I would run from the room when it came on. So far, the only bearable thing about the burglars was that they came and went unseen, like elves. *Would they come now?* I couldn't understand how a light could stop a thief. Would the man, Harry, turn the light on and confront the thief? Or—more comfortingly—perhaps the thief would simply run away? What would a *light* do, though? My mother and I were sitting in broad daylight. The someone on the roof clearly was not discouraged by a lack of darkness. *Would they?*

For the rest of the day I was afraid to walk past the kitchen. I shadowed my mother around the apartment, which ordinarily might have driven her crazy, but she let me. I remember sitting on the toilet while she put on her makeup in the mirror. It must have been early afternoon; my mother didn't need to turn on the bathroom light.

"Is the man gone?"

"Yes, he's gone now."

"Did the police get him?"

"Yes, they got him."

"Will he come back?"

"No, he won't come back."

What else could she have told me? As she comforted me, she must have pushed down, crushed, her own distress. My mother was not one to be cowed, but throughout her life her instincts served her. She'd step off an elevator if she did not like the looks of the man traveling with her. She'd cross the street when she did not like the looks of the scene she was approaching. And something about the looks of the man on the roof had caused her to pick up the phone and call the cops.

In the menacing idleness of the neighborhood, in the menacing idleness of noontide, we sat in the apartment on some days. I remember the living room curtains drawn, the apartment dim, if not cool. One afternoon I found my mother crying silently in the living room. These were not my tears, children's tears, the tears of dramatic affliction, and I had trouble believing that they were what they were. But I asked, astonished that my mother could cry. A headache, she said.

I don't know how happy or unhappy she was, or what made her happy or unhappy. I thought of her strictly in relation to myself: whether she was pleased with me, or angry; whether she was feeling generous or stingy, permissive or confining. To remember childhood is to remember an existence as a different species, highly keyed at all times and in every situation to its perception of well-being. But that's not to say that my mother's sadness had no effect on me—she and I were one being, her equilibrium was my equilibrium, her pulse my pulse. I have remembered my mother's tears that afternoon, the tears she never intended for me to see, for fifty years.

As an adult, when I had become wary of her, it was easy to forget both the unhappiness that had finally overwhelmed her, transforming the mainstay of my earliest years into an ailing recluse, and the indivisibility I'd once felt from this person with whom I had, in her last decade, sometimes gone for months and years without speaking. And during those silences, while I lived my life as a father, a husband and ex-husband, a friend, a teacher, a writer, and my mother filled her days in complete solitude, I did not think about what made her happy or unhappy; I felt only that my own unhappiness with the situation was the price for having escaped from confinement within the narrowest definition of what it was to be myself, a definition of me made by someone else, even if it applied only during the time it took me to phone, or during the isolated afternoons I traveled alone to her apartment to see her. Even that was too much. When my mother and I eventually found a way to remain on speaking terms—because, finally, we had come to the tacit agreement that to talk was happier than not to—I decided that it was time to end the battles we'd waged intermittently from my adolescence

until after my father had died; I allowed her the pyrrhic victory
of becoming her boy again, agreeing with her, listening to her
uncritically, allowing her to raise and drop the subjects, to decide
when we would sit at the table and when we would move into
the living room, when we would talk about the past (usually),
the present (preliminarily), the future (rarely). What difference
would it make for me to assert who I really was? From my earliest attempts it had rarely worked out happily, and for the last
eleven years of her life my mother never observed me *in situ*. She
never met the woman I lived with throughout that period. She
never met my stepson, whom I have helped to raise from birth.
Never visited any of the three apartments I lived in during that
time, never met any of my friends. Never celebrated a holiday
or a birthday with me. Never showed more than token interest
in the trips I took, the people I met, the work I published, the
courses I taught. These things were impermissible in her world,
and for me to acknowledge them in a more than cursory way
would have imposed them on her. When reality necessarily did
intrude, the gap between what she believed and what was real
usually was surprising to her. A year or so before she died, someone's name came up and my mother offered that my father had
thought this person was "pushy and ambitious." (Derided as he
was, my mother nonetheless often deferred to my late father's
opinions.) I gently explained to her that for the prior three years
this person, a steady supporter, had done more than anyone else
I knew to keep food on my table. But for the most part, I was
willing, finally, to avoid imposing reality upon my mother. This
came at some expense, but with the recompense of feeling, for

the last four years she was alive, that I had a mother who loved me, or an idea of me.

Was my father my predecessor in turning out, in her eyes, not to be who he was supposed to be? I'm fairly certain that this was the case, although having somewhat impulsively ended a marriage myself, and survived the complex, disillusioning, painful, and expensive aftermath, I am still not quite able to figure out why my mother, who periodically threatened to divorce my father, never got around to doing the same thing for what appear to have been far more solid reasons. "The worst marriage of all time." "We were terrible together." "Your father's job was to drive me nuts." "Ach—your father," this last with a dismissive wave of her hand. As we sat across from each other at her dining table, my mother would say these things to me, sometimes on the slightest pretext, and then she would tell me a story: about how my father had isolated her from her friends, about how my father had never done housework, about how my father had prevented her from accompanying him on a trip, about how my father had screwed up this opportunity, or gratuitously pissed off that helpful person, or alienated these old friends, or simply had been exactly and utterly predictably himself for forty-five years, finally refusing, over her objections, to seek treatment for the cancer that killed him anywhere but at the storefront medical establishments and third-rate hospital available locally, in Bay Ridge, where they had settled in retirement, also over her objections. "Your parents were co-dependent," my therapist once explained—an enlightening enough diagnosis, but reductive, I suppose.

Assume the diagnosis as a baseline, then, a starting point: my mother could not bring herself to leave my father, was talked out of it by him, did not want to be a single mother, was afraid of a deeper poverty, of being alone, thought my father could be changed, that her job was to change him, was gratified by the act of attempting to change him, by her own sense of grievance in his failure to change—a hundred reasons. But the boy in the living room—four, five years old?—saw only the unhappy woman, the monarch of his days, crying and wishing for something else. What did I think? What did I say to her? I'll tell you what I said: "Did I do something wrong? I'm sorry, Mommy."

Outside, chaos. Avenue B took on that appearance of threatening vacancy that thoroughfares in bad neighborhoods get. First, storefronts were boarded up. Then entire tenements. Around Halloween, older neighborhood kids would smear ashes on their faces and, roaming in groups, accost the adults, "trick-or-treating" by demanding spare change. They would do this whether it was actually the day of Halloween or not. The threat was implicit. One winter night junkies set a fire on our roof, just twelve feet over my head, and the firemen evacuated our building. I woke up in a stranger's kitchen, a bowl of cornflakes in front of me on the kitchen table. A woman who lived across the street had taken us in when she saw my parents holding me, in my bathrobe and pajamas, on the sidewalk. My father started carrying a kitchen knife with him when he took me to the park. The adults talked about crime: relatively lighthearted anecdotes, like the one about how Tuli Kupferberg had his "own" mugger who would approach him and call him by name—"Gimme the money, Tuli"—and grave stories, like the one about the woman, some vague acquaintance, who had been raped in her apartment. We listened to the radio. We sat on the broken furniture. We watched the black-and-white television with the hole in the screen. I liked *Walt Disney's Wonderful World of Color*.

School, in one form or another, programs run by settlement houses and philanthropic institutions, began to peel us apart from each other. For my mother it must have been a relief—even to be able to address the pedestrian facts of her day without having to take me into account, set me up with a suitable distraction, accommodate me somehow. I don't know what else she may have done, where she went or who she saw. I doubt that she missed me, not for the three or four hours that we may have been apart at these times. But for me, the reality, the definition, of my mother was her presence, when I felt it was time for her to be present. After spending my life having her within the sound of my voice, in view, suddenly she was gone. I would think of her, feel her absence acutely at times—at which point my rituals for summoning her were as focused and single-minded, as chanted and as sung, as those of any priest calling for the appearance of his god, although the consistent failure of these rituals, I later realized, was one of the principal lessons of early education, perhaps its point: people separated, and they survived. And when I had no need of her, it was as if she didn't exist at all.

For a while I went to preschool at the Educational Alliance down on East Broadway. I remember coloring line drawings of sinister-looking men offering candy to children on tree-lined suburban streets. This seemed like a less than immediate threat. A kid lashed me in the face with his book bag one day and cut my eye, giving me a scar I still have. My mother yelled at the teacher who, after I'd shit in my pants, flushed my underwear down the toilet: a brand-new pair of briefs! She yelled at the school bus driver who hadn't waited for her to arrive to pick me up before depositing me on the corner of Fourteenth Street and First Avenue and driving off; she made sure to be there waiting the next day to let him have it, started yelling as soon as the doors opened, climbing the steps into the coach deliberately, one by one, as she yelled, drawing intimidatingly closer to him. My mother's displays of her displeasure embarrassed me, sometimes scared me, but this was how it worked. This was how you got the lean piece of meat. This was how you got the fresh piece of fish. This was how you got the landlord to repair the broken stove. This was how you got the junkies in the vestibule, the importuning bum haunting our end of the park, the man following you down the street, to go away. Here, long before people commonly spoke of establishing boundaries in their relations with others, it was necessary to rigorously police the ones you had: the right you had to not be ripped off, to not be neglected, to not be abused. People pushed; you pushed back, or you pushed first, and those were the only two alternatives in the Hobbesian environment of the Lower East Side. For my mother it was important never to relinquish, in public, her aloofness, the irascibility with which she demonstrated her authority. She could be as sharp-tongued with a counterman who was trying a little too familiarly to be friendly as she could when confronted with a clear threat. She had no interest in preserving the appearance of friendliness. She

did not care if people thought she was a bitch. I saw people literally take a step back from her. She guaranteed that for as long as
I was riding that route, the bus driver would never once depart
from that stop without making sure that I had been safely picked
up. She guaranteed it without complaining, without threats to
report him to his superiors, without negotiating or applying any
leverage other than the display of her formidable anger.

This was not uncommon. The women my mother be-
came friends with came from all over. Some, like her, had been
working-class, some had been middle-class, some had come from
money, all had arrived at that particular patch of ground with the
idea in mind of not being whatever it was that had been expected
of them. (When, during the early '80s, stock images of the 1950s
began to resurface, appropriated for ironic purposes—grinning
housewives presiding over spotless suburban kitchens, and so
on—my mother could only roll her eyes. For her, the menacing
prospect of her young womanhood was not that she might be
brainwashed into living a bland domestic situation comedy, but
that she might willfully defraud herself, end up like so many of
the girls she'd grown up with, stuck in the Bronx with a petty
domestic tyrant, begging him for money, reading nothing, seeing nothing, knowing nothing, going nowhere, dreaming of new
drapes.) Defending themselves, their right to live undisturbed
and unmolested, was something they had learned to do: they
had defended themselves against the onslaught of disapproving
parents, in-laws, siblings, hometown boyfriends; of judgmental
physicians, clergymen, teachers, social workers. Self-defense already came naturally by the time they arrived on this inhospita-
ble ground, where the limits of this ability would be tested and

finally reached: every one of these families eventually left as the neighborhood deteriorated.

On May 13, 1968, shortly before my fifth birthday, my parents got married. I imagine it as a nice day, a day I spent with my best friend, Drew Bailey, in the company of his mother, Lillian. The wedding ceremony was performed by a deputy city clerk with a pronounced speech impediment, the source of much hilarity when the story was told and retold. It was witnessed by Mort Lucks, a painter friend who, summoned to the Municipal Building at the last minute, attended the ceremony wearing his soiled painting clothes and left immediately afterward to return to his studio. My parents had lunch at the Cedar, the new Cedar at Twelfth and University, and then my father went to work at Grove Press next door, while my mother, presumably, went home to Thirteenth Street, or to Lillian and her husband Mel's apartment on East Third Street to pick me up. I wasn't aware that my parents had gotten married that day. In fact, I was unaware that my parents hadn't been married to begin with. I'd assumed that you had to be married in order to have children.

As she was about the beginning of their relationship, my mother was unsentimental when discussing the exchange of vows. They had married, she later explained to me, because she was afraid that if they didn't I "would be taken away from" my father if something were to happen to her. Whether or not this was an urgent response to a developing situation, I don't know, but I do have a theory about this dire threat. Throughout much of her pregnancy, my mother had remained married to poor George Bradt, who would therefore legally have been presumed to be my father. (Under these circumstances, my father could not lawfully have signed an Acknowledgment of Paternity after my birth, but he later told me that he did so anyway, suffering an earful from the notary public who witnessed his signature and felt compelled to urge him not to sign away his freedom. My ambiguous status seems to have inspired a lot of officious advice: my mother recalled angrily that a social worker had visited her in the hospital shortly after my birth to assist her in making "arrangements" for me, probably standard operating procedure circa 1963 in the case of single mothers.) Since I never found anything among my mother's papers suggesting that poor George had ever made any claims concerning me one way or the other, I suspect that he may recently have died and that my mother was worried that his parents might have a valid claim to custody in the event that she herself died. It's possible that my mother thought that by legitimizing her relationship with my father she was further legitimizing me as my father's son.

Alive or dead, poor George Bradt seems to have faded away completely, obligingly permitting himself to become a perfect cipher. Using what little hard information I have and otherwise dependable online resources, I'm unable to find any definite record of his birth or of his death. What I have are two photographs of him that show a mild-looking, slender man, bearded and with large, rather melancholy eyes. I have a copy of the certificate of my mother's marriage to him. I have a copy of their divorce decree. I have a completely battered copy of the *Betty Crocker Cookbook*, inscribed "Merry Christmas to Vicki / Mother & Dad Bradt / Dec. 1957." That's it. Presumably more evidence of their lives together, my mother's and his, was lost in the storage locker debacle—another act of self-erasure on his part. My mother had felt that loss, she complained about it on more than one occasion, but it was poor George Bradt who was put out with the garbage along with my mother's photos and sheet music.

What is it about him that makes him simultaneously so fascinating to me and so indistinct? The life my mother lived with him lasted for only a brief period, when she was unimaginably young. Our conversations about him were always ones that she started, the details sharp but spare. She had left him, but circumstances had forced her hand. It was him or it was life: straightforward, but my mother's choice was one that a lot of twenty-two-year-olds might not have made under the circumstances. Who knows what the regrets were? It's enough to know that there were regrets, lingering ones, ones that must have raised implications about the life she went on to live, the one that had my father, and me, at its center: that it might not have needed to be what it was; that it was as a result of an unfortunate chain of mishaps, chance encounters ("that fucking Alex!"), misguided longings, bad decisions, belated intuitions, that she was now where she was, with whom she was, doing what she was, and it all might have been different.

My mother told me that he was killed in an auto accident when I was little. (Could this have been the cause of my mother's tears that afternoon?) It seemed a perfect end for the out-of-focus fuck-up who represented him in my head. But after she died, when I spoke to my cousin Denise to ask what she thought about my arranging a high requiem mass for her (she'd left the Church years earlier, but in going through her apartment I'd found crucifixes, rosaries, miraculous medals, keys, and other Catholic objects, all recently acquired), Denise told me, "You know, I'm a little surprised that you're asking. I know Titi Vivian had a real problem with the Church. Because of George." When I asked what she meant, she said, "They wouldn't allow him to have a Catholic burial. He committed suicide, you know."

6

I was enrolled in the kindergarten program at P.S. 61 that fall. I was a morning kid, returning home at noon with my mother. In Mrs. Falk's class, I was envious of the black and Puerto Rican kids, crew-cut and sharp in their cheap off-the-rack suits and clip-on ties. My mother viewed this way of grooming and dressing one's children with undisguised distaste, just as she viewed with distaste the way some of the white parents allowed their kids to appear—unkempt hair, torn jeans, T-shirts with slogans on them, ripped sneakers. My own school clothes were button-down shirts, corduroys, and Hush Puppies. There was a strange in-betweenness that I occupied. Already I was aware of one difference between my mother and others (a difference that came to life when she spoke Spanish), but there was no way to put a finger on how, or whether, that defined me in any way. Kids in school spoke Spanish, but it was a different Spanish. They spoke English with an accent I didn't share. They did not have an Italian last name and, most significant, they often had skin darker than mine. It was clear that my mother was happy to leave unacknowledged whatever affinities we may have shared, but the world from which they had come was not so completely different that it was unrecognizable.

The odd equilibrium of the park, maintained by the unseen hand of the mothers, had kept us apart, but P.S. 61 thrust us together. Here, at school, those kids had an urgently scrubbed look; wore polyester suits, clip-on bow ties. Patent leather shoes with white socks. I can imagine, now, the shine of those sad, cheap fabrics, the shine of cheap communion suits passed down from older brothers. But I saw only the drabness of my own clothes, was pulled toward the finery on display. I began to hound my mother for a suit of my own. I would see them in shop windows on Fourteenth or Delancey Streets, miniature suits on miniature mannequins. My mother finally bought me a blazer, probably at Klein's or Mays, which appears to have been her forceful riposte to my own ideas of elegance—a navy-blue woolen, double-breasted, with brass buttons. I refused to wear it except under extraordinary duress, and it became—until, mercifully, I outgrew it—part of the humiliating outfit my mother laid out for me on "special occasions": a T-shirt with thick navy and white horizontal stripes (or, in winter, a white turtleneck), a pair of navy wool short pants, a pair of navy knee socks, and black Buster Browns, topped by the blazer.

The thinking process that had cooked up this wretched ensemble, cooked it up out of private school pretensions and some archaic memory of the way well-dressed boys had appeared in old movies, reveals a certain neither/nor-ness in my mother's attitude toward the world: I would not be dressed like the barrio kids my mother abhorred, but I would not be dressed like those slovenly white children either. My entirely reasonable objections to the outfit appear to have been part of the point: the very idea that children should be dressed in impractical clothes that they hated and that made them feel self-conscious seems to me to have originated not just in my mother's sense of style or propriety but also in her conception of childhood as submission to the arbitrary will of an all-powerful adult, a conception no doubt passed on to her by Dora decades earlier. Every child's first tautology—*Why? Because.*—takes on shape and meaning, stops simply being synonymous with no, as that child learns to reason, as the adult bias against *justifying things* to children becomes less defensible. My ability to reason was already well on its way by the time that my mother insisted, in the face of all the easily observable contrary evidence, that hers was the only way for a boy to dress nicely.

But throughout her life my mother insisted on things she couldn't justify, raised vehement objections whose rationale she couldn't articulate, denounced things that couldn't possibly have made any difference to her. In this she was joined by my father, who had developed a similarly preposterous set of ideas that he'd carried out of a similarly working-class background.

Class presented itself, in our daily lives, as a set of internally lived contradictions. My parents lived a bohemian life, but they were not especially bohemian in their approach to it, and our household ran with a clockwork regularity that any workingman of the time might have appreciated. As I've said, my mother viewed ostentatious nonconformity as either a middle-class affectation or as the pathetic and reckless behavior of pitiful souls who had no idea how to cope with life. In their attitudes, their way of solving

problems, of persevering, of economizing, of meeting obliga-
tions, of forming judgments about others, my parents remained
essentially blue-collar throughout their lives. At the same time,
my father—and, by extension, my mother—had ideas about art
and culture, and their relation to it, that can only be described
as elitist. My father had disdain for the idea that what he did
was *craft*, an act of skillfully performing a useful task with the
materials and tools at hand. Art was distinctive in its uselessness,
not its utility; it was transcendent, not practical. The moment
that it began to concern itself with appearances, with prevail-
ing tastes—the moment, for that matter, that it began to desire
to *appear* creative—art became bourgeois. And so my parents
lived in the area suspended between the blue-collar (the solid
basis from which they met life's obstacles) and the aristocratic
(an exalted ideal of permanent values); more than anything, they
wanted to avoid falling into the middle-class pit they imagined
yawning below.

And yet the world of the artist—with real wealth mostly inaccessible to it, and the cultural expectations of the unsophis-
ticated anathema to it—has more in common with that of the
educated middle class than with anything else. Middle-class art
may be questionable, but middle-class life is an understandable
goal. Certainly to me it is, since in the end my parents, despite
themselves, raised me to be middle-class in my expectations. Despite themselves, no matter how many abstract paintings hung
on their walls or how many volumes of poetry were ranked on
their shelves or how many LPs of Morton Feldman's or Albert
Ayler's music spun on their turntable, they found that sooner or
later they needed to buy a new pepper mill or some coffee mugs

or a comforter for their bed, and when they did it was to the same selection of goods favored by any reasonably stylish housewife in Westchester or Bergen County that they turned. Despite themselves, they looked to Craig Claiborne and Julia Child for interesting new recipes. Despite themselves, my parents discovered that the middle-class world had begun to catch up with their tastes and habits to the exact extent that their tastes and habits had begun to seek gratification in a middle-class way.

For my father, living this contradiction was reasonably easy to finesse: he simply transferred his identification to those books he was reading and writing and the rest of the world fell away, gradually at first and then precipitously. My mother, though, had no such outlet through which she could assert what she saw as the absoluteness of her difference. The esoteric, highly stylized system of values—truly, an aesthetic—that had taken shape in her mind found its expression in other ways including, I am sorry to say, dressing and grooming me in a way that often was absurdly inappropriate for the time and place in which I was growing up. It couldn't have occurred to me that my mother was expressing her *refusal* of something entirely separate from me and my desires. Nor could it have occurred to me that her race—whatever it may have been officially or otherwise—was the odorless, colorless agent spurring her on: she did not want to be a Puerto Rican like the Puerto Ricans who lived on Avenue C. But she could not bear to be white, either.

And yet "white" was precisely the identity that the girl with the birth certificate labeling her BLACK had cultivated. As a very young woman she may have felt that she'd escaped it—being "black," being Puerto Rican, being other, being working-class, being Bronx, being anything; may have felt that the Manhattan cosmopolitanism in which she draped herself armed her against judgment, that cosmopolitanism itself was to be beyond such judgments. But it was a trap. It was a trap whose dimensions became apparent to her only once she had taken on the role of *wife*. Not the wife of poor George Bradt—the bride blessed with weekend trips and surprise Broadway tickets and lavish gifts and an apartment across the street from Central Park and the freedom to call it quits—but the wife (legally married or not) of Gilbert Sorrentino: mother of his child, cut off from travel, from evenings out, from lavishness of any kind; living in a drafty, insecure tenement apartment in a neighborhood that rapidly was turning into a nightmare; expected to make common cause with a group of women whose uniting characteristic was that all of them were expected, in good weather, to spend the bulk of their days sitting on a bench in Tompkins Square Park overseeing their kids—after finishing the housework, of course. Like convicts in a prison yard. Here again she was her origins—running the vacuum, running errands, putting supper on the table. To me, it was life; to her, life had ended the day I was born.

In my mind, a chasm exists between my mother's history with poor George Bradt and my mother's history with my father, and with me—but I remind myself that between her first marriage and my birth are only five years, two of which were lived at an age when another young woman might have been experiencing her junior and senior years of college, an option for which my mother's intelligence and inclinations surely qualified her. My mother barely had a chance to catch her breath between fatal decisions. One of those late nights when, in anger, she left my father's apartment to walk diagonally across Tompkins Square to her own place, she should have kept walking. But something pushed her toward entanglement. Somewhere she had to have been taught that she couldn't make it on her own. And now there I was, reminding her that whatever she may have wanted from her life, she would never have it. Here again she was her origins— without even the refuge of the sewing machine to which Dora had ridden the subway each morning to escape Charlotte Street; without even her first language, living surrounded by neighbors who spoke it, lest she betray herself as something she was determined not to be.

7

My parents informed me that we were moving to Greenwich Village when I arrived home for lunch one day in April 1970. I was in first grade now, and I navigated the two blocks to and from P.S. 61 on my own each day. These trips taught me all I needed to know about what the Lower East Side had turned into; I was routinely hassled, usually by boys only two or three years older than me. It was not playful, it was not a social transaction or a rite of passage. Yet I remember crying when I heard the news; the bleak and blasted neighborhood was all I really knew, and the Village was as vague to me as if it had been another country. "What will you miss?" my mother asked me. We sat at the dining table, now located in the alcove. Stuck for an answer, I replied, "The East River." My parents laughed. "There's another river," my father said. "Right across the street."

That was something. There was a strong sense of anticipation, generally. Things would be better: that was the promise. The new place was this, the new neighborhood was that, I was told. A new school, where I'd start in the fall, after finishing out the year at 61. The building had an elevator; in fact it was so big it had *three* elevator banks with a total of six elevators. The apartment itself was huge, a duplex, both floors flooded with light through giant windows. A loft, but everything brand-new, plumbing, appliances, everything. Lots of kids my age. It was in a new development, Westbeth, a subsidized housing complex for artists in the former Bell Laboratories buildings located on the far West Village block bounded by West, Bethune, Washington, and Bank Streets.

Moving day was May 1; I left for school in the morning and returned to five empty rooms. The only thing remaining by the time I walked in were the windowshades in my room, and they were staying, I was told. The defamiliarizing effect was spectacular. The same sunlight, but different, falling into the apartment and lying straight and unbroken across the bare floors. Outlines of dust where the pictures had hung. The echoes of our voices.

For my father, things had come together perfectly: almost simultaneous with our move, Grove Press laid off nearly its entire staff and doled out a surprisingly generous severance which, combined with unemployment, took care of money worries for the time being. Having entered first grade, I was out of the house for seven hours at a stretch. Suddenly, my father could spend uninterrupted days sitting in the study he'd made for himself at one end of the giant open space of our new apartment's lower floor, and there he began the most productive period of his career. During our twelve years at Westbeth, he wrote six novels and three books of poetry.

But for my mother, Westbeth could not possibly have been a congenial place. It was an *artists' community*, with all the built-in amateurism that the need to assert such a thing implies. My mother, as I have said, had no artistic pretensions and little tolerance for those who did. Certainly having been around artists for fifteen years had given her an eye for the difference between the bullshitters and the real thing. Certainly her experience with poor George Bradt had made her leery of arty ambitions and posturing, the fatal conflation of the work and a way of living that was believed to accompany it. And amid the complex, conflicting feelings she had about my father was a sense of what his work required of him. At Westbeth, people walked around saying, in effect, "I am an artist" to one another. It was a form of plumage. Mainly, these were the sort of people who were good at that most prized of New York skills, *getting things*—not paying retail, skipping lines, avoiding the higher interest rate, being upgraded to first class, all the crumbs from life's table—basically an admirable quality as long as fraud, coupled with insufferable conceit, isn't involved. Essentially, Westbeth was one of the lesser scams of the '60s counterculture. Someone had convinced various people and entities to subsidize a place where grown-ups could pretend to be crazy artists, setting it in Greenwich Village, that symbolic locus of America's avant-garde spirit, although it had long since become a nice middle-class neighborhood, about as avant-garde as *The New Yorker*. It was here, among these "crazy" "artists," that my father settled down to his work, unencumbered for the remainder of his life by a nine-to-five routine, and it was here that my mother abruptly had to figure out all over again who, in relation to this place and these people, she was, and how she fit in.

But while my father could just get to work as if programmed to turn out novels and poetry, comparatively untouched by the frauds, such people looked down on my mother, the mere *house-wife* whose prideful sin was in refusing to lie about nonexistent artistic accomplishments. I suspect that no sooner had she gotten the lay of the land and realized that these people and their pretensions were the dominant movers and shakers at Westbeth than the place began to drive her crazy. For all its problems, the Lower East Side had been a genuine bohemia. In exchange for leaving, we received an ersatz, bourgeois bohemia, located in a safe, picturesque neighborhood. On the Lower East Side we'd known people who went about their business without feeling any compulsion to enact a nonstop performance of radical nonconformity. We received in exchange ersatz rebels who couldn't do anything without considering it in relation to the way the straights might do it. On the Lower East Side we'd known people who'd committed themselves and their families to an ugly, down-at-the-heels neighborhood because it was undiscriminating enough to allow them to live however they wanted and cheap enough to allow them to pursue their vocations while living on whatever pittance they managed to earn. We received in exchange ersatz fellow travelers who had selected Westbeth because it suited their idea of themselves as *artists* deserving of an appropriately *artistic* setting and milieu, while relieving them of any shame or embarrassment they might have felt had they been forced to compare themselves to genuine artists and their genuine sacrifice and devotion, to say nothing of their achievements.

There were many real artists at Westbeth, of course—Diane Arbus, Merce Cunningham, Gil Evans, Mary Frank, Moses Gunn, and Hans Haacke are a few of the better-known names that come to mind—but they tended to keep to their work. Certainly their real community wasn't to be found among these clowns. The *community* aspect of this *artists' community* was overseen by the posers, the hobbyists, the minor league careerists, who were quick to commandeer any building activity that promised an opportunity for self-congratulation. At Westbeth, it was *very artistic*. It couldn't afford to stop being *artistic* for a minute. People dressed *artistically*. The building's galleries held vanity exhibitions displaying the tenants' *artistic* excreta. The place itself looked *artistic*, with half-moon-shaped "fire balconies" overlooking the intrusively ugly sculptures in the courtyard, interior walls painted in primary colors like a Scandinavian lunatic asylum, sensuously undulating acoustic ceilings, and seven-foot-tall wired glass windows with iron sashes. A disused railroad track—once part of the West Side Elevated Line, since amputated—picturesquely drove through the eastern facade of the building, finding its terminus at Bank Street. A set of iron gates on West Street opened onto a small porte cochere where a lucky few had managed to finagle permanent parking spots for their cars. The residential charm of the West Village pretty much ceased abruptly at Washington Street back then, yielding to *artistic* surroundings: warehouses, factories, truck lots, prostitutes patrolling the street corners after dark, a furtive gay demimonde in West Street leather bars and under the West Side Highway, splintering piers on a derelict waterfront. If you wanted to live a conspicuously *artistic* life in famous Greenwich Village, this was the perfect place. The setting did half the work for you.

So my parents arrived at Westbeth with a refugee mentality, feeling as if they'd escaped something, and were greeted with an orgy of complacency. My father, as noted above, registered this and then turned to his work for the next twelve years, but my mother had to contend with a new *community*, an *artists' community*, which, by the time we arrived, had already evolved a very specific hierarchy and a set of social rules of behavior.

I wasn't particularly happy either—new school, etc.—but happiness in childhood is a matter of sheer luck, and probably temperament. The unhappy child can always say, "One day, I'm going to get out of here." The unhappy adult says only, "How did I end up here?" This had to have been the question for my mother. In laying it on thick about Westbeth, I've given my father a break, actually. All the things that operated to make his life work exactly the way he'd always wanted it also operated to let him impose his will upon my mother, who might eventually have found ways to enjoy her new surroundings and routine had my father still been heading to Grove Press each morning while I was spending my entire day at school. It must have driven her up the wall to have raised me to the point at which I no longer needed her at my side only to have another demanding presence substituted for mine. If she wanted to invite one of the neighbors over for coffee, there was my father working at one end of the the large lower floor, needing not to be interrupted. If she wanted to listen to the radio while she cleaned or folded laundry, there was my father working at one end of the large lower floor, needing silence. If she decided to make herself a cup of tea, suddenly my father would appear, companionably (but unwelcomely) asking her what she was doing, whether she'd put some tea on for him, did she feel like a sandwich. In short, my father wanted to be able to avail himself of my mother's presence when he felt the need, but

otherwise wanted it to be inert. At around ten each morning he
would rise from the breakfast table to go into his study at one end
of the large lower floor. At one o'clock he would have lunch. At
around five thirty or six he would stop working to make drinks
for himself and my mother. First he would begin to whistle, announcing his reentry into the rhythms of the household. Then
he would begin to talk. He would talk to her. He would talk to
me. He would talk about: politics, local news, baseball, the book
review he'd read that day, whatever book he was reading, who
he'd talked to on the phone, what he'd heard from or about his
ex-wife or my half brother and half sister, what his agent had to
report, what the commentator on the radio was reporting on at
that very moment. He'd read aloud from the paper, from letters
he'd received from friends, from examples of absurd or egregious
prose that had caught his attention. I took everything he said
seriously, and assumed that he was always right, and would ask
questions that afforded him the opportunity to expatiate on any
subject at length. My mother, on the other hand, was weary of
the grooves he'd fall into; well-versed in his various prejudices,
biases, and complaints; annoyed by being read to. Her answers
ultimately were designed to discourage further conversation. By
the time supper was over, she was tired of the sound of his voice.
They would watch television for a couple of hours, and then my
mother would climb upstairs to go to bed and my father would
sit in his study and read until he himself went to bed at around
one. This was how my father lived, day in and day out, from May
1, 1970, until he died thirty-six years later. When in 1982 he was
appointed to his professorship at Stanford University, his iron
routine absorbed without faltering the workload of teaching,

advising students, and performing university service. He never took a vacation. A lengthy, unavoidable disruption—moving to California, or returning to New York twenty years later—would bring him to the verge of what appears in retrospect to have been psychosis. When he was dying, he managed to get to his desk to finish the novel he'd been working on when he became sick. I can say confidently that the majority of my father's working days— which were the majority of his days—were spent doing the exact same things in the exact same order. Utterly reliable. Had my father been my mother's car, he would have been perfect. As a husband, he must have been maddening. My mother became a maddened person. My father was an invalid, a writing invalid, an invalid that she had to care for unless she wanted his condition to devour her. But it did devour her. The feeling of claustrophobia must have been overwhelming. My father had no interest in traveling, and he never did it for pleasure. We took no vacations as a family. He did not attend the theater, or opera, or the ballet, or poetry readings, or live performances of any kind. He rarely went out with friends, or to parties. The implication always was that although these things *had* been a regular part of his life he had put them away, as in 1 Corinthians 13, in order to focus with near-exclusivity on his work. He did very little, and what little he did he subjected to a routine that emphasized invariability and increased his productivity.

A discussion of my father's peculiar and fixed habits, the rigid, self-annihilating discipline he exercised throughout the period of his life when I knew him, is for another day. The point is that those habits, that discipline, required the people in his orbit not only to behave equally predictably, but to submit to his compulsive sense of control as well. The giant apartment in the newly renovated building in the pleasantly different neighborhood became not the center but the scope of my mother's world. That she acquiesced in this fascinates and depresses me. Was there a reason this had to be the case?

Something I haven't mentioned yet is that one summer afternoon in the late '60s my mother had come home exhausted and feeling sick after spending the day in the sun. The next day, a rash appeared on her face, the butterfly rash that spreads its wings across the cheekbones and rests its thorax on the bridge of the nose. It was the first visible symptom of lupus. By the time we moved to Westbeth, my mother's chronic condition of illness was well-established in our house. In addition to being a burden, lupus would become a liberation from the challenges life posed, the principal challenges being (a) my father, (b) me, and eventually (c) everyone else. My father's invalidism was countered with her own, which had the advantage of being powerfully ratified by the medical profession, whose members would devote themselves for years to controlling her illness and its symptoms, which would in time be joined by other illnesses, other symptoms. From the time I was small, my mother couldn't be expected to *do things*, so all the *things* she might conceivably have done once I started school—completed her education at what was then a free City University system, for instance—she did not do. But I think the lupus played only a small part in that. Something else had crushed her impetus, something that had intensified once we moved from the Lower East Side. Did she have ambitions? I can't imagine that she didn't, but by the time this occurred to me, to have asked her what they were would have been cruel. It was predictable that her life would temporarily have halted with my arrival when she was twenty-five, but it had never started again because she had chosen a man who was completely satisfied with the life he was living. *And hadn't they chosen that life together?* I suppose that might have been a reasonable question on his part, when they argued about their lives. But they never did. They argued about everything else—small, bitter arguments about petty domestic matters that clearly stood for the larger problem of their essential incompatibility—but never, in my hearing, about an everyday existence that suited him perfectly but couldn't possibly have suited the person on whose complicity it depended.

And yet she was complicit. What might my father have said, if they argued about this? "You are complicit. This works for you, except when it does not, and then you blame me. Who's stopping you from doing what you want? Not me." He might have said, "You criticize what you see as my complacency. But I'm simply trying to survive. I'm struggling for my very life. This is what I do." He might have said, "I sit and I write and I've always arranged my life to permit it. You knew this. I sit, and I write, and in order to support doing it I worked in stockrooms and on loading platforms and on docks and in offices until I was forty-one years old and had the opportunity to stop doing those things." That's certainly what I would have said—and in fact over the years I've said things like it to women who found themselves unhappy with me. To be honest, it makes perfect sense to me, as arguments go. Ask for anything, but don't ask for *this*, because my answer will be no. My unhappy partners have responded, generally, in one (or eventually both) of two ways: by doing what they wanted without me, or by leaving. I'm not suggesting that these represent ideal solutions to the problem of an intractable mate, but none of them ever simply gave up, as my mother did, to watch life diminish into the passing of the hours.

Or did she? Here's a memory that crops up every now and then. When I was about eight, my mother decided to take me and my friend Jennifer Wyland, who was spending the day with us, for a walk on West Street, perhaps to the Morton Street Pier, a seedy structure that in those days passed for a waterfront attraction. It was a sunny, warm day. As we were walking, a young man approached us. He was clean-cut, pleasant looking. I distinctly remember that he was wearing an Oxford shirt, open at the neck. He casually put his arm around my mother's shoulder and said, smiling, "Hey, don't I know you from somewhere?"

"No, I don't *think* so," my mother said. We moved on. The man didn't say anything else, didn't follow or call after us.

"Who was that man?" I asked.

"Just somebody who thought he knew me," said my mother. For years I thought of this as just one of those odd encounters from childhood. It was devoid of menace, lasted an instant. Clean-cut, pleasant, smiling, casual, familiar. *Familiar*—that's what got me much, much later. The guy's whole approach was familiar, not like he'd just up and decided to come on with the world's most hackneyed pickup line to some stranger walking down the street with two elementary school kids in tow, but like he knew my mother and decided to cut through the awkwardness of the unexpected meeting by approaching her in a jokey, isn't-this-weird way. My mother played it OK in front of her audience of eight-year-olds—who knows what we might have said later in front of my father had she stopped to chat, even innocuously; who knows what questions might have been raised—but not so well before her middle-aged son, bearing witness across the span of decades and with his own history of sexual duplicity to draw on. The sexually cynical son says: Something off in that exchange. The tone wasn't right. That familiarity was like a spoor in the air. I mean, honestly: I don't know. Some people have a talent for illicit affairs and others don't. I suspect my mother would have been good at it; the concealment part, at least. Other than anger, she held her emotions close. I suspect that my mother, who later would sometimes say, her words heavy and dark with meaning, that the early '70s were "a terrible time" in my parents' marriage, might perfectly well have found herself in the dilemma of the philandering mother of young children: how to make this Thing that can't be everything be *enough?* How is it that this Thing intended to alleviate a Condition ends up underscoring the intolerableness of the Condition? And, finally, do you end up resenting the person (me) for whom, nominally, the Condition is endured because that person (me) is impossible to conceive of within the Thing?

Now I approach the beginnings of my psychological and emotional split from my mother. I think I indulge in speculation about her possible affairs not (just) because the possibility seems both plausible and exciting, but because it seems like a place to anchor my fixation on the idea that she held me responsible for what became of her life. But a number of things that contributed to our gradually increasing distance from each other began to coalesce after we moved to Westbeth. For one, there was my father's fixed presence in the house, after years of going to work each day. My mother and I had talked about many things over those years, naturally, but her attitude had often been businesslike, in the manner of mothers of small children who need to be bathed, dressed, fed, prevented from allowing their messes to engulf the house, kept occupied, exercised, socialized, put to bed, etc. In other words she was often issuing instructions rather than conversing, she was distracted much of the time, and—probably unfairly—the task of administering correction overwhelmingly fell to her. My father, on the other hand, was always delighted to talk to me, and, because I took tremendous interest in everything he had to say and in everything he did, he took pains to explain a lot of it to me. While my mother often seemed irritable or impatient, my father rarely did. This is not entirely fair to my mother. I would be asking her about some chore that, as mysterious and fascinating as it might have been to me, represented to her only something boring and necessary that needed to be gotten out of the way as quickly as possible. On the other hand, I would be asking my father about what he did at his desk all day, about what he talked about when he taught, about the books he was reading, about what was written on the tablets and in the notebooks he kept, the stacked manuscript pages, and ultimately about writers, poetry, and fiction.

The dynamic in the house took on a triangular configuration. Two against the father, two against the mother, two against the child. It went around and around to suit the political requirements of the moment. My mother and me versus my father was generally tongue-in-cheek, conspiratorial, a remnant of the years the two of us had spent in each other's company and my father's presence in the evenings had been all but superfluous. We would make him the butt of our humor; mocking his habitually parsimonious behavior (a true child of the Depression, my father inverted nearly empty ketchup bottles until the end of his life, wore his clothes until they fell apart, saved Jiffy bags that he received in the mail, and was fond of quoting the wartime motto "Use it up, wear it out, make it do"), or seizing on one of his occasional malapropisms and turning it into a family joke that we referred to for years afterward. Between my father and me, on the other hand, was an unspoken agreement that we understood each other; that I was adopting—inheriting, really—his interests, biases, and allegiances in exchange for his unstinting affection; that, united in this and in other ways, we endured my mother's temper, her rigidity, her icy silences (had these things always been there?). In this way my father usurped my mother's dominion over me, became the ultimate authority in the household even as she remained its overseer.

But the sinister alliance was between my parents, who clearly had agreed to use *any means necessary* to keep me in line and within the fold. With Tompkins Square Park behind me and my school days stretching before me, I began meeting people on my own; after years of carefully curated friendships with the kids whose parents my mother could get along with, I suddenly had been left to myself to make sense of the social landscape, both at school and, especially, at Westbeth. These kids, like all kids, had social criteria, criteria that I was determined to meet, although my mother made it strikingly difficult, sometimes impossible. Having mostly given up on the idea of accepting new people into her life, she affected incomprehension of my own need to be accepted. Neither of my parents wanted me to turn into someone they didn't recognize as one of them.

I don't know how to describe what being "one of them" consisted of without reference to language typically used to describe cults. You were in or you were out. To be out essentially was to be anyone else, and to be anyone else was to be no one at all. By now, my parents' friends shared the common characteristic of not posing a threat to their self-esteem. They were the fuck-ups, the has-beens, the unconnected, the ones with bad luck or bad timing, the mentally disordered, the drunks, the unambitious, the admirers, the ready acolytes. Those who didn't end up fitting the role my parents had cast them in—who succeeded, or who married well, or who willfully overcame adversity, or who found fulfillment somehow, or who grew up and developed ideas of their own—were excluded. All of the doctrines preached by my parents concerning any subject, even those about which they knew very little, had to be accepted without question. There was no such thing as healthy debate. At any sign of heterodoxy, you were subjected to the withdrawal of affection until you repented. Very few people repented. Being dependent upon them, I didn't have the luxury of being recalcitrant.

My indoctrination was divided evenly between them. Time, place, duration, and method of enforcement was up to my mother. Like most enforcers, she misused her authority. Certainly what she *wanted* she would obtain from me ruthlessly, using physical force if necessary, and it never seemed fair; there are few episodes from my childhood when I recall my mother's discipline with the sense that I had earned it. She never tried to make me feel guilty—emotional correction wasn't her stock in trade. I don't think she particularly cared how I felt in these moments of confrontation, whether I loved her or hated her, whether I was angry or scared or chastened, whether I ended up seeing the ferkakta wisdom of her position or not. She wanted to adjust me the way she adjusted askew piles of magazines, or toilet paper hung the wrong way on the spindle. She corrected behavior, on the spot, and if she needed to hit me to do it, she did so unhesitatingly. She didn't spank me, there was no time for dread, she struck suddenly—the head, the face, the upper arm, my ass, my thigh. Whatever she could reach. It didn't happen frequently but it happened frequently enough.

As I said, this was a bad time. My mother told me so, on several occasions, when rehearsing her life to me as we sat across from each other at her dining table—not that she needed to wait. Here's a story. When I was seven, in 1970, my mother had gotten pregnant again, and miscarried on Thanksgiving night. Every now and then, for years afterward, my father would become nostalgic about this pregnancy and talk about how I would have had a little sister (the imaginary child was always a girl). "She'd be ten years old now," he'd say in 1981. "She'd be graduating high school," he'd say in 1989. And so on. One night in the early 2000s, my wife, Nelle, and I were eating dinner at my parents' apartment in Brooklyn and my father started up. "She'd be thirty-two," or whatever it was, he said. My mother, in the act of lifting her fork to her mouth, allowed her hand to drop to the table with a crash.

"For Christ's sake, Gil," she said. "I was going to get rid of it any-way." I never heard my father mention my imaginary sister again.

So she and my father were not getting along. What was going on between them? Who knows. I already floated the affair hypothesis. This was '71, '72. It must have dawned on her after a year or two at Westbeth that my father had settled in; that he had no intention of doing anything differently, ever. I feel not as if my mother had done an about-face at this time (it's not like she'd ever been an easygoing person) but as if every antisocial tendency she had—to speak with unwelcome candor, to lose her temper abruptly, to shut down a conversation that wasn't proceeding to her liking, to withdraw into her own thoughts, to insist on microscopic control of her physical environment, to insist on having her way in matters that couldn't realistically have been important to her, to belittle people behind their backs, to distance herself from acquaintances, friends, and family—accelerated from this point on, leading to her years of social isolation in California and finally to the extreme apparitional reclusiveness of her widowhood in Bay Ridge, Brooklyn, of all places. Was it Westbeth's sophomoric pretensions, its gilding of bourgeois life with faux-bohemian trappings? Was it my father's subtly domineering presence? Was it my increasingly insistent push for autonomy? Was it depression that somehow went undiagnosed for her entire life, despite the well-documented connection between the condition and lupus?

Perhaps when I was very small she hadn't hit me as much or as hard. Perhaps the company of others—her friends from Tompkins Square, of whom she had now been deprived—and their possibly gentler example had been an influence. Her discipline was predictably capricious. I would whinge one time too many about some diktat that had come from the knee-socks-and-woolen-shorts part of her brain—no you can't watch *Batman* no you can't wear workboots no you can't have a banana bike no you can't have a shirt like that no you can't let your hair grow no you can't put posters on your walls no you can't have high-tops no you can't read superhero comics no you can't have a toy gun no you can't shower in the mornings no you can't wear sneakers in the winter no you can't have a looseleaf notebook—and *bam!* She would lash out, then send me away. Later I would be forced to apologize. Sometimes the apology had to be repeated: the first was insufficiently sincere.

One thing that was happening was that I was becoming a quick little kid. How not? I'd been steeped in a hyperverbal environment, the thrust and parry of combative conversation. I knew how to talk back, and I was beginning to recognize the occasional nonsensicality of the adult policies that directly afflicted me. My mother once typed up a daily schedule for me, which I wish I'd kept, and taped it to the door of my closet, where anyone could see the amount of time that had been allotted for my breakfast, the time of day my mother had set aside for my bowel movement. In a sense, my mother was the truly adventurous writer in our house, for this daring document, which broke down, into fifteen-minute intervals, the degree to which she felt that my existence had to be carefully regulated in order to preserve her tranquility, was a self-portrait of madness. It was the product of a deranged mind frustrated by reality's failure to comply with a highly detailed vision of perfection. So she created a blueprint, and so I asserted myself in all the ordinary ways of a child recognizing his own distinctness, recognizing the relationship between independence and the formation of the character he wants to present to the world. It was a fight for independence. It was often a stupid independence, I'll admit, the independence of mindless but desperate conformity. I grant my mother her point: No, the perverse desire for a looseleaf notebook or a pair of workboots hadn't originated with me. No, I didn't *really* want those workboots, I wanted to have what the other boys had. But my mother wasn't going into the hothouse of a new school in a new neighborhood every day, either. My mother wanted me to belong to her, not to the other kids I came into contact with every day. In fact, I'm pretty sure that my mother wanted me to be unacceptable to them, because they were not what we were, and to be what they were was to reject what we were. I refused to believe that it had to be one or the other, or that the choice was out of my hands entirely. So the appeal my mother (both my parents, really) made was not to my sense of guilt, but to my sense of loyalty: was I one of them, or was I an outsider?

Around when I was in second grade, I became friendly with a boy I shall call Eric, who lived three floors below me. Eric's parents were theater people—his mother no longer performed, but his father still worked as an actor and stage manager, and the apartment they lived in with Eric and his older sister, Melissa, was cluttered with mementos of their life on the stage: photos, framed posters and programs, a row of theater seats. Like a lot of Westbeth families, they took a casual attitude toward things like housework, television, and mealtimes, an attitude I appreciated given the scrupulous regimentation with which our household

ran. At home one evening, I made a complimentary reference
to the way things were done there, probably in connection with
something Eric was allowed to do or was not made to do. We
were sitting at the supper table.

"Christopher," my mother said, "Eric is an android."

"What do you mean?"

"I mean he's an android, Chris."

"No he isn't. What about Melissa?"

"Melissa is an android."

"What about his mom and dad."

"Paul is an android. Maggie is an android. They're *all an-droids*, Chris."

"Really?"

She wasn't smiling, wasn't struggling to keep a straight face.
The tone she used was the familiar one of peevish instruction. I
think she believed it. I think that, in the way that a convincing
metaphor can overtake the reality it represents, overrule it, she
herself believed they were androids. She didn't even understand
the conventions of the genre. Androids were tortured creations,
impassive yet torn by their yearning for human experience. They
didn't sit down at an old upright and bang out show tunes. And
yet there was my mother, telling me this. So I believed it too:
whatever *android* happened to have meant to me before that day,
its definition now shifted, conclusively, to accommodate whatever it was that my mother was trying to express about her feelings toward these people. That much I got: something about
them bugged her, and the quickest and most direct way she could
tell me that they weren't, in the sense that mattered to her, real or
authentic was to describe them like this. I haven't seen Eric since

I ran into him in a bar on St. Marks Place more than thirty years ago, but to this day, whenever I think of him, I automatically remind myself that he is an android, the way I might remind myself if he had been fitted with a glass eye.

8

By the time I was in fifth grade, things had gotten better. The crisis—whatever its cause—passed. Westbeth felt less alien. My mother let up on me. My father got a Guggenheim and money once again temporarily stopped being a problem. Could it all have been about money? I suppose I know as well as anyone that a lack of money can be more than enough, but something else had lifted, although I can't say what it was. Living with my parents exposed me to the contradictory twists and turns of the enduring marriage, but did little to reveal its mysteries. Living in a marriage, you realize how much of it is spent testing the bond, sometimes gingerly, sometimes forcefully, proving to yourself again and again that two individuals remain individual. The holy myth of the soul mate is easily dispelled by the most jejune discovery: "What do you mean you don't like Dylan?" "What do you mean you hate the Red Sox?" One can only adapt to marriage, successfully or unsuccessfully. Adults usually are lousy at it, which is why my mother's signature refrain, when remonstrating against my father, comically updated itself to mark the passage of time: "Ten years I've been telling you not to..." "Fifteen years I've asked you to . . ." "Twenty years I've been saying . . ." "Twenty-five years and you've never once . . ." Neither of them adapted. Thirty years, forty, forty-five. And then the tolling stopped.

When I was nearing the end of fifth grade, in 1974, my grandfather became very sick while he and Dora were visiting Uncle Jim and his family in Oklahoma City, where Jim was stationed at Tinker Air Force Base. The call came on a weekend morning; I remember that a friend, Michael Horowitz, was at the house and we were about to go out to the yard, which was what we called the plaza fronting Westbeth's Bank Street entrance that formed itself around a large circular fountain that usually was inoperative and clotted with garbage. Everything moved very quickly in response to the sudden bad news. My mother bought a plane ticket, packed, and headed to the airport. She was off to OKC for the duration, or until my grandfather stabilized, whichever came first.

I recall this overall period—roughly 1973–75—fondly. I liked school, was reasonably popular there, had pushed my way into view among my peers at Westbeth, and was able to concentrate productively on trying—since I was not to the manner born—to improve at being a proper little West Village shit. The lightened mood in our house had begun to make its clockwork routine dependable and comforting, rather than onerous and containing, but it is the weeks that followed my mother's departure that I remember as one of the happiest times of my life. My father and I talked constantly. We watched a lot of baseball together. We went to movies at the Quad (*Sleeper* and *Bananas*) and the Greenwich (*The Poseidon Adventure*) and then for pizza at La Marionetta. We ate takeout. We played catch in the yard. That was the extent of our indulgence; otherwise everything ran pretty much the same way. The difference was the absence of a certain atmosphere. Even at this best of times, when my mother was around one was always apprehensive that something might set her off. One might, say, cut some butter from the "wrong end" of the stick. One might, say, try to wear one's favorite shirt two days in a row. One might, say, put something on the "wrong shelf" in the fridge, so that my mother "couldn't find it." My father was looser, more relaxed. His self-involvement was purer; compulsive as he was in many ways, he had no interest off the page in combat and he lacked an overbearing need to control his surroundings. I don't mean to suggest that he lacked the need to control his surroundings. Only that he lacked an *overbearing* need to control his surroundings. His imperatives were expressed as suggestions, not as commands, and, easily propitiated, he would move ahead as if nothing had happened. Even at this best of times, my mother always began from a state of boiling resentment. The quickest and most penitent move to right things wouldn't necessarily mollify her. Sometimes she just wanted to pick a fight. If you attempted to be good-natured and understanding, she would say, "Don't patronize me." If you didn't understand the substance of her (often obscure and deeply personal) complaint, she would say, "Stop being disingenuous." At that age, I didn't face her with defiance. I faced her with fear. I was pliable, and I wanted to be loved, but sometimes I didn't think being loved by her was worth the price: being despised by her. Even at this best of times. At night, when the rates were low, she and my father would talk on the phone. I could hear her voice on the other end of the line, complaining about the way things were down there.

My mother came back. My grandfather's mysterious ailment, I learned, was leukemia. He'd become strong enough to return to the Bronx, where he would resume treatment at Montefiore Hospital on an outpatient basis. My mother seemed happy to be home. But this was when things faltered, at least from my perspective. Years later, I can see how it was all a blink of an eye, that the lingering happy period I remember was actually a brief interlude which came to an end when my mother realized that her father was going to die and that Dora was going to survive. She was going to lose her father and be stuck with Dora. She didn't say this at the time, not to me, and in fact she never did cop to having felt that way, even years after she had revealed her bitterness toward her mother. She didn't have to, really. It was precisely the way I felt when my father got sick and I realized that he was going to die.

My mother had to find a job. I'm not sure what happened, but money became scarce again. It was not something she wanted to do, not at thirty-seven, twelve years out of the job market. I'm not sure my father was happy about her going out and getting a job either, although it beat the alternative: his going out and getting a job. I thought it was extremely exciting—my mother would be going to work! Just like a normal person! I was disabused of this idea one afternoon when I ran into her on Bethune Street when I was walking home from school with some other kids. She was with another Westbeth mom, chatting with her before they went their separate ways at Hudson Street. My mother had scheduled a couple of job interviews for that week, and when I saw her I burst out, "Hi, Mom! Did you get a job yet?" Instantly I knew it was the wrong thing to have said. Her face changed in a way imperceptible to outsiders but which signaled, to me, forcibly controlled rage, as did the dread "reasonable" voice she assumed when she answered me: "Not yet, Christopher. Go home and I'll speak to you later."

Imagine "later."

So it came to pass that my mother went to work at Industrial Photo Products, Inc., at 74 Fifth Avenue. For a hundred and thirty-five dollars a week, gross, she answered phones and did typing and other clerical work from nine to five each day. For free, she came home each night and complained to my father about the day she had just endured. My father would sit in a chair with his drink, and my mother would sit opposite him on the couch with her drink, and she would talk until she was finished about all the ways that the job and the people she worked with were making her miserable. Similar debriefings had taken place after my grandfather got sick and my mother was forced to deal with her family, particularly her mother, on an everyday basis. Then, my father had been solicitous; now, faced with the ritual daily outpouring of complaint about work, he became utterly and un-precedentedly receptive. He spoke only to sympathize or when my mother made rhetorical space for him to prompt her about what happened next. I think he knew that if she had to endure that, he had to endure this. He helped too, of course. Lingering over a second cup of coffee in the mornings, reading the *Times*, he would make little check marks next to stories listed in the paper's "News Summary and Index" that he thought she might like to read.

Often enough, I listened too. To me, the grievances were incomprehensibly obscure, dealing as they did with procedures and protocols that literally had no meaning or import beyond the seedy premises of Industrial Photo Products, Inc. I had trouble understanding how people as paltry and insignificant as my mother made them out to be could have such an effect on her. But for the first time, after years of having seen representations of "work" on TV, in comic books, at the movies, I grasped that these caricatured depictions had an authentic source, a point of origin in these offices where the soul spent its day skulking, seething, stifling protest, faking cheerfulness, finding relief wherever it could. When I eventually experienced it firsthand, it all seemed familiar, somehow: *Not that, this. Not over here, over there. Not now, later. Not later, now. I don't care if I told you to do it that way, now I'm telling you to do it this way. You know perfectly well. If you don't know then you weren't paying attention. Don't ask questions. That goes in a red folder. This goes in a blue folder. Never use the green folders. What do you mean we're out of folders? Who said you could order folders? I said by two o'clock. I said on my desk. I said in my in-box. I said in my black in-box. Take that down. Put that up. Don't wear that. Never. Always. Sometimes. Later. When I say so. What do you mean no?* You *work for me!* Going to work was like dealing with my mother. For my mother it must have been like dealing with her mother. For Dora it must have been like dealing with Doña Ana. And so on, all the way back to some intransigent single-celled creature mitotically reproducing its own pain along with its issue.

On the weekends, she would take the subway up to the Bronx, either to my grandparents' apartment on Marion Avenue or, when my grandfather was hospitalized, all the way to the end of the D line, 205th Street, where she'd get out and walk up to Montefiore. The hospital visit is a specific genre of experience, salubrious and misery-making, conscience-cleaning and guilt-inducing, sickening even as it makes you thank God that you are well. For my mother, these visits that came at the end of a long week were another kind of job, unalleviating because in addition to seeing her beloved father she also was seeing and dealing with Dora, whose diligently faithful attendance at his bedside was mocked by my mother, who claimed that it looked as if she were "trying to win a prize." My grandmother had recently retired from her job working as a Spanish-language interpreter for the State of New York and infuriated my mother by becoming an unpaid volunteer at Montefiore, a job she performed so well that eventually she was offered a paid position.

But this was it. By the time my grandfather came home for the holidays in 1975, cancer ostensibly in remission, the sense that this was to be his last Christmas was so strong that we actually went up to the Bronx twice, once on Christmas Eve and once on Christmas Day, something I'd forgotten until, looking at photos taken at the time, I noticed that everyone in them is captured wearing two different outfits. On what I take to be Christmas Day, the second day of visits, my grandfather didn't bother to change out of his bathrobe and looks gaunt and exhausted. He would soon enter the hospital for—what? The rest of his life? The home stretch? The last time? What cliché captures the contagious, institutional loss of hope that being admitted to a hospital to die consists of? He went to the hospital to wait for oblivion, he went to the place we reserved, in the twentieth century, to keep our homes free of death. Many years later, sitting opposite me at her dining table, my mother would say, "They'll have to carry me out of here feet first." And so they did, although only after she died did it occur to me how much this sentiment may have been influenced by my grandfather's, and then my father's, lingering goodbye to the world of the living amid the stinking, nauseous, blaring, glaring, pain- and fear-ridden environment of a hospital ward in a major U.S. city. As disgusting as the discovery of her corpse, like the neglected and blackened peach at the bottom of the bowl, had been for me, it may have been a gift to herself. I never have figured out why my mother, in the midst of the crisis that killed her, did not press the button activating the medical alert system she had subscribed to for years. I think this may have been why.

He died on July 24, 1976, while I was at Camp Talcott, a YMCA facility in Huguenot, N.Y. He was a gentle man, with a low, soft voice. He was unsure of his English even after fifty years in New York, and spoke it with a heavy accent, considerably heavier than my grandmother's. When I went to see them, I liked to go on walks with him alone, because it was always quiet, but he always found something he wanted to point out to me. He was very tough, and must have lived his entire adult life conscious of the loss of status he had chosen, first in leaving home and then in marrying Dora. When his sisters would visit the mainland, they would intimidate my grandmother and my great-grandmother with their refined speech and sophisticated manners. My mother told me that she was fascinated by them, her aunts, for the same reason that her mother's family found them intimidating, and out of an unmistakable pride in her father for having come from *that* rather than from *this*. My grandfather's background and upbringing proved to her that her dream of Manhattan, of the life poor George Bradt temporarily would provide, had an unimpeachable justification: that she was not one of *these* people, who couldn't possibly belong, but one of the people who could belong, who did belong, who always had.

My mother's letter arrived while I was laid up in the camp infirmary with a bad case of impetigo. It said, in pertinent part:

> I'm afraid I have some bad news for you, which
> I hate to have to tell you. Grandpa died last Sat-
> urday, and was buried yesterday, Tuesday. It was
> a very peaceful and a painless death. He really
> just slipped away, first into a coma, and then very
> quietly into death. I wish I could have given you
> the news face to face. If you want to we'll talk
> about it when you come home. Of course, we
> were all expecting it, and the whole family has
> reacted very calmly. Grandma will be leaving on
> Saturday for a trip to Puerto Rico where she can
> relax and visit with the family.

I read the letter alone in the infirmary, where I was the only pa-tient. It was the first death that had touched me. He had been sick for so long. My mother's reassuring modifiers—*peaceful, painless,* and *quiet*—collided softly with the inescapable reality, death. They were probably there for her sake at least as much as for mine, but I was, in fact, reassured that it was easier for him to be dead than it was for him to go on living. He had been relieved, and the distinction between relief and nonbeing was not yet something I was equipped to consider, so I considered it calmly, as my mother had suggested.

Calm—yet this was when the process of my mother's purging of Dora from our emotional lives began. Later it occurred to me that death could begin an unraveling; that people themselves, their presence, held things together in ways that the memory of them never could. For my mother, my grandfather's death marked the end of everything worthwhile. I doubt that she knew it at the time. She had just turned thirty-nine, probably anticipated the forty-one years she had stretching ahead of her, and probably also figured that something would have to come along to redeem them. "Something always comes along" is one of those bromides that I seem to recall growing up with, fatalism disguised as hope. The idea of something coming along would have been crucial: neither of my parents was good at making things happen. They excelled at making sure that nothing happened. (When they did make things happen—when my father pursued the job at Stanford, for example, in 1982—the consequences were disastrous.) Death, however, invariably qualifies as something that happens, to the living as well as to the dead, to the survivors who keep turning the big change over in their heads: One minute he was talking, now he'll never talk again. One day I took her picture in the garden, a week later she was buried under the same soil that nurtures the flowers. Did I say what I needed to? Did they somehow carry my feelings with them when they went? Does their love for me survive? Is there a penultimate stage when they're a little more alive than they are dead, a little less dead than they are alive? Where does the threshold lie? Where have they gone? Can I communicate with them? They can't really be dead. They aren't really dead.

I don't know how my mother felt about these things. It was not in her nature to wax mystical, not with me anyway. That was the way other people defended themselves against grief, dreaming of the cottony-soft acres of Heaven where the dead went, vindicated but essentially untransformed. My mother came down from the Bronx and went back to work.

Later—but not too much later—I would hear a fuller story of my grandfather's death and funeral than my mother had included in her letter to me at camp. My mother, I would learn, never ran out of things to tell me about her mother. There was always more to tell. I had written down her grievances about my grandmother's behavior immediately after my grandfather's death, but then I deleted the passage. What's the point? There's no point. They're all dead. For our purposes, I am the distillation of the combined efforts of that little family group, their decades of work, of privation, of resentment, recrimination, sadness, jealousy, grief, despair: one middle-aged, middlingly successful writer. That's what all that struggling yielded; I'm the one to tell their story. Aren't these stories always the same anyway? Don't they happen in even the happiest of families? Under the turf, the earth, the tangle of vegetation, the dead serenely untroubled—"past love, praise, indifference, blame"—while all hell breaks loose up above. So the central point of the story of my grandfather's death is that the one person in the world whom my mother loved without reservation, and who loved her without reservation, died at the relatively early age of sixty-nine, leaving her stuck with an extended family she had little use for, and with my father, and with me. And this was not enough.

9

My adolescence arrived, which requires that this narrative skew toward me, at least for a bit. As far as I was concerned, my parents had become a single lumpen entity—hopeless, irrelevant, out of touch, embarrassing—while I became a slave to biology, which urged me, essentially, to reproduce and then do something that would cause my early death, neither of which things were likely to happen hanging around our apartment.

Adolescence began with my grudgingly allowing my mother to take Polaroid photographs of my fourteen-year-old ass in a pair of JCPenney Plain Pockets so that she could "prove" to me that I was not fat and ugly. She was trying, although her assurances couldn't mitigate the fact that I had no self-confidence, was terrified of girls, and hated what I saw in the mirror. But things would move swiftly away from such attempts at boosting my self-esteem. My mother later complained that adolescence was when "something" had "happened to" me. But initially, during the earlier stage of adolescence, I had been merely confronting the boredom that typically arrives when the things that have riveted your attention for years suddenly present themselves as dreary, parochial, immature. Comic books, *Mad* magazine, horror movies, *Star Trek*, baseball, baseball cards, the Beatles, science fiction—a psychobiography of my middle childhood would have to draw endlessly on these elements. Suddenly, I found them completely tedious. A sharper and hipper kid would have immediately started reading Baudelaire, or at least listening to Television, but I started going to a lot of old movies, listening to jazz, dreaming of becoming an abstract expressionist painter, and poring over the photos in my parents' old copies of Fred W. McDarrah's *The Beat Scene* and *The Artist's World in Pictures*. In the latter book, centered on the page opposite the copyright notification, was this:

THIS BOOK
IS DEDICATED
TO THE ARTIST

My heart! These initial gestures toward adulthood, if they were even that, should illustrate exactly how deeply my parents had gotten their hooks into me: that I would attempt to reproduce in my own life a cultural environment that hadn't thrived in New York since before my birth. But my parents had recited all the stories—about the Cedar, about Dillon's, about the San Remo, about Tenth Street, about the Five Spot; stories populated by characters with famous names; stories all about staying out late and getting drunk and having affairs and wiping clean the slate on which the world had been inscribed and rewriting it in a bold jagged hand—recited them many, many times. It was fascinating. Here was history, the history found on the walls of museums, pressed into the grooves of LP records, printed in the pages of books. I needed to believe that my parents had been at the center of everything and I needed badly to believe that my vicarious experience of this centrality bestowed a kind of specialness on me. Sometimes the stories even featured me. The time that a profoundly inappropriate Hubert Selby, Jr., babysat me and my parents came home to discover that I'd learned a profane new vocabulary from him. The time, riding the Fourteenth Street crosstown bus, that Sonny Rollins and I chatted. The time, at a New Year's party thrown at the home of our friends Dan and Jackie Rice, that my parents discovered me deep in conversation with Mark Rothko. "He was quite taken with you," my mother told me years later, recounting the story yet again. "He was listening to you very seriously." I couldn't have been more than five at the time. How not to carry anecdotes like these through life, wearing them like armor against the stupidity of the world? But where to take it, this alleged exceptionalism? Even if it did occur to me that New York City in the late 1970s bore no resemblance, in any respect, to New York City of the late 1950s, and that jazz and abstract expressionism, whatever their virtues, now had little currency, it never occurred to me that I was ignorant of what *did* have currency, or of what the city really was like below its surface. As was, and is, my habit, I thought I could will the world I wanted into being. And as was, and is, my habit, I set out to do it alone, via trial and error.

Here I am at fourteen. I'm wearing a Sweet-Orr corduroy jacket and a pair of OshKosh overalls that I have sedulously spattered with oil paint while taking summer classes at the Art Students League. I have parted my wiry and too-long hair on one side, forced it behind my ears, and treated the resulting knoll with a substance called the Dry Look to hold it in place. I wear thick eyeglasses in heavy black plastic aviator frames, need to shave my upper lip but nothing else, and religiously subject my face each night to the ministrations of something called the Skin Machine, a hand-held, battery-powered, rotating brush that scrubs oily pores to within an inch of their lives but still does a lousy job of preventing the large, sensitive-looking pimples, crested with white peaks filled with pus, that form on my face in constellations of four or five. I am smoking Lucky Strikes, which I have chosen as "my" brand because of the aesthetics of the package, which, as I will be happy to tell you, Stuart Davis chose to paint. I can identify the sidemen on a Thelonious Monk recording and can fairly accurately date, from stylistic evidence, any de Kooning from the 1930s through the 1960s. I am completely absorbed by the psychoanalytic analyses offered by Donald Spoto in *The Art of Alfred Hitchcock*, and accept them as authoritatively final interpretations of his films. Tell me the names of the stars of a movie produced before 1960 and I can probably tell you which studio is likely to have made it. My plans this weekend are to head—alone—to the Regency, or the New Yorker, or the Thalia, or the Carnegie Hall Cinema, or the Bleecker Street Cinema, or the Cinema Village, where I will see a double feature consisting of *Psycho* and *Repulsion*, or *Wild Strawberries* and *Tokyo Story*, or *I'm All Right Jack* and *The Man in the White Suit*, or *Les Diaboliques* and *Elevator to the Gallows*, or *The Lady from Shanghai* and

The Third Man. When I return home I'll relax with James M. Cain or Dashiell Hammett, or I'll watch Ernie Kovacs or Monty Python on Channel 13.

As far as trial and error goes, I count at least seven errors here. I was in some respects an impressive kid, in others, tiresome. I didn't intend to be eccentric. A few years later, I met a kid who wore nothing but vintage clothing from before 1940, and banned from his room all furnishings and decorations that had been made after then. Even his paperbacks and records were exiled to the hallway outside. That was affected eccentricity, with a controlled and disciplined design to it. Mine was chaos springing from my head, a bunch of ideas that I couldn't reconcile.

I was acquiring a lot of semi-arcane knowledge that often has proven very useful as I've grown older. What I wasn't getting was what everyone at that age desires: experience. Yet my mother, who might have known this from her own adolescence, didn't think it at all odd that I returned home immediately after school every afternoon, that the phone never rang for me, that I spent Friday and Saturday nights in my room. I was an excellent student of my parents' youth, but I must have seemed indifferent to my own.

My attitude preserved the peace, though. I was interested in my parents and, reciprocally, interesting to them. Both of them had ideas about me, for me. Their dream was that I would become a painter, because I'd shown a talent for drawing and an interest in art. (For decades, two promising but unformed oil wash sketches I'd done at fifteen—a still life of apples and a quick study of Vermeer's *Girl with the Red Hat*—hung framed on my parents' walls. That was as close to sentimentality as my parents ever got in their decor.) They were pleased when I was admitted to the High School of Music and Art in 1977, although the first year or so that I spent there, trying to make my "ideas" about art survive the translation into the sanctioned product of what was at the time a stodgy and uninspired fine arts program, is forgettable. Apart from the two pictures my parents put on the wall, none of the work I did then survives. There were kids there so much more talented than I was that I was embarrassed by my efforts. Lucky Strikes and paint-splattered overalls didn't help. I could feel myself drifting without even having the language to relate to myself what was happening. I began cutting school—alone, at first, and not that frequently, at first. I did it just to cut, to get away. I went to the movies. I went to the Museum of Modern Art. I walked around midtown, around Times Square, places I knew I wouldn't run into any adult I knew. One bitter cold day I found myself at the duck pond in lower Central Park. It was deserted and, without noticing that I was leaving the shoreline far behind me, I walked out onto the ice. As I drew nearer to the fieldstone bridge that crosses the pond, I realized that I was no longer on solid ground. I had no idea how thick the ice was; had no way to tell. But instead of turning around and going back the way I'd come I slowed but continued to edge forward, step by step. I wanted to see how far I could get before—what? Even I knew that plunging into freezing cold water in the middle of winter with no one in sight was likely to end badly. But I edged forward until I was under the bridge—which I then decided had been my objective all along—and only then moved to shore. This is who I was: a kid who, with eyes open, kept moving toward catastrophe until it either happened or, by some chance, didn't.

When I finally lost interest in my parents, at around sixteen, they took it as a betrayal. Both of them were sophisticated enough to be aware that adolescence was supposed to entail a vehement repudiation not only of childhood but of their way of being, but my mother rejected that. She seemed to think that the example she'd set was supposed to have preempted the hard wiring of teenage disorder. Is it possible that she believed she'd perfected motherhood? I can imagine her comparing her own upbringing to mine, and finding me ungrateful. Undoubtedly I behaved both ungratefully and in ways that inevitably seemed ungrateful. I lost interest in them, and, frustratingly for everyone concerned, often I had very little idea what did interest me. What I wanted, what I imagined for myself, what I thought was necessary to achieve it—my ideas along these lines were unremarkably vague and unrealistic. What was atypical, I think, was my parents' strategy of coping with my adolescence, which was either to fight me tooth and nail or to allow me to do exactly as I wanted.

In 1979, my father was appointed to a visiting professorship at the University of Scranton that paid the enormous sum of $45,000 for the year, more than quadrupling our household income. As strokes of luck go, it was huge. My father's career was in the ascent, then. Soon he would publish *Mulligan Stew*, still his best-known novel, and for a brief period he would enjoy a reputation as a significant writer, a reputation that ultimately would seal my parents' fate by inducing Stanford University to hire him as a tenured full professor.

The Scranton job permitted my mother to quit work. I imagine that her release from the obligation to hold a job revealed to her exactly how regressive her life had become. Their previous fixed roles must have begun to seem inevitable to my parents, given the financial urgency that had determined them: my mother went out to work in the mornings, and my father sat screwed to his chair at his desk, and one or two evenings a week went to teach his "dummies," as he referred to his students at the New School, where he taught in the continuing education program. His books were coming fast—after finishing *Mulligan Stew* in 1975, he immediately wrote *Crystal Vision*, translated the poems of Sulpicia, wrote the poetry collections *White Sail* and *The Orangery*, and then began writing *Aberration of Starlight* (at one point the three novels were circulating simultaneously, unsuccessfully seeking publishers). The books began to appear in the steady outpouring—1977, 1978, 1979, 1980, 1981—that wouldn't begin to let up until 1991. My mother, of course, had lupus to fall back on: work granted you the weekend, but lupus took it all back. The writer in *furore scribendi* and the woman taken to her bed—paired romances to explain the state of things, if I had questions, which I'm not sure as an adolescent I did.

She was about forty-one, had carried the household on her back for five years, and now, owing to his sudden prestige, my father had catapulted back into the position of family breadwinner without so much as a thank-you. His struggles, about which I eventually would begin to hear, and still continue to hear, from well-meaning others, would become mythically restricted

to his own efforts, his own neglect, his own courage, while my
mother—well, what about her courageous, effortful struggle? So
my father was not spoken of in the same terms as many of his
contemporaries—what about my mother's neglect? There she
was, after years of schlepping to the office, free at last—to vacuum, clean the bathroom, wash the dishes, do the laundry, cook
the supper.

I have no idea if she knew what she wanted, or if she knew
how to articulate it, beyond the fact that she wanted *something
else*, but she had us, and when she looked around at the rest of
the world she saw only what was contemptible about it. She'd
had no friends of her own for years; now whatever respite work
had granted her from the household was gone, as were the people she'd eventually become friendly with there. And friends my
parents shared began to fall away. This one married the wrong
person, that one said the wrong thing, the other one drank too
much, or was too neurotic, or too catty. The Westbeth syndrome
expanded, engulfed everything; people became unbearable. My
mother could smell their flaws the way a shark smells a drop of
blood in the ocean. Sometimes she was funny—she would pick
up on a physical defect, or a speech impediment, or some uncon-
scious tic, and mercilessly lampoon it, sending me into hyster-
ics. Other times she just seemed gratuitously judgmental, and
tenaciously so: even the few people who got a chance to make
a second impression rarely were able to reverse the judgment
she'd made based upon the first. An old family friend brought
a date to dinner at our house one night and my mother didn't
stop putting her down for thirty years. "That awful woman." Her
resentment grew. She became convinced, with some justification,

that people's interest or lack of interest in her derived from their interest in my father. She began to complain to him when people called, claiming that they were rude to her when she answered the phone, asking for him without acknowledging her. "Who doesn't say hello?" she would demand. She was right, of course, but what she wanted from my father was that he confront them about their rudeness. I once overheard him awkwardly and apologetically attempting just that with one caller. A sour atmosphere of indiscriminately spread blame saturated the house for the rest of the afternoon.

"She was a bitch," Gwen, one of the aging dowager duchesses of Westbeth, flatly informed me years later. I encountered her at a friend's father's loft on Allen Street in the early '90s. We were sitting on paint-spattered folding chairs in the living area of the big raw space and the small gathering suddenly got very quiet: I wasn't the only one startled by her own bitchiness, the virulence she'd pickled for the decade or more since she'd last dealt with my mother. I didn't press for details; never found out if my mother had in some way actively offended her or, more likely, remained unmistakably standoffish. Gwen almost certainly met my mother's criteria for the kind of person who did it all wrong.

Other people did things wrong: this lesson was inflicted early. It is still my reflexive sense of others, fought against constantly. The problems with such an attitude should be obvious. For one thing, it is the most primitive of social inaccuracies. It knows no bounds, for another. If you become obnoxiously self-righteous about the way that you wash a dish or the ingredients that belong in a salad, then other people soon become nothing more than the agglomeration of their various failings. Habits, decor, conversation, diet, spiritual beliefs, tastes, politics, dress, speech, cleanliness, child-rearing practices—each becomes an equal basis for forming a titanically dismissive judgment. My mother never shrank from such judgments; she lived within them as she might have within a fortress. As she approached the end of her life and we finally managed to come as close to becoming close as we would, I understood how deeply disappointed she had been in her own life, but what I never was able to understand was how she couldn't see that it was her obstinacy that had left her without resources or support, or why she found it impossible to make the slightest adjustment to alleviate her disappointment. The woman who at thirty-five perceived an inhuman mechanism operating beneath the surface appearance of our neighbors had, by middle age, pretty much determined never to catch such a glimpse again.

As she began to grow more isolated, my mother's perception of other people's hidden depths began to be tested only accidentally, by the happenstance of having to deal with them. There was, for example, Roger, the butcher, unhappily yoked to the shop his father had opened, whose modest dream was to go to work for a wholesale butcher, earn a good wage and work regular hours; there was Ira, the pharmacist, secretly gay, another storekeeper's reluctantly dutiful son unhappy with his life's path; there was Roy, who'd become a checkout clerk at D'Agostino's after developing ulcers working as a master bookbinder; there was Max, Westbeth's superintendent, endlessly snubbed and disdained by the other residents, always searching for a better job at a "real" apartment building (significantly, Max was one of the few Puerto Ricans outside the family with whom my mother was willing to converse in Spanish). At best I had a nodding acquaintance with any of these people; that I can remember these forty-year-old details says a lot about how far my mother got her nose into these strangers' lives. After a time, these were the only sort of people my mother really knew anything about. They became her truest, and only, friends, and throughout my adult life my mother regaled me with stories of the personal travails and triumphs of the various tradesmen, haircutters, dental hygienists, receptionists, deliverymen, and others with whom she regularly came into contact. Until just before she died she kept me up to date on the doings of the doormen and porters in her building. That was what she could handle: people whose lives were legible to her because she'd filled in most of the blanks using her imagination, working with the barest materials, wallet-sized snaps and stray anecdotes; people who asked little of her, who judged her using the simplest formula: she was nice to them. On the night that I discovered her body, I remember thinking, as I sat there chatting with them while we awaited the arrival of the police, how much my mother would have liked the two EMTs who had been dispatched to her apartment.

By the time my father was commuting back and forth between Scranton and New York, scheduling his classes so that he could spend the fewest possible number of days away from home, I'd dropped any pretense of wanting to be a painter. After three years of keeping to myself, I'd decided all at once not only that I didn't want to spend any more time in my own company, but that it was time to discard the strange pastiche I'd been attempting to live by. To adopt another one, yes, but one that made sense in the context within which I lived. What I wanted was to announce myself to the world, and was searching for the impenetrable disguise in which I could do that. I had started to learn to play the guitar, although it wasn't music, per se, that interested me any more than it had been workboots, per se, that I'd wanted to wear in fourth grade. What interested me was the fact that the people I'd begun to meet were interested in punk and new wave: in going to hear it played live, in dressing and behaving like the people who made it, in making it themselves. I was doing what I'd done since moving to Westbeth: escaping in reverse, tunneling from outside to inside, learning to be someone else. My mother, who must have recognized this process, distilled it into a motto that essentially blamed the guitar, investing it with magical, bewitching properties; she would remind me whenever it seemed appropriate to her: "You're no musician, Chris." This was the beginning of something new: this was not my mother's strategic effort to *shape* me into something recognizable to her and my father; this was not my mother's tactical effort to *correct* me when what I did interfered with her sense of order and equilibrium. I was already unrecognizable and uncorrectable; I had gone the wrong way; *something* had *happened* to me. Her assertion was an open acknowledgment that the philosophy she applied to everyone else—that what she did not accept as a legitimate pursuit was in fact completely worthless—now applied to me as well. It was only common sense, and if I couldn't see that, she could. "Let's be honest," she'd say, as if one of us had been lying, "you're no musician." Maybe if I'd thought of her spinet and sheet music, auctioned away after poor George Bradt neglected to pay the bill to store them, I would have burned less with resentment when she said it. But burn I did, and the first thing consumed was my capacity for sympathy toward her. My response was as blunt as a punch in the gut: "What are you? You're nothing."

My father's time in Scranton, minimized as it was, still left me and my mother alone together for three days each week. What did we talk about, I wonder. Remembering this period raises only the ghost of the apprehension I felt whenever my father headed for the Port Authority carrying his overnight bag. The emotional memory I have is one of tension and ingrained resentment, although it's difficult to say who was more resentful toward whom. I have little sense of what I was like to deal with, although at the time I was seeing a therapist each week, and the one aspect of his therapy I can recall was his regularly chiding me for the tone of voice I apparently habitually used—hostile, suspicious, mocking. My mother now spent much of the day in her bedroom—it was my father's bedroom too, but I always thought of it as hers. My parents had hired someone to come in to build a Sheetrock wall and frame a door, and my mother's bedroom became her primary retreat. She took her coffee there in the afternoons, often took her drink there in the evenings. She played solitaire, she read books and magazines, she listened to the radio. She smoked endlessly, cigarette after cigarette—I can still remember the distinctive sound of her lighting a cigarette: first a spasm of coughing, then the musical click of her Zippo. Tareytons, for a long time, then Gauloises now that my parents could afford them again. Fat, unfiltered, dirty-tasting cigarettes that I could barely finish whenever I stole one from her. This was, although I doubt that either of us knew it, to be the rest of her married life. When I think of my mother, I often see her sitting on her bed in the middle of the afternoon, a hand of solitaire spread out before her. The bed could be in New York, it could be in California. Solitaire and housework. Paperback mysteries and Dickens. *Ladies' Home Journal, Cosmopolitan, The New York Times Magazine.* Crossword puzzles. In New York I remember the twilight behind the river; the sky darkening until you could see the tiny pinpoint of light emanating from the torch of the Statue of Liberty. In California the dimming of the room under the condominium eaves; the shadows creeping down from the high "cathedral" ceiling. She would come downstairs to get her scotch at six and go right back up. For a long period she would take her coffee upstairs with her after supper. My father would sit downstairs in his study and read into the night. Confronted by her closed bedroom door when I needed to speak with her, I would sometimes freeze. There never wasn't a sense that I was interrupting a deep and melancholy solitude. This is unfair: Sometimes she was in a perfectly good mood, or a neutral mood. Sometimes she was busy with a project of some kind. But my expectations always were otherwise. I would knock on the door with pure timidity. Which reminds me of course of the last time I knocked on her door, on the evening of June 15, 2017, when I banged on it with my fist, loudly calling for her while my feet slipped on two weeks' worth of the *Times* encased in plastic bags.

My father went away to earn money and my mother and I suffered each other's presence. I spent most of my time in my own room, to be honest; two people behind closed doors at opposite ends of a large and otherwise unoccupied apartment. Meanwhile, I worked on the people I wanted to be with, who seemed to offer entrée to the things I wanted—other people, nightclubs, bars, parties, bands, girls, the vast range of the city, a life that seemed like it could be mine. I pushed and pushed, doggedly showed up, hung around until people told me to go away, showed up again, stubbornly repeated the routine until I was an accepted part of the scene, a leopard in the temple; the whole process a familiar one I would carry through my life from childhood: from making friends when I moved to Westbeth, to the overtures I made to people when I moved to California in my early twenties, to trying to break into the literary world at the end of the twentieth century, always—*always*—accompanied by the suspicion that I was operating under false pretenses, that I was merely imitating behavior that seemed attractive, that I did not belong, and, ultimately, that I did not really want to belong. Was this, I wonder, something I shared with my mother? A deep sense of unbelonging, of impostorhood? And in her case, from what did it arise?

I refuse to impose Tragic Mulatta status on my mother, not only because of its dubiousness (narrative and otherwise) but also because operating in my mother were certain elements of character and chemistry that I believe were specific to her. She was a difficult person, and she was a depressed person, and she would have been a difficult person had she not been depressed, and I believe she would have been a depressed person had she not been difficult. These two principal facets of her personality conspired to defeat her; she didn't have the emotional wherewithal to seek help for her depression and her arrogant lack of self-awareness blinded her to the reality that it was her own aloofness, and not the deficiencies of others, that had isolated her. She had the

unfortunate luck to pair with a man who either could not or
would not act to intervene as she gradually withdrew from life.

But still, can I really buy the idea of my mother as an otherwise assimilated white woman? Not only had she been labeled
BLACK from birth, and not only was she made aware early on
that her family viewed that as a taint, but how would she have
been encouraged to view herself by the world that had no idea
what was stipulated on her birth certificate? America may have
been titillated by the trope of the Latin Lover and doted on the
suave silliness of Ricky Ricardo, but *Puerto Rican* was a syn-
onym for urban lowlife from Day One. The lessons, obvious, are
American commonplaces: Don't talk like that. Don't call yourself that. Don't wear that. Don't eat that. Don't listen to that.
Don't live there. Don't date that. Accumulate enough of those,
keep your eye on the green light, and ultimately you may be
persuaded to tell yourself: I am *not* that. But you always are, I
think. There's a constant pressure that exerts itself at the low-
est of levels, a reminder, an underscoring of difference, a happy
willingness on the part of others to put their offhand prejudice
on display for you, a daft confusion that takes hold of you when
the "friend" who dresses and talks just like you, who lives in the
same neighborhood and shares the same frame of reference, asks
"What are you, anyway?"—and then, having received his answer,
says it for you: "No you're not." Not this and not that either—
an acute sense of this dilemma is surely a contributing factor to
my mother's self-conception, is what I'm saying. My mother ran
from every implication that might attach to being a Puerto Rican
girl from the South Bronx. Arriving in Manhattan, surrounded
by other people who similarly had made a break for it, she must

have felt that none of it would ever have to matter; may even have felt as if questions of "passing" or social climbing were irrelevant, since she wasn't seeking a bourgeois foothold on life, but an enlightened one. Westbeth was the first deep shock, and when she arrived eventually in Palo Alto, where matters of status not only were of paramount importance but came wrapped in the dubious prestige of newly made money, she must have folded.

I proceeded, sometimes beyond my parents' view, sometimes not. Bit by bit I was eliminating the Plain Pockets, the Adidas, the flannel shirts, the down jackets from my wardrobe, replacing them with black Levi's, All-Stars, ankle boots with elastic gussets, V-neck sweaters, club-collar shirts, and worn suit jackets or tweed overcoats that I scavenged from thrift shops and Canal Jeans. Chris Standora, a friend since seventh grade who one day had presented himself in public dressed in a motorcycle jacket, dog collar, shredded T-shirt, and engineer boots, recommended a visit to a salon on the corner of Sixth Avenue and West Tenth, where for the first time in my life a woman not my mother laid her hands on me, leaned me back in a chair, combed and washed my hair, and then cut it, following as best she could the directions I gave her. It was an odd, spiky cut with bangs which, combined with my hair's natural tendency to curl once it grew beyond an inch in length, provided me a more or less permanently uncombed-looking helmet.

My big social break came when school was canceled during the transit strike of 1980. I had a friend named Patrick Adams whose mother and stepfather had coincidentally gone abroad, leaving Pat's older sister Adrienne in charge of things at their recently purchased house on Bleecker Street. Adrienne was nineteen, which meant basically a round-the-clock open house. For the nearly two weeks that the transit system was shut down, I was able to spend my days and evenings there, getting in serious time with people who would become some of my closest friends. Pat's house at first filled with people who'd grown up in the Village and attended school there before dispersing to go to high school. Soon we were all bringing friends around from whatever schools we went to—Music and Art, Stuyvesant, Bronx Science, Art and Design, Performing Arts.

I lied a lot about things I'd done and places I'd been, feeling at sixteen the arriviste's urgent doomed need to pretend always to have been there, where it mattered; to be expertly aware. The last remnants of my late-'50s bohemian bricolage were purged. That was not me. That had never been me. I was always who I was now. One look at me in one of my homespun new wave outfits—some CPA's suit jacket from 1965, musty and greenish with age, a Black Watch tartan shirt buttoned up to the neck, a Casio watch, my hair that made me look like one of the Sir Douglas Quintet with a perm—and the game must have been up. A slightly older boy, a stranger, similarly but more expertly accoutred, once leaned toward me as we passed each other on the sidewalk and shouted in my face: "Poser!" He wasn't wrong, but what was he? We were all trying things on. Some people managed to get through without changing a thing about their appearance or dress, others remade themselves entirely. Very few people were committed to the ideological exclusiveness of punk politics and aesthetics. It wouldn't have been fun, and fun was the idea. Music was the core and the focus. Those who sought such a commitment soon peeled off and formed their own groups, threw their own parties, went to their own shows. You'd see them sometimes, sitting on a stoop on St. Marks, or on the sidewalk outside Cooper Union, grim and somehow self-impoverished. The rest of us listened to, and tried to play, British and American punk, post-punk, and new wave, '60s pop and soul, ska, reggae, disco, funk, and, finally, hip-hop, which had made its way into our awareness early, thanks in part to Music and Art's location in the center of Harlem and the semi-successful integration of its student body.

1980 happened. I made friends. My father wrapped up his year at Scranton and settled down to finish *Blue Pastoral*, a long and complicated novel whose composition apparently was barely interrupted by his weekly trips to Pennsylvania, he was on such a roll. My mother sat on her bed. Or so the tableau appears in my memory: I wasn't really paying attention. Home would snap sharply into focus on two types of occasion: when one or both of my parents was on me about something, which had begun to happen frequently, or when they were on each other, which also had begun to happen frequently. In the case of what was irritating them about me, I'll get to that presently. In the case of what was irritating them about each other, all I can think is that, once again, my mother had been thoroughly disappointed by my father. He was unchanged. He got up at eight, shaved, dressed, put on water for coffee, went to get the paper, returned, made breakfast for himself, and read the paper. He sat at his desk at ten. He rose from it at one p.m. "How about a little lunch, babe?" He did the daily crossword, muttering "Fuck you, Maleska" (directed at the *Times* crossword editor Eugene T. Maleska) as he dispatched it in a matter of minutes, working in pen. He went back to his desk, rising from it, whistling, in the early evening to make drinks. Repeat ad nauseam. His equilibrium fortified, his finances stabilized, his career an actual thing, he seemed to me to be completely content.

But my mother's disappointment was keyed to expectations that couldn't really have had her fulfillment as their predicted outcome. Disappointment itself had to have been the predicted outcome. She must have known after nearly twenty years that my father was a virtual automaton, that he had nothing inside of himself to spare for spontaneity, for accommodation of the unexpected, in his life. It all went into the work. Did he make her promises? OK, so he made her promises: so what? Who did she think he might spontaneously become? A non-artist? An artist who could put the work aside indefinitely (or even for a definite term) without beginning to shudder like a car that decelerates in high gear? And to do what? Take her someplace? Learn ballroom dancing? Take up contract bridge? If I seem unfairly to be taking my father's side here, it's not quite the case. It's more accurate to say that I recognize in my mother the signs of an unwillingness, within a relationship, to insist upon one's own fulfillment. There are all sorts of ways that people work out their incompatibilities successfully and without constant conflict, but this requires conversation and actions that do more than support the false ideal of marriage as a united front, closed against outsiders and outside influences, reinforced by the notion that deviation from the party line is a form of betrayal. Within such a structure, my parents were destined to wither, their emotional fate determined by the passive-aggression of one and the paralysis of the other.

My father did precisely as he liked while pretending to be agreeable to anything my mother wanted, while she grew increasingly incensed as she waited in vain for him to come around, unable to act on her own; unable, finally, even to speak. It was often blindingly clear what she wanted, but did she ever say? Unfathomable mind, now beacon, now sea. I don't recall a single conversation when I was growing up in which my mother expressed her yearnings, even idle yearnings, like, "I'd like to visit Paris one day." No, that wasn't what you did. That wasn't doing it right. If life handed you lemons, you drank lemon juice and felt superior to people who didn't know how to cut a lemon in half. It was the curse of the working class, taking shape seemingly out of nowhere in the midst of this pleasant apartment in Greenwich Village, filled with books and records, paintings on the walls; taking shape out of nothing but some shared idea, maybe the only idea they really shared, about the boundaries they imagined they had to live within, as if my father were a laborer and my mother had been born chained to the stove and the vacuum cleaner, as if that world beyond their door that *tried things*, that *went places*, that just said fuck it every once in a while and left the dirty dishes in the sink overnight, was something to be regarded with deep, reactionary suspicion. It was a house built on rituals, and even if serving those rituals made them both miserable, relaxing or changing the rules threw them both into a panic. Of course, the principal rule that couldn't be broken was the one prohibiting divorce. I don't know what rationale my parents used, individually or together, to justify continuing to be married. Love is not enough. I have no doubt that they loved each other, but since love is only quantifiable as itself—as randomly determined by whoever happens to identify their feelings with it—and not as a predictor of compatibility or happiness, of empathy or compromise, of understanding or even of agreement on what, exactly, has transpired between two people, it is not enough. It is mistaking the crucifix you're nailed to for a support.

Their outlet, then, was the argument, and it served them in the way that I suppose sex probably serves some other couples. Their arguments were monstrous improvisations, arising from misplaced items, overcooked food, untended chores, forgotten errands, spilled drinks, tossed-out leftovers, inadvertent discourtesies. My mother initiated them, all of them. It was her way, I think, of saying to my father, "Let's talk." It wasn't as if they never talked otherwise, but "otherwise" was simply my father turning on the tap and letting loose. He talked and talked. The days of my mother filling the air with her daily dispatches from the workplace were long over now; my father had reasserted his position as primary constructor of reality. Did he realize that he was living with someone who was slowly going crazy? My mother's grievances, or rather the extravagant way she expressed and apparently experienced them, were certainly unhinged. The secret message encoded at their heart never changed, though: I am dying, and you are killing me. My father's response was almost invariably "reasonable"—grindingly, infuriatingly, condescendingly patient, my father would humor my mother, adeptly responding, making the slightest regretful hints that, perhaps, possibly, my mother was mistaken? That maybe she could be misremembering? This would drive my mother into a blind rage, which was the point at which I would become very quiet and still—it wouldn't take much to encourage my mother to draw me into the argument, identify me as part of the conspiracy to torture her by forgetting to take the lamb chops out of the freezer or leaving the avocado on the windowsill to ripen for one day too long—and at which my father could now begin, with his enormous verbal dexterity, to play with her, to get in tiny jabs that passed and vanished before they fully registered, to allude to other instances in which my mother—possibly, possibly—had been *similarly* mistaken, and in which he had, despite every provocation she unreasonably threw his way, remained calm, civil, understanding, cooperative. It was really quite a performance on his part: brilliant, probably cruel, but also restrained and very self-aware. Every now and then, perhaps once a year, my mother would succeed in what I imagine was her goal of making my father lose his temper, *react*, and that was when the house shook. They could square off then for hours. I remember them pausing when they ran out of cigarettes so that my father could run to the store for more and then resuming the argument where they'd left off.

In the midst of all this, two important things happened: first, I fell wildly in love with G, and then, as I entered my senior year of high school, I made the ridiculous decision to stop attending classes.

My parents laid out their objections to G immediately: She was too quiet, as in *secretive* or *concealing*. She was rude. She was unattractive. She was unintelligent. My father dubbed her "Miss America" for what he deemed to be her cloddish embodiment of native tactlessness and crude taste, and my mother likened her movements through our apartment to those of a mouse scurrying along the wall. Not entirely inaccurately, they linked my truancy to my relationship with her, blaming her completely. Their ad hominem vehemence was confusing to me. Everything was going great, and now I had a girlfriend. I think it confused them, too, but they gave in to it completely, reflexively. The threat she posed must have been considerable; my mother, in particular, laid into me about her. Both my parents were no doubt conscious of the intoxicating allure an apparently unlimited supply of sex must have had to a seventeen-year-old boy. Of course: of all the things that I was discovering they couldn't provide, this was definitive. But it was stupid of them: the frontal assault had only the predictable effect of stiffening my resistance. I would have married her if I could.

Decades later, G and I reestablished contact and I made the mistake of mentioning it to my mother. By then, G was a middle-aged teacher at a prestigious private school, married for years and living in Westchester with her husband, but my mother spoke of her as if she was still the sixteen-year-old siren who had lured a fool to his destruction. I sat across the dining table from her and listened in frank amazement as she spoke earnestly of G's alleged shortcomings and my own susceptibility to her phony charms as if thirty years had suddenly disappeared. What meaning can life hold apart from that of your biggest failures?, my mother seemed to say; why move on? And I thought: When I went out with G, I decorated my room with pictures of musicians cut out of magazines. When I went out with her I needed to shave only once a week. When I went out with her I didn't know how to drive. When I went out with her I'd never written a check or charged something to a credit card. When I went out with her I'd never been to Europe, or to California, or to a shopping mall. When

I went out with her I'd never scrubbed a toilet or chopped an onion or ironed a shirt or shined a pair of shoes. When I went out with her I claimed in dead earnest that I hoped to die at forty. When I went out with her I'd never worried over a bill that I knew I couldn't pay. When I went out with her I'd never eaten sushi. When I went out with her I'd never seen a desert, or one of the Great Lakes. When I went out with her I'd never had an STD. When I went out with her I'd never been stopped by the police. When I went out with her I'd never assembled a piece of furniture, or unloaded a truck, or taped Sheetrock, or painted a wall. When I went out with her I'd never had a glass of good scotch. When I went out with her I'd never fired a gun or ridden a bus across the country. When I went out with her I'd never changed a diaper. When I went out with her I'd never spent the night in a hotel. When I went out with her I'd never read Hawthorne, Melville, James, Faulkner. And when I gaze, with perverse satisfaction, on this very incomplete list detailing my lack of worldliness ca. 1980, I think that to try crawling back inside that ignorant little head to revisit, however temporarily and incompletely, the parochial and insecure teenage mind feeding upon its claustrophobic, arrogant outlook, is to forgive myself nearly everything; and I think that falling in love with G was hardly a transgression—it was, in fact, one of the few things I did to move myself forward. And maybe this is why my mother, in particular—my father's disgust, predictably, was aesthetic—objected so strenuously, continued to object even after these events were years behind me. You hear family myths, sometimes, about things, big things, little things, that changed everything, pivot points in the grand plot of life. They're shorthand, they're an excuse for being stuck, they're the residue of some long-ago reached consensus, they're the *explanation*. For my mother, I think G was the *something that happened to me*. I met a girl and fell in love with her, with her body, with her eyes, with her smell, with sheets of a different weave in a brand-new bed. Sooner or later this sort of thing was going to lead to an entirely different life than the one my mother, with her daily timetable of my bowel movements taped to the closet door, had carefully groomed me for. I might pick up all sorts of ideas out there in the wider world standing beside people, especially another woman, of my own choosing. I might take a shit whenever I felt like it.

I made a point of cutting class now. I began to have drunken mishaps that landed me in the emergency room, where I'd call my parents, waking them in the middle of the night to alert them that I needed to have broken bones set or my chin stitched up. Cut slips would arrive in the mail. Teachers and administrators called home. I managed to get suspended twice during my senior year, once for drinking beer in the alley that ran between Music and Art and the City College campus and again for hanging out with my friend Missy in the girls' bathroom. These were called warning signs. Mr. Cooney, the dean of discipline, would ask my mother what she was going to do to get me back on the straight and narrow. "What do you want from me?" she'd say. "He's bigger than I am." Mr. Cooney tried to schedule a meeting with my parents but my father refused to take a morning off work to travel up to Harlem. My mother refused for her own reasons—the above-mentioned pointlessness of attempting to right me, and perhaps spite: let me fall on my ass and see for myself what happened. In any case, neither of my parents did much except half-heartedly point out that what I was doing wasn't such a great idea. I went out every night, stayed out. Neither I nor my friends had the slightest interest in attending college. Manhattan belonged to us. What could you possibly do at college that we weren't already doing? We'd met the hopeless rubes who went to NYU. They knew nothing, came from places where they hung out at the 7-Eleven and where the bars—if they could even get inside—closed at two a.m. Even the bridge-and-tunnel kids were hipper. And what could we learn, since we already knew everything worth knowing? Yet it soon became obvious even to me that each of my friends, exerting minimal effort, was going to graduate.

Although my mother couldn't get me to go to school, she could get me out of her face, and she began throwing me out. One of us would pick a fight—our preferred time was late at night— and my mother would tell me to capitulate or leave. We were both seething; I often felt very close to violence in general, and my mother, who would never back down, knew exactly what to say to me to escalate things. Escalation was part of our dance; it was easy to get from me the indignant rage my father only rarely granted her. I would leave, stuffing underwear and a toothbrush in my backpack and strolling out into the city. If it was too late to call someone I would simply walk around. The first couple of hours felt weightless, free, and then I would recall just how long a night could be. If I had some money I might go to a coffee shop. If I didn't I might ride the A train or the D train to the end of the line and back. One time G's mother called my mother to tell her that I was safe and sound at their house. "You didn't have to bother," she reportedly said. "I knew he would be just fine." This happened several times; usually after three or four days I would call and beg to be allowed to come home. It always turned out that, like Dorothy in Oz, the power to return had always been mine, I just had to offer up the right incantation.

I dropped out. I dropped back in. G and I broke up, a protracted event. It was 1981, fall, and I was repeating my senior year. And one day my father got a call.

10

Years later, as we sat opposite each other at her dining table, my mother sometimes enjoyed recounting for me the various opportunities my father had blown or squandered over time: the book column in the glossy magazine that he'd been offered but had turned down; the proposal from the president of Brooklyn College to award him an honorary doctorate that was withdrawn after my father, who had left the school about twenty credits shy of his degree, somewhat petulantly suggested that he should be awarded his BA instead; the spurned opportunity to buy a Soho loft at a bargain price; the invitations to conferences and meetings in interesting places that he declined; the friendly overtures from far more successful writers that he politely rebuffed; and so on. My father's being appointed to a full professorship at Stanford University was the one time when he played his hand shrewdly and successfully—and it was a disaster. I'm tempted to look at it as an ironic cosmic rebuke to his typically disdainful neglect of the material and social side of his career. It was an incredible windfall of prestigious luck that could not rationally be refused, yet it happened to precisely the wrong person, and it marked the absolute end of my parents' functioning as socially normal human beings. Creatures of habit who never traveled, my parents were permanently disoriented by the move, which they approached with the same sense of irrevocable removal that nineteenth-century immigrants might have felt traveling in steerage from the old world to the new. But there was no question of their integrating themselves into the rhythms of life in a new place surrounded by new people. They were there to do time. For the duration of their stay in California they lived aloof and apart from their neighbors, from my father's colleagues, from the community, and from the region as a whole. From the moment they arrived until the moment they left twenty years later, they expressed their yearning for New York, yet they would rarely take advantage of my father's academic schedule and their new relative affluence to go back, returning only once or twice for brief visits. The luminous vision of New York, awaiting them at the conclusion of their long sentence, might have wavered and disappeared if they'd allowed themselves to be less miserable.

How did they end up in California? The story of the pettiness and academic infighting surrounding the hire, while worth recounting, is for another time. Here, what I'll say is that things moved quickly. My father was interviewed by Stanford at the MLA meeting in New York late in December 1981. Within a couple of months my parents had been flown out to California for the usual grueling array of tasks, meetings, and events that an on-campus interview comprises. I don't think that either of my parents had been aboard an airplane in years, but somehow the possibility, the opportunity, that had begun to take shape in their minds must have filled them with an extraordinary spirit of adventure. What the job meant to them is obvious: steady income, the chance to put away money, excellent health care for my mother, a predictable schedule larded with plenty of free time for my father. It's obvious now, anyway. The Stanford appointment delivered on all of these promises, delivered my parents from the most grinding kind of uncertainty, and for years I resented them for taking advantage of it. Only midway upon the journey of my life, with none of those promises in hand, did I really understand exactly how impossible it would have been to refuse Stanford's offer. What I've never understood is why they treated it like a prison term.

My parents returned from their California audition optimistic (I'd refused to go). From my point of view, they were facing what was starting to look like their future with infuriating equanimity. I knew it was my future, too. Three years devoted to hanging out had bought me a second crack at twelfth grade, which I was repeating as lackadaisically as possible at the alternative school to which I'd transferred after earning an overall 07 average (a passing average was 65) at the High School of Music and Art for the term ending January 1981, with forty-two absences. Even if one had been willing to admit me, I still had no interest in college. I had no work experience; I had no work ethic. Realistically there was nowhere to go but with them. They were sensitive enough to my feelings to warn me of the evident likelihood of the move. It was definitely a warning.

My mother bought a copy of a Sunset Books guide to Northern California. I flipped the pages, stared at the pictures. Big Sur. Lombard Street. The Golden Gate Bridge. The Marin

Headlands. Sausalito. Sproul Plaza. The Stanford Memorial Church, its facade gaudy against the sandstone of the quad, brown foothills climbing the horizon to a sky so blue it looked burnt.

My mother revised the history of this later on, telling me that her intention always had been to remain in New York, at Westbeth, while my father went to Stanford. That's what she presented to him, she said. He would go, she would stay, and they would decide then either to separate permanently or for my father to spend the academic year there and return to New York periodically and in the summers. In describing it to me, as we sat across from each other at her dining table, she actually used the term *perfect opportunity*. I—my mother went on—would of course have been free to live with whomever I had chosen. But my father refused! He refused to leave New York without my mother; said he would turn down the job if she declined to come. And so she had been forced to agree, had been forced into making the move against her will.

What do I even make of this fantastic story? Can it be made to make sense? Either my mother wanted to divorce my father, in which case she could have done so whether or not he moved to California, or she just didn't want to go, in which case she simply had to stay and let my father decide what he was going to do. These are events I remember very well, this was an emotional climate whose tensions and stresses broke out into the open in all the usual ways, and I'm convinced that this is not how things played out. But I confess that I experienced a jolt of anguish when my mother laid out the fanciful scenario my father is supposed to have adamantly denied us: I could have stayed! I might not have had to go! The eighteen-year-old in me writhed. It was depressing. I returned home from that visit with my mother thinking about the eighteen-year-old who still, apparently, was waiting for satisfaction of the grievance that had left him frozen in place inside the middle-aged man that I'd become. Time to go, I told him. The only person who wants to talk to the eighteen-year-old is the forty-five-year-old stuck inside my septuagenarian mother. These two time travelers are made for each other.

Of course I wanted to get rid of the teenager who made a shambles of things. The teenager who couldn't sit still to read a book, who couldn't finish what he started, who did things half-assed, who never considered the consequences, who left everything to the last minute, and who, more than anything, believed that he knew it all. Banishing him was a snap. I knew he didn't really know anything, that beneath the bluster was anxious desire. Like Chekhov and his slave, I squeezed him out of myself drop by drop. But what about his mother, my mother, whose removal isn't quite so easy? My mother still had the old aura of authority. For years she was a god, even when I held her in contempt. Even years after I began to pity her, she could summon up an imperiousness that silenced me even when she made the most ignorant pronouncements. When she told me of her life, as we sat across from each other at her small dining table, I listened with particular attentiveness, because even her inventions contained startling truths. She was not telling me that day about the way she ended up in California, but about the crowning tragedy that California turned out to be: about an entrapment, perpetrated by my father, that in retrospect had shown itself to have played out in

careful stages: first by his having seduced her; then by his having
impregnated her; then by his cajoling her into moving in with
him and becoming financially dependent on him; and finally by
his forcing her into drudgery to support the household while he
cultivated the career that eventually led them both to California
exile. She hadn't mentioned all of this that day, had mentioned
only—and for the very first time—the fictional story of my father's refusal to allow her peacefully to remain in New York,
but like every other myth I learned from the people who raised
me, it could assume its entire shape from even its smallest part.
The story of my mother's sadness and defeat is overwhelming,
considered this way, considered as a whole whose parts, related
separately and sometimes at intervals of years, seamlessly join in
my head without the least prompting. I feel overwhelmed typing
it out even now, more than a year after I spoke to her for the last
time. Even if I could *prove* that my mother's stories were false,
there is no way to reduce her sadness and defeat into nothing-
ness. Even now that she is dead, her sadness and defeat remain,
looking for their cause.

I worry about inheriting her eerie fatalism, well concealed
behind an appearance of hard-edged unconcern; I worry about
the need to blame. My mother let things happen to her, drifted
into situations she hated and became stuck until some force dis-
lodged her and sent her on her way again. She would endure in
silence but finally she would lay blame. Laying blame for the
thing she endured was always the delayed reward for having endured it. Rare was the complaint that didn't raise a deeper, older
complaint. Her willingness to ride the old line out to the end
of the past, sometimes stopping at every station along the way,

sometimes only specific ones, was unfailingly unnerving. At every stop, I would feel implicated in some way.

For the next few months I lived in a kind of vague hope that something would come along and rescue me. I changed my behavior very little. After I graduated high school in June 1982, I got a job working as a foot messenger through Chris Standora. The messenger service was brand-new and had few customers. I would sit with Chris, their dispatcher, at their rented desk at a shared office space in Chelsea and shoot the shit. As dispatcher, Chris earned six dollars an hour to do this. Working on commission, I earned virtually nothing, particularly since Chris, honorably enough, assigned most of the runs to those messengers—older men, mostly black and Puerto Rican—who actually depended on the money for their livelihood. I didn't care. For me, "working" evidently held some symbolic value tied neither to money nor labor. I don't know for whom the symbolism was intended—the gods? If I got ahold of a dollar, I spent it immediately. Meanwhile, my parents had crossed the threshold beyond which the move ceased to be speculative and had become something that needed to be implemented. Things were packed up, discarded, sold, or given away. One thing that was gotten rid of was my cat, who was gone when I came home one afternoon.

"Where is he?"

"Your father took him to a nice couple."

"Who?"

"[Name of a friend, unmentioned for many prior years] put us in touch."

"You just took him to the shelter, didn't you."

"No, Christopher." By now my mother was speaking through gritted teeth. My father fluttering somewhat helplessly at the edge of things.

"Yeah, who are they? What's their name?"

"They're a couple, they're nice, that's all you need to know."

"Bullshit. Where? Where do they live?" This addressed to my father.

"They wanted an adult cat," my mother said.

"You just took him to the ASPCA. You fucking killed him."

"Don't talk to your mother that way."

"She fucking made you, didn't she?"

And so on. What's the point? We had a lot of conversations like this. My mother's unrelenting, totally unsentimental matter-of-factness, exhibiting none of the reluctance she would claim more than thirty years later, made me crazy with frustration. In fact, she seemed to take satisfaction in my own blatant unhappiness. After all, I had no one to blame but myself, as she frequently reminded me. If I hadn't gotten involved with that fucking Miss America. If I'd gone to school. If I'd applied to college. If I'd gotten a job. If I didn't stay out all night. If I didn't drink so much. If I could make a phone call or arrive somewhere on time or remember an appointment or save money. But I hadn't been able to manage any of that, had I? I had fucked up and they had not.

In retrospect, I don't think my parents were at all equable about the whole thing. At first they must have been stunned, acting quickly to nail down this move they weren't sure they wanted to make, without thinking too much about the consequences of what they were doing. As they began systematically to prepare to leave, the terror was so close, it must have been important to hold it at bay. Distance was real, then. No email, no text messaging, no social media, no Skype, no cheap long distance, no way to follow regional news from afar. The feeling of displacement was more or less complete. My mother's unsentimental efficiency was the old one of performing hard tasks without hesitation. She'd always done it. I always admired her for it, really. It couldn't have been easy, and if, ten years after my father's death, she felt she had to blame him for everything that had happened, then I had to indulge her. I couldn't hold the old grudge, couldn't remind her that while the house had filled with boxes and been emptied of furniture there'd never been a moment when, yielding to the terror pressing against her, she'd admitted, This is hard for all of us.

I was a good boy to the end. I always was. That's the big asterisk attached to the story of me and my parents; the fact that when they told me to do something, made it plain what their expectations were, I always listened. For years and years this was the case; for years and years my life, my habits, my attitudes, took on a shape strikingly like theirs. It pleased them, and, for me, I guess being kept in the fold was its own reward. I'd seen too many people excommunicated for sins against my parents' capricious orthodoxy. But I think it's kosher to point out, here, that what they didn't tell me back then was to go to school. They didn't tell me not to drink. They didn't tell me not to stay out all night. They didn't tell me that college was necessary. I suspect that they found attentiveness to be inconvenient. But they did tell me that I was going to accompany them to California, that this was what was right for me; this was the way to correct the mess I'd made of things after having been left to my own devices since tenth grade. So I went. I considered running. Maybe I should have, but I doubt that it would have worked out. My parents had not been incorrect in pointing out to me my unpreparedness for adulthood.

Finally the day arrived, August 28, 1982. The movers came and took everything away. I said my goodbyes to the random friends I'd found to hang out with on a late summer Saturday and obediently headed to the emptied apartment where my parents were waiting. We walked to Hudson Street together to catch a cab to take us out to JFK, where we were to spend the night in an airport hotel before our morning flight. It was the damnedest place to say goodbye from, an anonymous space set down in featureless land. To save money, we all stayed in one room, and before we went downstairs to eat at the hotel restaurant I began to cry. "God damn it," my mother said. "Stop it. Stop it right now. I don't need this. You stop it."

11

From "New York Day by Day," *The New York Times*, Monday, August 30, 1982:

Never Mind Degrees

From a working-class boyhood in the Bay Ridge section of Brooklyn to Brooklyn College and on to "beat" Greenwich Village in the 50's and a Westbeth studio for the last 12 years—Gilbert Sorrentino has been a compleat New York poet, novelist and book reviewer.

Critics have described his dozen-plus volumes as comedic, experimental, nostalgic, scornful, vulnerable, and "passion mixed with dyspepsia." One also decided he was "obsessed with the colors orange and blue."

Not so attached to New York's colors, evidently, as to keep him in New York. Mr.

Sorrentino, who never picked up a university degree but often taught in City University schools, left yesterday for California and a full professorship, tenured, at Stanford University.

"It just fell on me—just one of those things," he said. At Stanford, where he will teach creative writing and English literature, departmental heads said they had received 200 applications and "interviewed the whole world."

"In New York we went to the Writers' Congress last October and to publishing houses and magazines," said John L'Heureux, novelist who heads the writing program. "Who in New York circles was a superb teacher, a brilliant writer and still writing? He was out in front."

Academic degrees? Said Mr. L'Heureux, "Sorrentino is a very learned man—we weren't for a second concerned about a Good Housekeeping Seal of Approval."

The Palo Alto where we arrived in 1982 was a complacency factory that derived an unearned sense of superiority from the proximity of the great institution in its midst. It imagined itself to be a center of culture and was fascinatingly self-congratulatory about some things—the weather, for example—over which it had neither influence nor control, while being punitively or prohibitively angry about others that any big-city dweller would take in his stride: smoking, public inebriation, the mentally ill, panhandlers, the poor generally, people of different races and ethnicities, graffiti, raucous teenagers hanging out, cars with loud exhausts, dogs with expired licenses, garbage, unsightly front yards, fortune-tellers, pawnshops, nonresidents using its public facilities, airliners flying directly overhead on their approach to SFO.

Technically speaking, Stanford was where we were, a little unincorporated patch of Santa Clara County between the foothills, tinder now as the dry summer reached its halfway point, and El Camino Real. For our first few days, Arnold Rampersad, then on sabbatical while working on his biography of Langston Hughes, lent us his place in the Pearce Mitchell development on Mayfield Avenue, a short walk from the campus. After that, we moved into a rented condominium in the brand-new Peter Coutts development, which sat on a hilltop that had been bulldozed naked and overlooked Hewlett-Packard and much of Silicon Valley. The development was raw-looking, its common areas planted with fragile-looking saplings and still unsodded. Construction was ongoing in parts of the complex, and the whole still smelled of paint, glue, cedar, joint compound, new carpeting, asphalt. For the first few days, my parents would ritually say, "It'll weather nicely." One day, the pale bright shingles siding the buildings would darken, the saplings would grow into impressive shade trees—one day. They were looking for relief in the distant future. Ritually, I would say in response, "I won't be here."

Members of the English department invited my father to functions and parties early in our stay. A deliberate effort was made to include me and my mother. At first, both of us went.

At one gathering I rapidly got drunk and, apparently stuck for an answer, told anyone who asked that my mother "worked with computers." This was because at her last job she had as one of her duties operated a big Burroughs billing machine. Soon, I noticed my mother glaring at me whenever I happened to catch her eye. When we left, after climbing into the tiny Pontiac my father had rented, she said, "For Christ's sake, Chris. Why did you have to tell them that I was involved with computers?"

"Weren't you?" I asked.

"Not like that."

"Like what?" This wasn't disingenuous. I had absolutely no idea of the region's association with computer technology and had in fact been bragging about my mother's abilities, figuring that it sounded better than saying that she seemed to sit around the house all day long.

"You know exactly what I mean."

"I don't."

"Gil," my mother said, "I'm going to throttle this little prick."

Whatever my father said in response is lost in the crypts of time. It doesn't matter. By then he had long since learned to keep far away from my mother's disputes with me. Otherwise, we would take a break from tearing into each other to turn on him. At this point, I don't think either of us felt that we had anything to lose by fighting—we were *out here*, weren't we? How much worse could things get? Anyway, assume he made a noncommittal conciliatory noise as he, a brand-new driver at fifty-three, struggled to navigate home without incident from wherever the party had been.

"Don't *say* anything about me to these people."

"What'm I suppose to do?"

"Just keep your god damned mouth shut. That shouldn't be too hard, should it?"

"Shit, Mom. What do you, want me not to say anything at all when they talk to me?"

"You can make conversation without bringing me into it."

"They're not interested in me. I'm just the kid."

"They're not interested in me, either," she said, bitterly.

In a crude sense, I'm sure she was correct about this: my father was the one who'd been hired, and people primarily were curious about this nonacademic New Yorker who'd suddenly vaulted to a senior position in their English department. But my mother, already sensitive about what she took to be her invisibility within my father's shadow and thoroughly out of practice in dealing with new people, took it to be a permanent obstacle, founded on a principle of excluding her. Defensively, she'd already made up her mind that she would have nothing to do with any of them. Some, women in particular, reached out to her, offering to take her to lunch or to shop for the furniture and housewares that my parents needed, but after a few uncomfortable encounters my mother soon became expert at keeping them at arm's length. Once again, her illness came in handy. Soon enough, my parents would trundle out the awkward excuse of her illness whenever either of them wanted to avoid something. Soon enough, my mother's illness would become the sole characteristic for which she was known. Soon enough, it would become the central fact of her existence.

✦

My mother's illness. How it thrived in California. In New York, she had mostly treated herself, wary of the expense, I imagine, and probably also mindful of her family's belief, expressed most baldly by Doña Ana—now in her nineties—that "doctors make you sick." In California, the family mantra found a new application. In New York, my mother had learned to live with illness; in New York there were the familiar streets to walk down, the familiar errands to run. In California, where everything was new, lupus must have seemed like an old friend with whom she could finally spend some serious time. We suddenly had excellent medical insurance, its premium largely subsidized by Stanford. Nearby there were Stanford University Medical Center and the Palo Alto Medical Foundation. My mother became a patient. The doctors were eager. My mother was eager. For all I know, she thought that it would make her better—I mean in all respects; that is, I mean in terms of her seeing no one and doing nothing and going nowhere. My mother was no fool and it's likely that she made a connection between living with lupus and whatever had steadily drawn her away from the world. I think she was very aware of it. The problem with my mother was that her awareness didn't extend to the crucial moment when she would be able to identify her resistance to meeting the world on its own unpredictable, frightening, exhilarating terms as the main obstacle to her reentering it. She never arrived at that moment. Even years later, when confined for several weeks to a nursing home, where she dealt with and even enjoyed the unfiltered encounters she was obliged to have day after day, she was not ultimately able to say, "I've been doing it wrong, this is the better way." Of course, by then she was seventy-five and her opportunities were few. It took confinement to an institution to force them upon her, and when she was discharged, she soon found herself back where she'd begun.

But when she arrived in Palo Alto, my mother was still a young woman, forty-five. I didn't realize how young until I reached that age myself and thought, with a clarity so simple as to be almost stupid, "My life isn't over yet—why was hers?" It was a thought I would have at the most unexceptional times—swimming in the ocean, eating with friends, flying in an airplane; it was a thought I would have while doing things my mother hadn't done in years. Was lupus the answer? Was California? My father? Or was it her own intractability? At least one of the internists, cardiologists, hematologists, rheumatologists, pulmonologists, and other specialists with whom she consulted over the years must have asked her how she was doing. Fished a little, just to see. Chronic illness sufferers generally, and lupus sufferers specifically, are prone to depression.

But that damned stone face—the one who packed half her life into boxes and gave the rest away, the one who substituted a heavy club and a slum apartment for poor George Bradt when she left him to live on her own, the one whose response to her beloved father's death was to say, in a typewritten letter to her thirteen-year-old son, "of course, we were all expecting it, and the whole family has reacted very calmly," the one who began to sing after her mother struck her in the head with an iron skillet, the one who freely expressed anger but never sadness—admitted nothing.

Not even I knew *really.* There was never a conversation about loneliness or isolation or boredom. There were many conversations about what my mother couldn't stand, about what she believed

was ridiculous or false or stupid or pretentious or boorish or un-
sophisticated after my parents had lived in Palo Alto for a while,
but the point of comparison, the something or someone or someplace better, smarter, or truer that was longed for, never appeared.

She rejected not only friends and family, she rejected the idea
that friendships and family bonds were the foundation of social
life. She rejected not only psychotherapy and antidepressants,
she rejected the idea that they were effective and that the people
who sought them out were genuinely seeking to alleviate the way
they felt. She missed New York, but very quickly the New York
that she and my father spoke of bore little resemblance to what
New York City had become; bore little resemblance, even, to the
New York City they'd left behind them. They retreated, finally,
into the oldest old stories, stories of an extinct New York, of old
hangouts and events, the New York City of friends long since
moved to Woodstock and Los Angeles and Cape Cod and the
cemetery, of old lovers long since married, of married couples
long since divorced, of the dead and the destroyed.

We always seemed to be angry at one another at the rented condo
on Peter Coutts Circle. Partly this was because my father, whatever misgivings he'd had about the move, now did what always
came naturally to him: established a new unbreakable routine and
went to work as soon as possible, picking up where he'd left off
some months beforehand. The condo had an open loft that overlooked the main living area, and that was where my father set up
his study, which my mother nicknamed "the command post." As
he had while at the University of Scranton, he figured out very

quickly how to arrange his duties at Stanford around his real work and his other habits, and once he and my mother had finished unpacking and furnishing the place he began every morning to climb the carpeted stairs up to the loft, just as he had removed himself to the study at one end of the large lower floor at Westbeth. And my mother, what about her? She'd endorsed the move, or accepted it at any rate, even if what she would later claim about her thwarted attempt to stay behind in New York was true. Assume that it was true, to the extent that she'd privately expressed her apprehensions to my father and he'd said, It'll be different, babe. It'll be great, it'll be beautiful, it'll be away from all this bullshit— whatever he said. We'll buy a car and see the natural wonders of the golden west. I'm sure a conversation a lot like this happened, probably more than once. It's the conversation I'd have, the pitch I'd make: Don't worry, it'll all be OK. And what does OK mean? For my father, it meant climbing the carpeted steps up to the loft and working on one of the eight books he would write during their twenty years in California. How burned did my mother feel, watching his ass retreat up those stairs? She was irate. Here we go again. Once my father's equanimity had been established, nothing could be changed. She sat marooned in the stifling condo—most of the floor-to-ceiling windows faced west and the place would be flooded with pitiless sunlight each afternoon. There was nothing to walk to. Nothing to look at through the windows or from the deck but the turned earth of the development and the construction taking place on identical units in another sector of the complex. She took a driving lesson but apparently it didn't go well, and so that was it for driving. Because it was something she couldn't do, couldn't face doing, it became another thing not worth doing,

something vaguely contemptible. And so she waited: she waited
for my father to finish working, she waited for him to return from
campus, she waited for him to take her to University Avenue or
California Avenue or the Stanford Shopping Center or Town
and Country Village or Kepler's or Draeger's. And she waited
for him to fuck up so that they could yell at each other for a few
hours. These California fights were special. I remember them the
way I remember specific shots in certain films—indelible beyond
context. The only context was California, and misery. I stood
in the kitchen. I stood in the hallway. I hid in the bedroom, the
bathroom. I covered my ears. I fled the premises and returned
hours later to hear the shouting as I parked my bike outside. This
was the entire history of their association being reviewed piece
by piece, day by day. Both of them lectured. Both of them complained. For twenty years this, for twenty years that. You can't,
you won't, you always, you never. Divorce was the answer, but they
couldn't divorce: not anymore. I doubt that serious thoughts of
divorcing my mother ever crossed my father's mind, but I wonder
if that's what occurred to her as she stood there on the deck in the
late afternoon, seeking relief from the heat inside the oven of our
unit, listening to the mourning doves calling: that in agreeing to
come to California, she'd agreed to be bound to my father for life.
"Hey, don't I know you from somewhere?" Sometimes I think of
that man we ran into on the street, more than forty-five years ago.
Was he her lover? Would I eventually have forgiven her if at that
moment she'd turned me and Jenny Wyland around, told us to
scoot back to Westbeth, and just gone with him and never come
home? If she had, would she eventually have forgiven me for fucking her life up for her? What would she have done with a man who

was willing to get on a plane, take a vacation, go to a show, drive to the country, eat at a new restaurant, try a new brand of soap, sit in a different chair, take a few days off, eat in front of the TV once in a while, throw a party, change his mind? Or would she just have realized how well my father's limitations complemented her own? All I know is that at that point, newly in California with all bridges smoldering behind them, they must have realized that one of them would die first, and for the other that would be either the best or the worst thing to be hoped for. All I knew then was that I had to get out of there.

Mourning doves have migrated to New York City in recent years, and the sound of their calling always puts me in a melancholy mood.

I did two things almost immediately: I learned to drive and I got a job. The job, at a Jack in the Box on El Camino Real, was my introduction to complete invisibility. In a polyester shirt that stank of grease no matter how frequently I washed it, I served shitty food to people who didn't actually see me or my coworkers, who were mostly from ghettos like East Palo Alto or East Menlo Park or from déclassé Peninsula towns like Mountain View and Sunnyvale. On several occasions, people to whom I'd been introduced upon our arrival at Stanford came in and neglected to acknowledge me when I greeted them by name. This bald-faced refusal to engage, which I dubbed "the California hello," has since spread around the country. Maybe it was always there. Naturally I blamed California. I hated the place. That was my real job, had been my job since my parents had announced their intention to move there. I began to save money as soon as I started getting paid. Within a month or so I'd left Jack in the Box to work as a temp, using my skill as a typist to double my wage. Soon I was working for the City of Palo Alto at its Animal Services Division, a shelter and clinic on East Bayshore Road, on the other side of the freeway. Rain or shine, I rode there on my bicycle, where for about seven dollars an hour I worked answering phones, assisting customers, processing animal adoptions, helping in the spay and neuter clinic, administering inoculations to dogs, assisting with the weekly euthanasia, adding up the daily deposit, dispatching animal control officers via two-way radio, and other miscellaneous duties. Every two weeks I received a check for a little under $450 and banked $400 of it, my getaway money. I was going to return to New York after a year: that was the plan. I saw no one. I did nothing. I went to work and I came home. I spent money on cigarettes and little else. I was going to go home. I wrote letters to everyone. Amazingly, they mostly wrote back. Sometimes, someone would begin a letter to me at a party and pass it around so that everyone could contribute. (Years later I would discover, in one group letter, a greeting from my future wife Nelle, then fifteen.) The letters, both to and from, sustained me and kept me focused. I still keep the ones I received, stored in two manila envelopes. What I wrote in my outbound letters, I have little idea. I sat and pounded away on my Royal portable. Here's what's wrong with this place, I'd write. Don't forget me, I'd write. What else would I have had to say?

"Christopher." My mother was waiting for me one day. "I don't want you sending my pictures off to your stupid friends without asking me."

"Pictures?"

"Don't be disingenuous. The ones I just got developed."

"I didn't."

"I had them set aside. Right there." She pointed vaguely at a built-in bookcase in the dining area.

"I didn't even, I didn't see them."

"Don't bullshit me, Chris. I'm telling you what I want. I'm telling you what you're not to do. Is that clear?"

"But I didn't do anything."

"Damn it, don't you think I know what you're up to? I know you've sent pictures to your girlfriends."

"That was other pictures. They were mine."

"What pictures? You don't have any pictures."

"You gave me them."

"And now mysteriously the pictures I set aside are gone."

"I didn't take them. Why would I?"

"How should I know. To show off. What do I care why. You always turn everything into a song and dance. You can't ever just apologize and admit you were wrong."

"You're the one who's wrong."

"Don't contradict me."

"Well, you are. I didn't even see them."

"Stop lying to me. If you didn't, then where are they?"

"Pictures of what? What are they of?"

"Oh, please. Of you. You send them to your little girlfriends. You're like a mail-order bride. I pay money to have them developed and you just send them off."

"But I didn't."

"You just admitted it."

"I did it one time. With my pictures you gave me."

"Mother of God, help me to go through. I'm sick and tired of the bullshit. What did you do with them if you didn't just send them off? They were right over there and now they're gone."

"Where?"

"You know perfectly well. Over there." She pointed again at the built-in. It wasn't exactly a bookcase, more like a set of deep shelves for dining-related tchotchkes. I went over and found the pictures where they'd fallen behind some cookbooks from where she'd perched them. Pictures of me in a yellow polo shirt and chinos that I never would have sent to my friends.

"Look. Here they are. See? They were here the whole time. I didn't take them. OK? You go accusing me and you don't even know what you're talking about."

"You put them there."

"What?"

"You just put them there right this minute. Don't fuck with me."

"I just went over there. You watched me."

"You had them in your pocket and you put them there. What kind of idiot do you take me for."

"Well, at least you stopped me before I sent them to my friends. They're fucking shitty pictures."

My mother had a particularly annoying habit of freezing in the midst of whatever gesture she'd been making while asking an all-but-rhetorical question and gazing accusingly at me while holding the pose in silence. Maybe it was something she'd learned during her year at the High School of Performing Arts. Usually I just remained quiet and she would gradually relax and move on to the next complaint. But now she pursed her lips and narrowed her eyes and drew back her hand—which had been extended to indicate the photos' phantasmic journey from there, in my pocket, to there, on the built-in shelf—and hit me hard across the face. Blood spurted from my nose onto the dining table she hated.

Did I threaten her? Did I burst into tears? Both? Did I storm out? As I recall, my brain stopped functioning correctly, flickered a little, when my mother presented her utterly paranoid explanation for the sudden reappearance of the photographs. I probably didn't actually make any pithy remarks about the quality of her snapshots. Very likely, I just told her that she was insane. My mother was sensitive to any intimation that her mental state was not at its best and could be counted on to react angrily—for example, when I suggested gingerly that she "talk to someone" while she was taking care of my dying father day after day with no assistance, she said, "You're always telling me I'm crazy!" But she was crazy. I do remember at that moment appealing to my father, who had remained silently present throughout all this, asking him to somehow impose sanity on the situation. He couldn't, though. There was no sanity to be had. That was the situation. In the months after arriving in California, the three of us maneuvered through our daily lives in a state of hysteria. My mother, in particular. She devised elaborate systems for when the curtains were to be closed, or opened, and by how much. She taped three-by-five index cards to the inside of the kitchen cabinets on which she made minute notations tracking when the lightbulbs had been changed, how many rolls of toilet paper we had gone through. She raged around the unit, searching for "her" pencil. She sank into the one comfort she had, which was to completely dominate the only thing over which she had any control, the running of the household. She had resigned herself to living unhappily, and my father had resigned himself to being unhappy about her unhappiness. This was life, according to them. Happiness was something the smart money wasted no time pursuing. I had affronted them both by refusing to go along with it. I had expressed the belief that there was an alternative to being unhappy and that to pursue that alternative was sane, sensible, true to myself. There was nothing secret about my plan to return to New York. I advertised it whenever possible. In effect, it was the same as calling them crazy every day.

I was just twenty, about the age my mother had been when she married poor George Bradt. My own bad decisions were ahead of me, and I was in a hurry to make them. I believe my parents actually thought, or at least hoped, that by rising early each morning and going to work, saving money compulsively, denying myself luxuries and other indulgences, I was *growing up*. But I did not have the slightest regret or second thought about quitting my job when the time came, about buying an airline ticket, about heading to New York and whatever couch I could crash on. It was not a plan at all. All my industry and discipline had been tactical, an act of elegantly delayed self-destruction. I had what seemed to me to be a lot of money—I think it was around six thousand dollars—and my strategy, it turned out, was the same as it had been a year earlier: I would resume my drift through life, my arrogant confidence that something special would have to happen to someone as special as I was. Almost a year to the day after arriving in California, I left for the airport one morning in a taxi. I wouldn't see my parents again for almost two years.

12

During those nearly two years in New York I did very little. My attempts at employment were comical—New York partisan though I may have been, I was intimidated by the pace, the brusque impatience of my supervisors, at the Manhattan offices where I accepted the occasional temp assignment. California's passive aggression had spoiled me for New York's blunt directness. I very conveniently fell in love with a girl, F, whose mother, Dianne, and her boyfriend Larry were not averse to my staying with them indefinitely. Dianne ran a failing sewing shop that took in piecework from clothing designers, and Larry was nominally an electrician, though I would later discover that in fact he worked mainly at being a heroin addict. They were constantly behind in the rent on their apartment, a chaotic dump on St. Marks Place, and in arrears on their utilities payments as well. I was eager to ingratiate myself with my new family, as perhaps I thought of them, and took it upon myself to pay off the debts they owed to the New York Telephone Company, Con Edison, and Mr. Frietsche, their landlord, while also regularly heading to the Key Food on Avenue A to stock the refrigerator and cabinets with groceries. The apartment, which lacked heat, hot water, unbroken windows, and level floors, also was filthy from front to back, its kitchen sink overflowing with dirty dishes, its bathroom crusty with grime and stains, forgotten plates of food left to rot in the corners of every room. Roaches thrived. The basic organizing principle was the mound: sliding, shifting, avalanching masses of papers, textiles, books, record albums, tools, street finds, garbage. Repulsed, I instituted a cleaning regimen. Dianne and Larry had triggered the latent orderliness my parents apparently had programmed into me. I was astounded by the way they lived. Inadequate adults previously had presented themselves to me in the form of faintly neglectful or absent parents, people who despite their flaws were able to function passably as grown-ups. While Dianne and Larry's unfitness may have astounded me, it didn't astound my parents. They were precisely the type my parents despised above all others—vaguely bohemian, lapsed bourgeois who always seemed to have money for takeout or taxicabs but let their telephone and electricity get cut off; who scoffed at convention in all its forms but faithfully worshiped at the shrine of the Christmas tree and the Mother's Day brunch. During my year on St. Marks Place, my parents energetically but utterly ineffectually expressed their dismay as F and her family blithely allowed me to deplete my bank account on their behalf. I think I thought that I might serve as an example to them, although all I was doing, really, was spending money. In my inability or unwillingness to earn any, I was the same as they were. That made the money seem magical, simply there, and so they felt that they deserved it. Maybe they did. Eventually F's father, an amiable drunk and quasi-vagrant, arrived to spend a night on the sofa and never left, and so, at age twenty, I found myself providing material support to F and all three of her parents while my money dwindled. Meanwhile, my relationship with F—only superficially plausible to begin with—disintegrated, and I was unceremoniously jettisoned from the household more or less coincident with the moment when I no longer was able to fund it. A valuable lesson. I bummed around New York, staying in various places, for another ten months before giving up, boarding a Greyhound Bus bound for San Francisco in July 1985 with four ham-and-cheese sandwiches in a backpack.

As usual, I had been waiting in New York for the unmistakable opportunity, announcing itself in blazing neon, that was supposed to carry me off to something better. For ten months I sat and brooded in my room in Palo Alto, consumed with what I viewed as my defeat in New York, still hung up on F, angry about having ended up back where I'd begun. Although at the time the investment in F had seemed a necessary risk, it was difficult for me to justify my expenditure of grief. "At least you didn't marry her." My mother's judgment seemed gratuitous, given how things had turned out. My parents had been right all along. Of course, I wasn't mourning F's loss exclusively. I'd messed up completely. I hadn't done anything right. My friends had gotten sick of me— of my kvetching about F, of my sponging, of my loutish, drunken behavior. The shame was intense. I didn't feel as if I could set foot in New York until everyone had forgotten me (it would be five years before I returned for a visit). I'd thrown my money away and failed to do anything to replace it. I'd put myself in a position where I was at the mercy of weak, immature, selfish people who, ultimately, owed me nothing. Well, how could I have known? I had no experience. For my mother, who had married and divorced in her early twenties, the answer was simple, like the proverbial doctor's response when told "It hurts when I do that": So don't do that. "At least you didn't marry her." "Thank God you didn't get married." Those were my mother's consoling words. I'd cut my losses before it had gotten a lot worse. Feeling heartsick, humiliated, deceived, abandoned—these were as nothing compared with extricating yourself from a legal entanglement, apparently. That was so awful that my mother had been able to face it only once.

During my time in New York, my parents had decided to buy a unit at Peter Coutts, larger and better-appointed than the one they'd rented on our arrival in 1982. Filled with new furniture and lamps, with their art framed on the walls and a fire in the hearth, it reads in photographs as a pleasant and comfortable place. Comparing it to the apartment at Westbeth in photos taken just a few years earlier, their life looks remarkably, and conventionally, middle-class. They were living well. The marathon fights had ceased. They seemed calmer, more at peace with each other. But now tensions were rising again. My sullen presence threw things off—not that I spent much time considering my parents' feelings, given my focus on my own abundant feelings. For ten months I would get up late, piss the day away, and then at about four or five o'clock I would get on my bike and ride down to campus, where I slouched around Tressider Union or the bookstore or the Green Library, feeling as if I radiated imposture. I certainly didn't belong there. The people there who were my age were Stanford students and therefore, as my mother liked to remind me, accomplished. They certainly looked better. Photos of me taken around the time of my arrival back in California are a little startling. Two years in New York had caused me to drop about twenty pounds. I look tired and dissolute. My skin is pasty, and my hair has been savagely cut. A punk rocker at last. There are no photos where I'm not holding a cigarette— gesturing with it, drawing on it, putting it out, lighting a new one from an old one.

And yet I went to campus nearly every afternoon. My mother would complain as soon as she saw me gathering my keys, wallet, and cigarettes: "You're a vampire!" She seemed to be under the impression that I behaved as I did deliberately, to annoy her.

"Who knows where he goes just as darkness begins to fall," she would narrate. "A total mystery. Suppose you were to go out while the sun was still shining in the sky? It'd kill you, or what? If you had a normal schedule maybe you'd have some friends. I hear people going by outside, young people on their way somewhere, and I say to myself, 'Why isn't that Chris?' But no—my son's a vampire."

What exactly was my mother, though? My depression was simple. It had been triggered by identifiable failure, by loss you could pinpoint. It was mending. I could feel it mending even when I was in its midst. It would end and I would be returned to the world. But my mother had become a stranger to the world. She still could fluently recount the ups and downs of the UPS man, the Peter Coutts landscaper, the cashier at the local market, the nurse who worked in the office of her primary care physician, and her other local favorites, but she hadn't crossed a friend's threshold in years.

One day, an old family friend from New York announced that he would be passing through the Bay Area and that, on a Sunday afternoon, his business would bring him to the South Bay. How would it be if he dropped by? My father, who spoke with him on the phone, said that it would be all right—although we might be out. Odd as this offhandedness must have seemed to the old friend, who hadn't seen my parents in several years and didn't typically travel to the West Coast, it was insufficiently vigilant for my mother, who became angry at my father for not simply lying and saying that we would be out of town. And so began one of the most peculiar adventures I ever had with my parents.

The friend had said that he would try to drop by in the early evening. At about four in the afternoon on the appointed day, my parents, under the direction of my mother, sprang into action. My father went out to make sure that the car was inside the garage with the door lowered. My mother went around closing the blinds on the ground floor, where the windows were giant walls of glass, two of which looked upon the large patio at the rear of the unit and the other upon a smaller patio off my father's study. The front door was closed and locked and, as a final deceptive touch, the porch light turned on, as if no one would be returning until after nightfall. I was rousted from my bedroom lair, where I suppose I might have been spotted by a determined caller, to join my parents in the living room, to smoke and sulk over the weird inconvenience of it all in a chair across from where my parents sat huddled on the couch as if awaiting the knock of the Gestapo.

Every now and then my father or I would begin to say something and my mother would violently shush us, bringing a finger to her lips and raising a hand, palm out.

I'm not sure how long we sat there, but the room grew dark as we waited. Nobody came to the door; the phone didn't ring. The old family friend apparently had picked up on my father's ambivalence—was ambivalent himself, who knows. Finally my mother gave the all-clear, and she and my father went around the house lighting the lamps while I disappeared back upstairs to do some hiding of my own in my bedroom. Now whenever I'm tempted—as I often am—to avoid people, to neglect friendships that no longer seem to have any immediate point, to withdraw for too long from the day-to-day, I think of that late afternoon, the shadows falling in our silent living room, as we sat in a state of heightened alertness, hiding from one of my parents' oldest friends.

When would I get a job? Would I enroll in the local JC? Apply to a four-year college? Would I stop moping around? Why couldn't I just get it together? My parents' attitude was perhaps understandable. I was an adult living in their house who, from their point of view, refused either to work or to go to school. That the very idea of facing people drove me back under the covers in the morning was something they attributed solely to laziness.

One afternoon they went to the Stanford Shopping Center and when they returned my mother had a gift for me: two neckties. It was a marvelously pointed gift, subtle and unsubtle at the same time. Unsubtly, it announced, "Get off your ass." But on another level, it said, "You think you need so much to actually function as an adult. You're telling me that you can't manage it, that you're not equipped. But here's all the equipment you need: men knot them around their necks each morning and are deemed presentable. Shave your face, put one of these on, and see if it doesn't make the difference. See if it matters at all to anyone how you feel, what you think you're capable or incapable of coping with, whether you want to cry or hide or wander aimlessly around the grounds of a great institution. This is part of the costume people wear to hide the fact that they're falling apart inside. That's what normal people, competent people, do: fall apart inside while taking care of business. Get hit with a skillet, sing. See all your personal possessions auctioned away, clap. Give away your cat, whistle. Bury your father, dance. Put on the tie or *you'll* be like Dianne and Larry, falling apart on the *outside*, standing in a phone booth on the corner in frigid January weather to make your calls or running an extension cord from the outlet in the hallway outside the apartment to power your TV. You'll be the one working harder to con your landlord into letting the rent slide for another month than you would to actually earn the money to pay it. People with a whingeing, wheedling, grasping reality. You're surprised they fucked you? Of course they fucked you. That's how people like that get by. They fuck other people to make up the difference between their inadequacy and what's normally required of adult human beings, and then they tell themselves that it's just what they were owed."

That was the lesson of the neckties, at least as I understand it now. It was my mother speaking to me loud and clear. In a weird way, it was her at her best. She was actually giving me the lesson of her experience as well as she could. Of course no one wants to be like Dianne and Larry. Larry committed suicide years ago; he was maybe forty. F's father died young too. Dianne still lives in that apartment, and F lives with her. One of the ties was brown, woven with dark stripes of maroon and navy, and the other was a gray knit. I wore them both for years.

13

For the first half of the next ten years, I lived an ordinary and somewhat aimless life. I moved to San Francisco, kept New York far from my mind, went to work in an office, earned a decent amount of money, and lived for the satisfactions of the weekend. My view into my parents' lives was minimized by my not living with them. I no longer saw them critically: they just were. Their strangeness had little effect on me. I had done what I always do: made myself presentable to the members of the group I deemed most desirable as friends (my coworkers) and infiltrated their ranks, feeling, as I always do, a vague sense of imposture. Then came my awakening, so to speak, and for the second half of those ten years I learned to be a writer, shed nearly everyone I'd met during the first half, and, untroubled by second thoughts, happily prepared myself for a life of devotion to Art.

Some people spent time in both halves of this decade with me—K, for example; K, who finally left in baffled disgust over what I was doing with my life. My parents had liked K the same way they liked everybody—their dealings with her were like a sustained interaction with their favorite supermarket checkout clerk, carrying the same expectations. I think they may have suspected that my life, at around the time that K came into it, was somewhat thin and insubstantial, and they would have been right. They were probably just happy that I was on my feet again. I was a callow twenty-four; a girlfriend seemed like a good idea. But as nice as K was, as time passed I found it increasingly difficult to be nice to her.

She and I had gotten together in 1988 while I was working as a claims adjustor for a small professional liability insurer, and her stifling ambitions for us eventually would become a contributing factor in my determination to become a writer. That is, the vivid glimpse her dreams afforded of the fate that awaited me if I did not step off the track I was on provided powerful motivation to do so. She did not understand why I didn't want to wear a pressed suit and a crisp shirt and tie to work every day, why I resisted my boss's suggestion that he sponsor me, despite my lack of a bachelor's degree, for a place in law school, or why eventually I quit my job and accepted a friend's offer to sublet his Williamsburg railroad flat for a year, while he went off to grad school, so that I could write a novel. I identified her with a class of people with whom I no longer felt I shared any common ground—those who had no artistic or creative ambitions—and I identified a creative or artistic life as being one of perfect fulfillment.

I should probably have just broken up with K and gone into a different line of work—advertising, say. The world would be down one novelist and I would have found my way to a secure and satisfying life. But blood tells. The decision to become a writer had arrived, after a vague and groping period of unfocused dissatisfaction, not like a calling, but as if I'd been activated by a posthypnotic trigger to do some undreamt-of harm. The ambition came to me full-blown; there was no intermediate, tentative period during which I decided to *take a shot at it*. I urgently started writing a novel and urgently started reading fiction and that was that. I was just parochial enough to see things in Manichaean terms: K and a Sears bedroom set vs. total satisfaction. No middle ground, and God knows no idea of satisfaction or fulfillment deriving from friends, family, raising children, taking part in community activity, travel, gardening, hobbies— whatever the fuck civilians did. *This* was how it was done! Would I be poor? Would I be lonely? Would I be obscure? Would I be disaffected? Yes! Yes! Yes! Yes!

At any rate, our time together, K's and mine, particularly after my Brooklyn sojourn, was a period of mutual bafflement that somehow dragged on for five years, until late 1993. K wanted the suburbs, a partner who steadily advanced in his chosen profession, Saturday night double dates at Chevys. I wanted—suddenly and incomprehensibly, from her perspective—to remain in the city, scratching out a living at temp jobs and spending my evenings and weekends at my desk, writing. Each of us responded to the other's recalcitrance with ungenerous resentment. Her ambitions and desires convinced me that she was stupid, which she was not. My ambitions and desires convinced her that I was crazy, which I was not. We'd both been cheated out of happiness by the illusion of who I'd seemed to be. When we came into direct conflict, the result could be terrifying. Shortly before we broke up, there was an incident in our kitchen in Noe Valley where she waved a chef's knife in my face, ranting that she was going to kill me. Of course I thought of my mother's rages at my father. K at least had a firm sense of self-preservation. She left before her frustration drove her to stab me to death. She was right that the life my choices were forcing upon her was crazy, for her at least, just as the life my father's choices had forced upon my mother was crazy. For my mother, her own mysterious choice was not to leave—but then, K had not had a child with me; she had never placed her livelihood in my hands. So she found an apartment, informed me (not ungently) that she would be moving out, and was gone.

Both of my parents had reason to be apprehensive about the life I seemed to be pursuing, knowing its perils as well as they did. So I had declared myself a writer: what, exactly, did I think I meant by that? I had finished my first novel and it was being turned down by publisher after publisher, while the shorter pieces I was mailing out to the usual magazines and journals were being rejected as well. I felt perversely validated by this process and displayed the rejections on my refrigerator. Sooner or later, I figured, someone would see what I was doing as good and publish it. I was not part of any scene and, ignorant of the system of connections and institutional affiliations that help to make a literary career, I could sustain a Pollyannaish outlook in the face of odds that, in retrospect, look pretty daunting. For my father, this must have evoked the earliest years of his own career when, newly discharged from the army and based in provincial Brooklyn, he began the long slog of establishing himself as a writer while working various dead-end jobs. For him, disappointment had too often been the wages of his efforts.

My mother, though, was less concerned with whether I would be fulfilled or disappointed as an artist. I believe my mother was concerned with whether I would be fulfilled or disappointed as a human being. She knew better than anyone the limitations that my father had imposed upon himself, and upon her, in dedicating his life to writing. She knew the model I was working from. I had no other. The images of my father that I retain from my—as they say—formative years appear to me as a series of tableaux, a Via Crucis: my father rises and prepares himself to work; my father drafts his work in longhand; my father sits at his typewriter; my father scoffs, over lunch, at the rejection letters/bad reviews that have arrived in the mail; my father returns to his desk; my father sits in the battered easy chair, reading under the lamp until early in the morning. Even the way he handled unwanted mail—tearing it briskly in two before dropping it into the wastepaper basket—played its irreplaceable role in his days, and became something I assimilated unconsciously. My mother surely knew that there was no good reason for a man of thirty, unmarried and without children, not only to substitute artistic practice for life, but to pursue that practice in imitation of a routine, a protocol, a compulsion devised to stabilize and soothe one and only one person. But I couldn't be dissuaded—not by her, anyway. Again, I had only one model, and that model was a god, so why would I proceed otherwise?

Nelle had started at Music and Art the year I had left the school. I'd known her slightly at the time, and several years later, when she was in her senior year and I was at loose ends post–St. Marks Place, she and I had gone out briefly. I ran into her on September 29, 1994, at a reading in San Francisco given by our fellow Music and Art alumnus Jonathan Lethem, whose own first novel had just appeared. All three of us, it turned out, had been in the Bay Area for years. It was, for me, a significant night. In reestablishing my acquaintance with Jonathan I formed the first important friendship of my adult life, with someone as connected to the artistic world as I was isolated from it. With Nelle, I began a relationship that little more than a year later would result in marriage and a child. Both were linked to the past that I had never quite put aside; both pointed me toward the future that I wanted badly to begin.

I was living at the time in the small apartment on Dolores Street where I'd moved after K's departure. Nominally, Nelle was someone else's wife, but her marriage was shambling to its end, and by the end of the year she had moved in with me. Our affair gave my mother the opportunity to say things like "Christopher, a married woman!" and my father the opportunity to refer to her as "faithless." I sometimes wonder if my parents simply had a secret affection for the old-fashioned phrases, their old-fashioned sound. The fact was that even a married Nelle was a much more suitable partner than K, and she proved capable of dissuading me from blindly following my father's example. Nelle was—is—far more eager to live than most people I've encountered. Dedication she could understand, and as a kid raised in Soho she could understand art, but she rejected the monastic ideal that I had been determined to imitate. Under her tutelage, I learned a lot about how to live. In the abstract,

I think, this pleased my mother. When my parents finally met Nelle, they were utterly charmed, and all talk of her alleged character flaws ended forevermore. They greeted the news of Nelle's leaving her husband, of her moving in with me on Dolores Street, of her becoming pregnant, with equanimity. My mother in particular took to her. They remained close until my mother's death.

By this time, my mother's ideas about *how to do things* had become entwined with an exaggerated sense of duty—duty to some standard of behavior that she found sorely lacking in others, citizens of the Bay Area in particular. What defined it? I don't know. I know a lot about what she didn't like, and if I wanted I could begin torturously to draw plausible connections between those things and the moral turpitude of people who did like them; the decline of Western civilization; the erasure of taste, class, style, humor, wit, sophistication from culture and public life. Those were the big problems, or so I gathered, and lots of things contributed to them, were caused by them, or stood on display as symbols of them. You never knew what it was going to be. When I was about forty, my mother ridiculed a wristwatch I was wearing: "That's an absurd watch for a grown man." The remark arrived from out of nowhere; she delivered it as casually and lightly as if she'd been paying a compliment, and moved on.

Anyway, the conflict between this sense of duty and my failure sufficiently to honor it brought about the following incident, the precedent for the harrowing periods of estrangement that my mother and I would perfect in the years after my father's death. In the summer of 1995, Nelle and I, both of us already underemployed, decided to fly to Michigan and spend some time in Maple City, a tiny Leelanau County town between Traverse City and the Lake Michigan shore where Nelle's father and stepmother owned a farmhouse that came with a barn, several other outbuildings, and a hundred rolling acres of land. Our daughter Violet was due in October, and this would be our last chance to travel before she arrived. Before leaving, I called my parents to let them know that I would be out of town for a couple of weeks. I was thirty-two years old.

"That's nice, I suppose," my mother said.

"What do you mean?"

"Well, Chris. Do I have to say it?"

"Say what?"

"You have a baby coming."

"Yeah?"

"Is this the smartest thing you could be doing with the time you have before that happens?"

"What's not smart about it?"

"How the hell can you afford to take two weeks off work?"

"I don't really have any work right now."

"All the more reason not to go, then. Don't you think it would be a better idea to spend the two weeks going through the want ads and looking for a job?"

"No," I said. "No, I don't think that would be a better idea. I doubt I'd find a job over two weeks in August."

"Well, now you won't know, will you?"

"I guess not."

"Don't you think it's time you thought about what you're going to do for money? You're expecting a child."

"I know we are, Mom. We'll manage."

"It's a big responsibility. Babies aren't free—"

"I'm aware of that."

"If you'd just let me finish a sentence. Babies aren't free. Babies are expensive. I just don't see how you can even consider indulging in the luxury of a vacation."

"You don't have to see," I said. "I know what I'm doing."

"Oh you do do you."

"It's a vacation. People take them."

"*People.* Only in California would a person take a vacation when he's not even working. It's preposterous. Your father and I never would have dreamed of taking a vacation when we couldn't afford it."

"Well," I said, "you're you. I'm me. Don't worry about it. We'll economize."

"There are limits to how much you can economize. *It's a baby.*"

"I know it's a baby, Mom."

"Do you? Because it doesn't sound as if you really know what you've gotten yourself into."

"Gotten myself, what? Gotten myself into?"

"Neither of you has a real job. I don't want to hear about it if you find yourself in trouble."

"We'll be all right."

"If I were in your shoes I'd just take those two weeks to hunker down with the classifieds each morning and try to find work."

"Yeah, you said that."

"Well, Christopher. I guess I'm saying it again."

"I don't have to ask your permission, Mom."

"How dare you," she said. "How dare you."

Then I was standing there, holding the dead phone in my hand. Again, my brain experienced that slight flickering. I don't recall if I called back and my mother didn't answer the phone, or if I didn't call back. In either event, I didn't speak to my parents during the time we were gone.

I can't remember if Nelle had picked up on the peculiarity of the way that my parents lived and pointed it out to me or if, seeing them through her eyes, I was able at last to view them as others did, and to compare their lives to the one I was impatient to live. Before that, I had probably convinced myself that theirs was what I imagined to be the uneventful and slightly eccentric existence of the elderly (at the time, my father was sixty-six, my mother fifty-eight). Now that I thought about it, though, even my own abuela Dora, past eighty, was constantly packing her bag and traveling around the country, around the world: visiting family, on organized tours, as one of the seniors who hopped the jitneys to Atlantic City to play the slots. Now that I thought about it, Nelle's parents and stepparents were always seeing old friends, dining out, welcoming people into their homes. Now that I thought about it, everybody I knew was perfectly at ease with life as a source of plenty: plenty of places to go, plenty of things to do, plenty of people to see. It didn't really matter whether they were comfortable or struggling to make ends meet, didn't matter if they had books to write, businesses to run, jobs to go to, classes to attend. Now that I thought about it, the only people who lived like my parents—with each day carefully parceled out like a scarce resource, dedicated to precisely the same activities in precisely the same order at precisely the same time—were astronauts aboard a space station.

To Nelle, the Vacation Incident was the latest in a series of perplexities for which I couldn't offer any explanation. Why had my mother so forcefully resisted the suggestion that our parents get together when Nelle's had visited California? Why hadn't my parents traveled the ten minutes from their place to Printer's Ink bookstore on California Avenue to hear me read from my first book after it was published in April 1995? These things were confusing to both of us. As time passed, this kind of behavior became less unfamiliar to Nelle, but as she became closer to my parents, she also became more capable of being hurt by them. I remember one occasion, some years later in New York, when Nelle cried angry tears of humiliation when my parents at the last minute bailed on dinner plans with Nelle's mother—whom they never did meet—pleading my mother's illness, as usual. I was embarrassed, having been put in the position of needing to apologize to Nelle's mother for my parents' gauche and transparent lie, but I had been expecting it; Nelle had not. (That time, uncharacteristically, I called my mother to chide her—by which I mean very cautiously suggesting that what she had done was not necessarily OK. "Tell Nelle not to worry," she said, grandly missing the point. "I'll write her mother a note. It'll be fine." At the beginning of the twenty-first century, this was her social apparatus: a box of ecru notepaper and envelopes, and her old-fashioned Palmer handwriting, armed and ready to send her regrets.)

In 1995, I felt untouchable. One after another, things I'd wanted were arriving—more than that, things I hadn't realized I wanted were announcing themselves as available to me if I just reached out for them. And so I did. If my parents wanted to just sit in their stupid condo and wait for me to show up and tell them what it was like outside, then fine. But the Vacation Incident was different. As my mother had intended, it actually managed to cast a pall over the trip to Michigan. Nelle and I had sharp arguments about nothing. I found myself reflexively feeling critical of the way that Nelle's father and stepmother did things despite the fact that the way they did things while at their vacation home was as relaxingly unstructured as you could possibly want (I can see now that at thirty-two I had no idea how a vacation was supposed to work). I fretted about the financial ruin that awaited us when, having wasted time that would have been better spent mailing résumés to offices emptied of vacationing workers, we returned from this utterly frivolous trip as underemployed as we'd been when we left. And of course I brooded over the silence from my parents. Nelle, being of an entirely more pragmatic turn of mind, bought a picture postcard depicting downtown Traverse City, filled out the back with deliberately cheerful blather, and dropped it in the mail to them. Gradually, over two weeks, I managed to relax and enjoy myself.

We came home. I was half-surprised not to hear from them, completely surprised that my own outrage hadn't abated. Fucking assholes! I was livid, and I became more livid when neither of them phoned to smooth things over. It became a call-and-response routine between me and Nelle: *Who's in the wrong, me or them?* They are! *We're about to have a kid, shouldn't they call?* They should call! *I'm an adult, aren't I?* Yes you are! *I get to decide how I live my life, don't I?* Yes you do! Obviously, I wasn't entirely convinced, and as the weeks went by, I began to get nervous. It occurred to me that it was very possible that, if I didn't call them, I might never talk to them again. Nelle refused to accept this. To Nelle, this was an impossible concept. But I knew better. I knew my family history. I could call the roll of those who'd been banished. Not only was it not impossible that my parents would never speak to me again, it was probable. It was a likelihood even if I did reach out to them. I understood the coded subtext too well: my mother now knew that my intention was to live differently than she did, to live in a way that she thought foolish and found threatening. My frustration while living with K hadn't bothered her nearly as much as my happiness living with Nelle evidently did. My unhappiness had satisfied her. It had proven certain things to her about the fundamentally unhappy nature of life. K was the best I could hope for. K's limitations would make me as miserable as my father's limitations had made my mother. But then everything had changed so quickly. K had slipped out of my life and a year later I met Nelle. I was publishing my work. I was meeting other writers. I was going to be a father. Individually, these things might not have looked so bad to her. Viewed in a certain light, they might even, individually, have looked pretty good. It had taken the upsetting news of our trip to Michigan to restore my mother's sight. Soon I would be out of reach. *Michigan!* I might as well have told her that I was joining a cult on Mars. What would even be the point of talking with me when I returned? By the time I got back from this ludicrous trip, "something" would have "happened to me."

It was the old choice, the one you face time and again when dealing with people, relationships—work through it, eating shit occasionally, or throw it away. My mother always chose option number two. So tempting, and so easy that it feels like you've done nothing at all. She chose it until she was more alone than anyone I've ever known.

Fearful as I was of losing touch with my parents—specifically, with my father—I couldn't face hearing from my mother how ridiculous it all was, if I chose to tell her how it had gone in Michigan. I couldn't face not mentioning it, pretending it hadn't happened. Certainly I knew that Nelle's parents' lives, if I talked about the trip, would be held up to ridicule: their mismatched tableware, their scruffy furniture, their habit of block-printing designs on the walls and floors of the house, the amateur art that hung around the place, their ultra-casual housekeeping routine, their tendency to keep food in the fridge long after it had gone bad, their permissiveness with Nelle's two younger half brothers, their frowning on cigarette smoking, their whimsical dress, their enthusiasm for current bestsellers, their penchant for s'mores and singalongs, Nelle's stepmother's Seven Sisters drawl—I couldn't bear to hear her opinion on these things. I felt protective of them. As living with Nelle had, visiting Michigan had given me a view into another possible way of living—not *the* answer, but certainly *an* answer, at least to part of the question.

I waited until the day after Nelle's baby shower. My parents had been invited, but they neither responded to the invitation nor showed up. This was a different form of damage: that's my opinion as of right now, twenty-three years later. It was a harsh, childish, damaging snub that I can't imagine inflicting on any of my own children. Right now, twenty-three years later, I think that both my parents should have been thankful for the rest of their lives that I was willing to view it as—what? As a signal that they required assistance, as a call to me to intervene in a situation hazardous to their mental well-being. I spoke with my father.

"Hi, Chris," he said, his voice straining with the effort to sound nonchalant. "What's on your mind?"

"What's on my mind? I haven't heard from you in like a month and a half."

"We haven't heard from you either, Chris. We're very hurt that you haven't called."

My father has been deputized, I thought. Deputized to deliver the party line and prohibited, I thought, from calling me. I felt a surge of hatred for my mother, whose presence was palpable during this call. I assume she was sitting right next to him while he spoke.

"Mom hung up on me," I said. "She should have called."

"She hung up because you were very rude to her. She was very upset."

"I don't think I was rude. She was telling me how to live my life. I'm thirty-two years old. I think I'm entitled to tell her to mind her own business."

"I think," said my father, "that you owe your mother an apology."

"Well, I'm calling. Let me talk to her."

"She's in the shower right now." The shower was one of my mother's refuges in real life—for as long as I could remember she had lost herself in showers lasting an hour, an hour and a half—and also served as her standard excuse to avoid the telephone. I knew that. They knew I knew.

"I'm sorry if I made you feel bad. But you could have called anytime."

"We are the parents. It's not our job to call you."

"That's . . . that's silly," I said, at a loss. What could I say to that? It was a new rule, or an old one that had never before been articulated. Surely they'd called me in the past. I was certain my father had called me. Was he trying to communicate something to me, that he was under duress, that he also thought that this was silly, ridiculous? To be sure, his voice—the tone of which I remember a lot more accurately than I remember the verbatim content of our dialogue—sounded as if he wanted this episode to come to an end, as if he wished I would simply play the stupid game my mother had invented according to these supposed *rules* governing our respective *jobs*. I decided to change tack.

"And what about the baby shower?"

"What about it, Chris?"

"You didn't come. You didn't even RSVP to the invitation."

"*That? That* was the invitation?" Now, suddenly, my father sounded much less uncertain. Now he sounded like himself, when he talked about other people. Nelle's friend Jon had taken on the task of organizing the shower and had collaged a cheeky invitation, xeroxing it onto card stock and mailing it out. "We thought that was a *joke*, Chris. It was this cutesy *postcard*. You couldn't possibly have expected us to take that absurd thing seriously."

And abruptly I knew that my mother was not holding my father hostage here—that in his own misplaced snobbery he'd found the rationale he needed to agree with her. I was now one of those people who did absurd, vulgar things; who took unearned vacations, who sent tacky postcards inviting serious people to joke events. My father may have been in pain, but he wasn't suffering—he was seething, roiling in the anger my mother had kept stoked.

I don't remember what I did. My impression now—maybe tainted by hindsight—is that I was aware that this was delicate territory. My father may have thought that the vacation itself was OK, but it was clear that he shared my mother's angry misgivings about the strange, sociable turn my life was taking, my happy embrace of the tacky, the crude, the cretinous, the popular. I'd heard variations on this shit a dozen, a hundred times before— something would set my parents off, some poor sap's hat or wife or poetry collection or new beard or vacation photos or dissertation topic or shoes or fat ass or political opinion or enthusiasm for jogging or hobby or favorite saloon or taste in jazz or whatever it happened to be. The object of derision could be a stranger or a neighbor, a colleague or a friend. There was no way to win. It was like the Abbott and Costello routine where Lou asks successive passersby to direct him to the Susquehanna Hat Company on Bagel Street, only to find himself under physical attack each time when one or the other reference triggers a violent response. "Invitation? You call that an invitation? That's not an invitation! I'll show you an invitation!" I had two choices: either apologize or tell my parents that they were full of shit and take my place among the outcasts.

The conversation ended soon afterward. I don't remember if my mother called me back or if I had to call again. I know that I didn't see them before Violet was born—I called them from a phone booth at UCSF Medical Center on the morning of October 20, at a time when both of them almost certainly were at home, and left a message on their answering machine informing them that they were grandparents.* They were not among the visitors who came to see us on Dolores Street in the days and weeks that followed. When Nelle and I got married early in December, they did not attend our City Hall wedding.

My father and I managed to move past this incident and resume our ordinarily close relationship, but my mother never really warmed up to me again after that. When we went to Palo Alto, she dealt mainly with Nelle—who came out of the incident untainted—speaking to me only if it was unavoidable or when it would have been blatantly rude to do otherwise. If I called, she said hello and quickly passed the phone to my father. Over the next few months Nelle and I formulated a plan to move back to New York City, and in June 1996, we did.

---

* Actually, grandparents for the second time. My half sister had had a son in 1985. At the time of Violet's birth, my parents had never met him.

14

Between 1996 and 2001, about eighty letters went back and forth between Palo Alto and Brooklyn, where Nelle, Violet, and I had moved into an apartment on Smith Street. They're illuminating in the way that old letters can be—particularly the ones coming from me, which are slightly less dumb than I feared (I dreaded rereading them) but reveal an ingratiating fealty to my parents' ideas that I'm pretty sure I adopted largely to communicate to them that I remained a loyal son. The question of whether I was a loyal son or not remains open. Actually, the question is how concretely disloyalty could possibly have manifested itself under the circumstances. By the time the correspondence ended, a few months before my parents, following my father's retirement, returned to New York in early 2002, I was thirty-eight years old, married six years, with two children (Nelle and I had a second daughter, Penelope, in the summer of 2001). Surely I could do and think what I wanted without feeling the need to reassure my mother and father that I still did and thought things the way that they did. Surely, living my adult life three thousand miles distant

from them, I could not really have believed that it was important.
But the letters say otherwise.

Actually, the question is how I'm defining loyalty even now,
more than a year after my mother's death and more than twelve
since my father's. While in the abstract I probably felt throughout this period like I was doing what I wanted, in practice, "what
I wanted" looked a lot like a flawless combination of both my parents' habits. I got up at four each morning to write for a couple of
hours and took care of Violet and the household for most of the
rest of the day while Nelle went to work at her father's company.
I felt virtuous—undoubtedly the way my parents felt, precisely
performing various duties day in and day out. I'm not sure *virtue*
covers it, though. If it does, then the lesson I've taken away from
those years is that virtue is frustrating and breeds resentment. I'd
gone to New York to become a writer among writers and instead
I was isolated in Brooklyn—which had not yet become, I want
to make clear, the Brooklyn that has since inflamed the world's
imagination—mopping the floor, changing diapers, killing time
on the playground, reading picture books, and trying to make
sense of my second novel, which I would eventually abandon. I
didn't really know how to do either thing—write the book or
raise the kid. Having already written a novel, I'd fooled myself
into thinking that the process would be endlessly duplicable,
easier each time out. I'd probably similarly fooled myself about
the demands upon a full-time parent. The Sisyphean chore of
writing an intractable book made its way into my letters, the animal frustration I felt being at the beck and call of a preschooler
did not.

✦

My mother remains a blank during this period because she did not deign to write, unless she was sending a note to Nelle thanking her for some thoughtful gesture (photos, news clippings, etc.), and she continued to hand me off to my father immediately if she answered the phone when I called. My mother's uninterest in me by now had become wallpaper, part of the landscape of my relationship with my father, as if he had a new wife with whom I maintained frosty but superficially cordial relations.

There's another way of looking at this, one fairer to my mother. The letters back and forth are dominated by Literary Matters: my father provides his opinions, *qui mihi discipulus*, and I eagerly offer my own. My mother's exclusion seems to have been written between the lines of these letters, which gloss books and authors she'd never read and had no interest in reading, not to mention what you might call a politics of literature and publishing. Later, as we sat across from each other at her small dining table, my father safely deceased, she could finally offer some of the opinions she'd formed from her own reading. She was quite literate, with a particular fondness for nineteenth-century English novels. "Ach, your father," she would say. "He was always *correcting* me."

Nor did it ever occur to me to write her to ask, in view of my own situation, what it had been like for her in 1963 to have me—inarticulate but never silent, powerless but domineering— abruptly grafted to her side as she went about her business day after day. Having been there with her, I probably thought that we shared the same perspective, despite my new and acute awareness that the parent's priorities, schedule, anxieties, needs, and desires diverge irreconcilably from those of the child, which almost always take precedence. Maybe I thought I was an easier kid than Violet (not at all likely); maybe I just assumed that my mother's purpose, uncomplicated by the holy calling of High Art, was to care for me. At that point, I had never heard of the famous pram in the hall and would have sneered at Connolly's suggestion that its destructive presence is felt by the artist only in those moments when his wife is being negligent in the performance of her duties. I felt it all the time; my wife's duties were to schlep to the office and work all day: that was the agreement we had made. The making of art in whatever interstices remained was my problem, not hers, we had agreed.

I never did ask her. Possibly I didn't want to know; didn't want to hear nostalgia for the child I'd been before I mutated into the monstrosity I'd become, certainly didn't want to hear pointed complaints about the way I'd infringed upon her life, her freedom. "Hey, don't I know you from somewhere?" I blamed, *blame* myself, but truly the path had been cleared for my mother to take a stab at a different kind of life years before—when I began my move toward the independence that so frequently angered her—and it always remained open to her. The mystery of her entrapment inside my father's particular neediness, her refusal to refuse him even as she showered him with her contempt and anger, will remain a mystery.

I began after a while to lean on my parents to travel to New York, a trip that they resisted, despite my father's constantly— and gleefully—referring in his letters to his short-timer status at Stanford and their professed eagerness to return permanently to the East Coast. My mother, though, was never quite well enough to travel, according to my father. Doctor's orders—this was their Get Out of Anything card. It was a form of paralysis: no matter what the circumstances, the conditions were never quite right. The famous trip was always referred to as something that possibly would be happening at some point in what they sincerely hoped would be the near future, God willing. And my father did like to invoke the will of the gods in this connection, as if the offering of a hecatomb preceded every successful vacation. My mother was silent—except to the extent that her illness spoke for her, saying no. It would be a flare-up, a complication, a debilitating medication, an onerous regimen, a stretch of follow-up appointments. At one point, clearly frustrated, I say in effect in one of my letters, Just book a flight and get on the plane. There's no responding letter taking me to task, but I must have heard about it on the phone. In my next letter I offer copious apologies.

One hot summer afternoon I returned home from Carroll Park with Violet and was approached by our upstairs neighbor, Awilda, as we stood on the landing while I unlocked the door.

"There was an old lady here, ringing the bell downstairs," she said. "She said she's looking for you."

"An old lady? Did she tell you her name?"

"No. I let her in the building and give her some water, but I tell her I don't think they're here. She said she wanted to see her granddaughter."

I thought: She did it. She said fuck it and got on a fucking plane.

"About five foot five?" I held a hand up. "Puerto Rican lady?"

"Yeah, yeah, I think so. But shorter, you know?"

Possibly she'd shrunk. Why not? She was getting older, weird shit happened to old people. At this point I hadn't seen either of my parents in a couple of years.

"I think that might've been my mother," I said.

"Where's she live at?"

"California."

"Far away. And you didn't know she's coming?"

I shrugged. "She didn't say where she was going, did she?"

"I didn't see her leave. I guess she got tired of waiting."

"I guess so. I'd better go figure this out."

"Yeah, you better." She started up the stairs to her apartment and then turned. "You're Puerto Rican?"

As we moved through our errands on the Lower East Side, my mother later told me, she would speak to me in Spanish and I would respond. "You spoke Spanish," she said. And then she offered the observation she sometimes would make about the mysteries that had clouded her life: "I don't know what happened." Neither do I. One spring, a couple of years before my mother died, Violet came home from college on break and I took her to my mother's apartment for a visit. I went to make coffee for the three of us and apparently banged things around too loudly. My mother wheeled to face me from where she was sitting at the dining table and said sharply, in Spanish, "Will you please stop breaking my kitchen?" I immediately responded in English: "I'm not breaking anything." Violet gaped at me. I was surprised also. Where had it come from? Only my mother seemed unfazed, sitting patiently, and somewhat pleased, while she waited for me to serve the coffee.

My mother was disparaging of her own abilities with Spanish—"I speak it like a seven-year-old," she once said—and I'm in no position to judge. Certainly she was ambivalent about the language, as was my uncle Jim, who never spoke Spanish in my hearing and who, according to my mother, pretended to have forgotten how to speak it. Like my mother, Jim pursued total assimilation, in his case in the Air Force rather than in Manhattan, and cultivated his own unimpeachably nonethnic accent. When I last spoke to him, after my mother's death, he sounded like a man who'd spent his entire life in the middle west. Would my mother and I have had a different relationship if we'd had a language of our own in which to communicate? Sometimes she would tell me a different story: that she would speak to me in Spanish when I was little and that I would respond by making fun of her. I think there may have been more of Uncle Jim in my mother than she was willing to admit. One day, in the mid-'70s, the two of us were walking down Fourteenth Street, west of Union Square. A man singled my mother out from among the dozens. He approached us holding a piece of paper in his hand. In Spanish, he said, "Do you know where the unemployment office is?" My mother waved him away, like this: "Sorry, I don't understand." In English. As we moved on, I said, "Mom, why—?"

"Shh!" she said.

Unemployed Puerto Ricans. Employed Puerto Ricans. Black Puerto Ricans, brown Puerto Ricans, white Puerto Ricans. Puerto Ricans who sat on upturned milk crates outside the bodega playing dominoes and drinking Malta, and Puerto Ricans like my family, conspicuously petit bourgeois, working away to buy the new sofa and to put one kid after another through Catholic school and then college. It didn't matter—not to the world, and, in the end, not to me or my mother. If I stuck out my arm and put it next to those of my great-grandmother, my grandmother, my cousins—it was the same color. But it didn't matter. I was white, and they were not. My mother was white, and they were not.

"Christopher," my mother would say to me, "you are *not* Puerto Rican." I know what she meant, although I think it was a cramped and unimaginative declaration, revealing a limited conception of what "being Puerto Rican" can consist of. My mother would probably have argued that it *should* be limited: I didn't go through the "immigrant experience," never had to learn English as a second language, was not routinely discriminated against, or subjected to stereotyping. I didn't have to struggle to break into a bigger and more sophisticated world, had no stifling faith to shed, nor was I raised amid a set of cultural traditions and expectations specific to Puerto Ricans or Latinos. The occasional Sunday trip up to the Bronx was exactly and only that, and what I found there—the console stereos and color television sets, the little sunken living rooms, the "good" china and everyday Corelle, the furniture laminated in plastic, the bedroom sets, the matched dinettes, the assembly-line still lifes and landscapes, the Book-of-the-Month Club bestsellers—I could have found in any aspirational lower-middle-class American household. I think as far as my mother was concerned, things had worked out exactly the way they were supposed to: two generations in, I was a fully invested American. Why should I want to be anything else?

I have spent years thinking about this, trying to figure out whether what my mother gave me was a gift or not, and whether she gave it to me deliberately or if it just happened.

Contorting the phrase's Christian connotations, James Baldwin writes of the "unspeakable light" that shines on black people throughout their lives, as if they live them onstage. That light can illuminate or it can be turned upon the audience, used to blind. You can impose the blindness through the way you speak, the way you dress, your tastes, the connections you make, the connections you refuse. That was the secret my mother had discovered years before. Her transformation of herself was no wronger, and considerably less absurd, than the New York City Department of Health's decision to declare her BLACK at birth. It was a counter to it. But Baldwin cautions against the incompleteness of the assimilated life; grasps that, in conforming to another's model, someone like my mother allows others to define her just as surely as they would have in applying the stereotypes she has mostly escaped.

Inside the apartment that hot summer afternoon, I found several messages waiting for me on the answering machine that began to explain things. My mother had called. Uncle Jim had called. My grandmother had called. It turned out that it hadn't been my mother who'd showed up, but Dora, who was beginning to manifest the symptoms of Alzheimer's and impulsively had decided to make her way from Co-op City to Brooklyn to pay a surprise visit and meet Violet. (In several years in New York I had made no attempt to contact her, owing, I suppose, to my mother's continued animosity toward her.) Soon after, Uncle Jim would buy a house in Virginia Beach for the two of them, sell my grandmother's apartment, and move her down there. So my mother hadn't managed to make it out of her pumpkin shell after all. It would be a while.

15

Bay Ridge is provincial: homely, backwards, filigreed with the occasional touch of garish pretension. Like large swaths of the borough of Brooklyn that sprawl south of Prospect Park, it is not a neighborhood seasoned in any way by its proximity to the city at large. On its best behavior it aspires to be "nice." On its worst it has an insolent and vaguely threatening atmosphere. One day, as I walked from my mother's place to the subway, a guy came cruising up Colonial Road in a Cadillac sedan, its windows down, blasting Bobby Darin. He wasn't old, either, just the kind of guy for whom a Cadillac and Bobby Darin were the perfect rebuke to a fallen world, and Bay Ridge absorbed him with a shrug of assent. One day, on Third Avenue, I saw two identical locals— overweight bruisers with high and tight hair and chin beards, wearing tank tops, baggy shorts, and shower sandals—pacing on opposite corners of the intersection at Ninety-second Street, like the twin figures that emerge from either side of the chalet when the cuckoo clock strikes the hour, each yelling complaints into his cell phone at some unfortunate woman and gesturing with his free hand, each unaware of the other. Hubert Selby once told me a story about visiting the neighborhood in the late 1970s, when his mother was still living there. He said that he ran into an old acquaintance of his and my father's, a man named Donato, standing on the same street corner where he might have been found twenty-five years earlier. "Hey, Cubby. Where you been?" he asked, like he hadn't seen Selby in a month rather than since 1955, then continued: "You seen Gil?" as if it had just occurred to him that my father hadn't been around in a while either. While kvetching about the place to my therapist a couple of years ago, I told her that I was surprised that the graffiti didn't take the form of cave paintings. My father wrote about it with unsparing precision in book after book.

I cop to my own elitism; it's an elitism given me by my parents. It's an elitism that reflects their own sensibilities, and it informed my advice and suggestions to them about places they might like to settle as I kept one eye on the real estate boom that began to accelerate throughout the city in the late '90s. Bay Ridge was not on my list, but when they finally arrived, ready to buy, it was to Bay Ridge that they made a beeline, and it was in Bay Ridge where my parents—and finally my mother, alone— ended up, eventually purchasing a modest four-room apartment in a doorman building constructed after the war. Years later, my mother would say, "It was all your father's idea. He got it into his head that this was where we were going to move and that was that. What does this place have to do with me? It could be any- where." More to the point, it could have been somewhere better than this. If the great leap of my father's imagination as a young man had been to see beyond the neighborhood's limitations, its great failure had been to return to them, a nostalgic gesture in the face of panic. And I do think they panicked, my parents. After twenty years they now knew the city only peripherally; the neighborhoods where they'd spent their adult lives had changed beyond recognition and were far too expensive for them to consider. But they were committed to returning. They couldn't stay where they were because they'd convinced themselves that there was no place worse. The dream of their eventual return had influenced everything. The last time I'd been to the condo at Peter Coutts, in the late '90s, the plumbing had begun to fail. The nap of the wall-to-wall carpeting had flattened, and the paint had yellowed from years of cigarette smoke. On the wall below the kitchen pass-through a long brown stain, like the vertical trail of pigment on one of Morris Louis's poured paintings, permanently traced the path of the spilled coffee that had formed it years earlier. Numerous earthquakes had caused cracks to appear here and there. The upholstered furniture, originally shades of cream and beige, had become grimy and threadbare. On the patio, they'd lost interest in tending the flower beds and other plantings they'd nurtured in prior years. Only the cotoneaster and the pyracantha that they'd planted right after moving in thrived. (My parents had been right, though: the cedar shingling had weathered very nicely, turning an autumnal reddish brown under a sky that never brought autumn, and the saplings had grown into mature shade trees.) My mother still kept the house impeccably clean and orderly, and these problems were the sort of thing that a decent supply of money can easily correct, so the unit's condition was a little surprising. But whenever

I mentioned it to her, she would always say, "Why bother? We're leaving."

So Bay Ridge it was. I can see the appeal of *the old neighborhood*, its verities of the kitchen table and the candy store. Such verities may be stupid—in 2016, several precincts in my mother's immediate area went for Donald Trump, and he amassed a respectable percentage of the vote in the neighborhood as a whole—but they may at least in a certain romantic or nostalgic light be seen as *real*. What my parents wanted was something *realer* than the anxious parade of Veblenesque status that they'd found in California, the facile, superficial civility with nothing beneath it, not even a hint of a promise of intimacy—in fact, the actual promise is that intimacy's approach will be halted permanently. Palo Alto's advantage is that it is portable, a moveable snack. Thrive there and I imagine you'll be equally at ease in Scottsdale or La Jolla or Highland Park or Wellesley. But the dense-packed neighborhoods of the boroughs are tribal in the extreme. If memory goes to affluent suburbs to die, it lingers in the neighborhoods, haunts them. Prove you belong: do you remember this and can you remember that—stores, bars, diners, local characters, teachers, cops, priests, schoolyards, empty lots, stored away in the tabernacle of the thousand remaining hearts that beat alike. My parents really didn't belong in Bay Ridge. My father, maybe, once upon a time, but my mother most definitely not, and her neighborhood, her Bronx, had burned to the ground thirty years earlier.

"Thirty years earlier" was where my parents really belonged. Make it forty, forty-five. They never "lived" in Palo Alto. Living was sitting around all night talking, arguing, laughing, making off-color jokes, in your face, drinking, smoking, turn up the music, close the bar, go to the party, to the opening, to the reading, going home with strangers, hollering up at the windows from the street to be let in, falling through skylights—that was what my parents missed. That shit didn't happen in Palo Alto (or if it did, it was draped in shame and the clichéd mystique of suburban discontent), so they blamed Palo Alto. Why not? Palo Altans couldn't risk misbehaving like that; they couldn't afford to do anything except amass insulating capital of various kinds. They had no feeling of the tribe. They were too worried about being exiled from the loose and interchangeable circle of the affluent anxious to which they'd gained entrée. It was a bonhomie at home everyplace where money and the most orthodox effusions of good taste may be found.

But those things didn't happen in Bay Ridge, either. I don't know if they happen anywhere in New York anymore. By 2002, when my mother and father finally returned to the East Coast, I was regularly hanging out with other writers and artists, and while the scene was stimulating, it had more of the tang of professionalism to it than that of bohemianism. Things—rent in particular—just cost too much to be able to not give a fuck.

They moved in on March 15. I stood outside their building, freezing in a stiff wind off the Narrows, keeping an eye on the truck as the movers carried in my parents' belongings through the service door. When they were done and I went upstairs, the apartment had been overwhelmed by the freight deposited in it, but my mother had already begun taking charge. Among the many neglected talents she possessed was a natural gift for interior design—she loved floor plans and blueprints, and for as long as I could remember she had, before making changes to a room, drawn a scale rendering of it and then cut out scale renderings of the objects she intended to fill it with, moving them around in various configurations to see what worked best. She had already laid out the apartment in her head, ordered custom-built bookcases to hold the couple of thousand volumes they had kept, and she put me to work finding all the cartons containing books (she had meticulously numbered and labeled them on all four sides and their tops, and kept a corresponding list to check against) and stacking them along the east wall of the living room—carpenters would be arriving in a few days to install the bookcases along the long west wall. By the time I was done my biceps and forearms were black and blue from cradling the heavy cartons as I moved them.

That same day, in Virginia Beach, Dora died at eighty-eight. The call from Uncle Jim came while we were in the middle of setting the place up to be liveable for the next few days. Not too long prior, the old lady finally had been institutionalized; her long life had in the end become needle-focused on daily crises of disorientation, outbursts, falls, infections. Engulfed by cardboard and crumpled newspaper, my mother irritably arranged to fly south immediately. Even my mother didn't dare skip her own mother's funeral. Even for her, that was a step too far. Fucked again by Dora!—that was her outward attitude. There was no sign of sentiment or reflection. For her, there was no complexity to the relationship, no significance to the death. They had "done their duty" to each other—that was the phrase my mother often used to describe her perfunctory dealings with my grandmother. This meshuggah instantiation of the Categorical Imperative, her sense of moral obligation to perform the role of the Daughter, suggests to me that she felt equally obliged to perform the role of the Mother (and also quite a bit about her expectations of me as a son), although she did manage to tell me, a few years before she died, that she loved me—reflexive and dutiful love though it may have been, it must have cost her to say it, and she never said anything of the kind about Dora.

As far as I know, Dora left her nothing—not even a keepsake. Or maybe my mother hadn't wanted anything. The expectation of an inheritance, the idea of my mother's being dependent upon or beholden to Dora for anything, seemed so incompatible with their relationship that I was surprised when, years later, sitting across from each other at her small dining table, she angrily announced that my grandmother had routinely stiffed me—that, for example, she had provided my cousins Paul and Justin, Uncle Jim's kids, with stipends while they attended school, while I had received nothing. I have no idea whether this is true, although I'll point out in the old lady's defense that not only had my cousins remained in touch with her (I don't think I spoke a word to her for the last four or five years of her life), but that Paul is now a successful attorney and Justin a successful anesthesiologist, while I had never progressed beyond the four semesters of college I attended at various unselective institutions. For what was I supposed to have been given money? Maybe my mother believed that if my grandmother had funded it, I would have gone to school as well—so, in other words, what she is blaming on my grandmother is what she perceives as my failure. This is the manner in which I overthink these things.

Whatever theory I'd had of life with my parents present in it, it was soon disproven. New York City did not liberate them. Bay Ridge pinned them to their apartment. Where was there to go? To do what? The nearest stores were half a mile away, the subway farther. The main drag, Eighty-sixth Street, was one of those dismally utilitarian strips of cell phone stores, appliance stores, sneaker stores, discount clothing stores, fast-food restaurants, and bank branches, the kind of place where a sensible person went with a specific goal and left immediately after achieving it. The locals did nothing of the sort, loitering and milling about aimlessly, with the usual look of sullen dissatisfaction written on their faces. Besides, my parents no longer could function normally. Shortly after they arrived, I made the mistake of inviting them to our apartment without first telling them that Nelle's father and stepmother would be there. This was not unintentional; I think I believed that it would be "good for them" to finally meet their in-laws. My father gamely but awkwardly attempted conversation; my mother sat there silently with a distant and unhappy look on her face until it was time to leave. It was excruciating. When I invited them to Thanksgiving dinner that first year, my mother got on the phone. "Is anybody else going to be there?" she asked, suspiciously. I told her I couldn't say for certain, and she turned me down on the spot. I found out later that my father had gone on Thanksgiving to a delicatessen and gotten sandwiches for the two of them.

We established a routine. Every month or so my parents

would come to dinner at our apartment. Sometimes I could persuade them to let us take them out to dinner at one of the new restaurants that had opened on Smith Street, but these places often were not to their taste. Every month or so, we would go to dinner at their apartment. Sometimes my parents would take us to one of the shabbily nice restaurants on Third Avenue, where my father would joke with the waiter who served us, his voice assuming the tonal colorings of the local speech.

Complaining to me as we sat across from each other, at the small dining table. Bay Ridge: what did it have to do with her? "Your father was insistent," she'd say. I have no doubt that, once the idea had taken hold of him, he was. But from this perspective—the way things looked from the dining table, seven, eight years after he'd gone—it sometimes seemed to me as if the entire operation of coming back to New York had from the beginning moved, under my mother's hand, toward this moment: when she could blame him for its outcome.

Death always punctuates life, but I'm looking, I think, to find a fatal significance in this particular period. It was the end period, after all. On some level my parents knew they'd arrived in New York City to die, no matter how much they may have thought that they'd returned in order to live. They returned to New York City for what would be the end of their lives and, starting with my grandmother, each year delivered new deaths to emphasize how much closer that end was drawing: my half sister, friends, former friends, family members, acquaintances, colleagues, bitter enemies, the lady on the seventh floor—death swallowed them all. For the moribund, Bay Ridge was the perfect stopping place, because it was itself moribund, or at least arrested in a state of Joycean paralysis. When death came for my father, he met it without resistance.

16

I don't think I really became a writer until I wrote *Trance*, which I began in the fall of 2000. Everything before that was, at least to some degree, dicking around—spare-time stuff. The only thing that kept me from thinking of myself as a hobbyist, a dilettante, was the fact that I'd published a novel. But hobbyists and dilettantes publish novels all the time. My father had a joke that he loved. It emblematized something important for him. A nice Jewish boy makes good, delighting his doting mother. One day, he buys a boat and shows up at his mother's house wearing a yacht cap with gold braid. "Look, Ma," he says proudly, "I'm a captain!" The old lady's eyes fill with tears and she reaches out to cradle her son's face in her hands. "Bubbeleh," she says, "to *me*, you're a captain. But to *captains*—you're no captain." I had wanted to be a captain among captains, and *Trance*, my four-year introduction to the discipline of putting an unfinished book before everything else, allowed me to become one. For the first time, Nelle and my children were exposed to the fundamentally demented state of the writer in the grip of a long project.

I was also in the grip of my parents' habits, the folkways of the Sorrentino Cult. Go nowhere. Do nothing out of the ordinary. Never deviate from routine. "See no one" did not come into play, because I was routinely going out in the evenings to hang out with other writers—often no farther than the four blocks from our apartment to the Brooklyn Inn on Bergen and Hoyt—but I did not permit my social life to interfere with my work. The rhythms beating beneath the predictability and the stability, uninterrupted since my childhood, served me well. For fifty weeks a year, I sat and worked. For two weeks, I went to Michigan with my family. Nothing else changed. I sat at my desk throughout the duration in a broken chair: I claimed not to want to waste time changing it, but in fact I was afraid to change it. I taped "FOCUS" to my computer monitor, but it was unnecessary.

The soothing pattern was familiar. I would walk Violet to school, then return home to sit with the paper and coffee. At around ten o'clock, I would go to my desk and work until one, when I would make myself lunch. At two thirty, I would head over to pick Violet up. After giving her a snack and chatting with her about her day and helping her with her homework, I would return to my desk until Nelle came home. Then I would make a drink and talk to Nelle until dinner was ready. (Booze had always been the great lubricant of my nonwriting time, and I started to drink a lot more of it while writing *Trance*, when I began to suffer chronic pain in my hip, lower back, upper back, shoulder, and wrists.) Later, we would watch TV, and often I would sit up and read after Nelle had gone to bed. After Penelope was born, accommodations for her—with the advance I'd been paid for *Trance*, we sent her to daycare—were smoothly incorporated into the scheme. *Trance* climbed to nearly 1,200 typescript pages, then I revised it down to 800 and delivered it for publication.

Unlike my father, I did not have another project to which I immediately turned. What I turned to instead were my highest hopes. Waiting for a book to be published is a kind of limbo of busywork—reviewing the copyedited manuscript, correcting proof, writing jacket copy, obtaining blurbs, etc. Within this anticipatory space, where the book seems to be of the utmost importance to everyone involved with it, writers may indulge their fondest fantasies. When *Trance* was published in July 2005, it seemed on the verge of fulfilling them. It was a decent book that was described as "breathtaking," "brilliant," "hilarious," "amazing," "transcendent," "a tour-de-force," "bravura," "powerful," "epoch-defining," "magnificent," "staggering," "heroic," and "a contender for Great American Novel status." It was with such amphetamine phrases driving the blood through my veins that I went with Nelle and the kids to Michigan in August.

We returned to New York and a couple of days later I called my parents to check in. The news was always the same. But not that day. My mother answered.

"Well," she said, when I asked how they were, "something a little weird happened." She sounded shaky. My mother never sounded shaky.

"What? What happened?"

"Your father went to the doctor, and he sent him for an MRI."

"An MRI? What for?"

"Well, he hasn't been feeling so good lately, you know."

"No, I didn't know. Like how do you mean?"

"Oh, he's been really tired. Dizzy. So he went to Dr. Gouvias to have it checked out."

"OK. So Gouvias ordered an MRI, OK. Where?"

"A place on Fourth Avenue."

"No, sorry—like what part of the body?"

"They took an MRI of his *brain*, Christopher." Her mild impatience made my mother sound more like herself. "Anyway, Dr. Gouvias just called with the results. Apparently there's a large growth."

My father's brain: what else was he? My mother was all body, a five-foot-five colossus, bodying forth her anger, her contempt, her flintiness; her presence depended on some aspect of the physical. Which is not to say that my father was somehow physically inconsequential, lacking presence, but that his mind was able to summon forth his essence—what he expressed directly, and whatever residue of himself went unspoken in the words he wrote. If I read notes and letters my mother wrote, she doesn't appear, some falsified equanimity masquerading in her name shows up instead. But when I read him—and there is so much of him to read—he is present, body and blood. In this way of never really having lost him completely, I feel his loss most severely.

The details were pedestrian: he would require surgery to remove the tumor. The surgery needed to be done as soon as possible, because the tumor was at risk of herniation, which could incapacitate, even kill him. Being my father, he wanted to think about it. My mother being my mother, she refused me when I asked to come to their place to see him. I wept and wept. For three nights

I drank straight bourbon whiskey and wept as if weeping were an unavoidable ordeal my body was going to make me endure, like passing a kidney stone or withdrawing from narcotics. I had never wept like that as a man and I had never wept like that as a child. The grief was breathtaking, and I seemed to have endless energy for it. I astonished Nelle and I scared the kids. When it was done, finally, I was done actively, or at least overtly, grieving. A kind of reckless, staticky anger settled upon me instead.

Finally, I was permitted to visit them in Bay Ridge. My father looked tired, a little thin, but was fundamentally himself—the surgery would mark the real beginning of his ordeal, his rapid diminution. I did no crying at their house. When my father went into the other room I asked my mother how she was. She sat at one end of the sofa, I at the other. She looked at me and her eyes filled with fear and anguish. A small, wordless exclamation escaped her throat and she raised her hands as if reaching out to me and then abruptly covered her eyes with them. I sat frozen before this display. I had never seen anything like it from her. Then she dropped her hands and looked away. She had regained her composure. "That's enough," she said. "No more."

My mother and I began jockeying for position almost immediately. Uncharacteristically, I was almost completely uninterested in placating her. She had the advantage of proximity, however, and I would have to deal with her vigilant policing of the territory she felt belonged only to her. So when I grilled Gouvias, my father's doctor, my phone rang within hours.

"Why did you call Dr. Gouvias?"

"I had questions for him."

"You have questions, ask me."

"I thought he would have more information."

"I am the wife, Christopher. Of course I have all the information."

"More than the doctor?"

"More than he's going to tell *you*."

"It depends on the questions, doesn't it?"

"Nu? You think I don't know what to ask?" My mother had a point: she'd been questioning doctors, sometimes to their great irritation, for twenty-five years.

"Look, I wanted to talk to the guy. What can I tell you? I don't know him."

"He was very surprised to hear from you."

"Oh, come on."

"You think I'm making this up?"

"No," I said, "I'm saying that he may not have expected my call, but it couldn't possibly have come as a surprise to hear from an elderly patient's son."

"You're making it sound like your father's not competent."

"That's not what I mean at all."

"Well, it *sounds* like that's what you mean."

"I'm sorry if that's how it sounds. I'm asking why would he be surprised. Why are you surprised? What's the harm?"

She couldn't articulate what the harm was. I imagine that partly it had to do with controlling the flow of information. "Ask me," she says. Well, Gouvias certainly didn't need any help playing his cards close to the vest. He had been guarded and wary when I spoke to him, as if I might be trying to trip him up, get him to admit liability for my father's tumor. It was like speaking to primary care medicine's press secretary. But I think my mother also had been bugged that my call to Gouvias had marred the smooth surface that she had imagined proceeding along, complicated it like a scrap of trash on a cleanly swept floor or a book that didn't sit at right angles to the edges of the coffee table it was on.

The weather was beautiful the day my father had the surgery. It was always beautiful out while my father died: the day I found out about his diagnosis, the day of the surgery, the days I went with my parents to the radiologist or to chemo, the day he went into the hospital for the last time, the day of his death. Golden during the waning days of summer, aflame during the fall, piercingly clear during the winter, lambent during the spring—the weather mocked us all year, the earth bursting with life as my father was transformed from a man into a corpse. My father had the surgery extremely locally, at Victory Memorial Hospital in Dyker Heights—a wretchedly inadequate place, now defunct. The waiting area for people whose loved ones were in surgery was, oddly, the main reception area in the hospital's lobby, and so throughout the morning and afternoon, while I sat there reading the *Times* beside my mother, I was able to observe the parade of humanity that crosses the threshold of an urban hospital, discovering that pathos has only a limited number of ways of expressing itself. The chronically ill, the crippled, the elderly, the developmentally disabled, the non-English-speaking, the addicted, the poor, the homeless—in presenting themselves to the gatekeepers of Victory Memorial (whether guards, nurses, or cashiers) all confronted abjection in the same way, all expressed indignation the same way, all submitted the same way.

It was in this public space that we submitted as well, to the inevitable. The neurosurgeon appeared after several hours and before an audience of whoever happened to be there told us, "The surgery's finished. It went very well. The tumor was well defined and close to the surface and I'm pretty sure I got it all out. He's recovering in the ICU now. I'm going to order a course of radiation to eliminate any remaining cells. You should know, though, that from the looks of things this is a metastatic tumor, from cancer cells originating in the lung, I'm pretty sure. I sent a frozen section to the lab for analysis, but before surgery I had some pictures taken and there's definitely a shadow there." His attitude was brusque, but not disagreeable. His business was in the operating room; as soon as he was done there, his involvement with my father's case had ended. His efficient omission of sympathetic gestures from his announcement was, frankly, welcome. He had the right idea. When he'd gone, I turned to my mother and said something, something reassuring.

"*Don't* try to comfort me, Chris," my mother said, physically recoiling. "I don't *need* comforting."

So this was to be the final ordeal for her as well. Life was pulling into port for both of them, and each of them had their job to do, my father's to die and my mother's to help him. When it was done, they both stopped. Her life would become a static and low-ceilinged shrine to the contemplation of the past—a contemplation that, thanks to the uneventfulness of the prior twenty-five years, could center on individual instances of the everyday, the sorts of things that ordinary people—contented people, at least—put aside and forgot. After he'd died, a great transformation occurred, one that I didn't recognize until it had taken place. For years I'd thought of my parents as essentially antagonistic toward each other, even as their ferocious quarrels ebbed with time. But after my father's death, I realized that my mother's allegiance had always been to the marriage, if not to the spouse. She may have been alienated from and unhappy within it, but it was the union she depended on for her survival, and while my father was alive she had defended it from whatever threatened. But now, with the means to her survival at last solely in her own hands, she was able to transfer that allegiance from the marriage—the unit that had both preserved and imprisoned her—to her own injured self.

But all of that came later. At this point, there were eight months to get through.

17

For years I'd held two incompatible ideas in mind: first, that my mother was indestructible and could survive anything, and second, that she would die first, since the limitations allegedly placed upon her by her various illnesses were observed so religiously by both of my parents that it sometimes seemed like life itself was a necessary risk she had to take. I assumed that it would take her a long time to die, because she was mean and tough and I'd never witnessed any debilitating aspect of her illness that didn't in some way work to her convenience. Her illness seemed to prevent her from participating only in the things she didn't want to participate in. Had my mother been born in the nineteenth century, she would have been diagnosed with neurasthenia and sent for a rest cure. In the late twentieth century, she simply stepped aboard the giant wheel of medicine and was carried in an endless circular course—counteracting symptoms with powerful drugs that gave rise to their own symptoms and side effects that were themselves then treated, and on and on. What I'm getting at is that my mother's vocation was that of a patient. She found her purpose in combating, temporarily outsmarting, rallying against illness; in enduring relapse after relapse, examination after examination, test after test, cure after cure; in following prescribed dietary regimens, exercise regimens, drug regimens. Her repeatedly surviving these occurrences was what fed my private myth of her invulnerability. Always imperiled, never vanquished. My mother's complicated history of specialists, diagnoses, prognoses, therapies, and medications was as daunting, as confusing, as the synopsis of a complex work of narrative art, like a long-running soap opera. The premise at the center of it was that the treatment of sickness was in itself a form of health—logical, if perverse. Treatment was endless, but it was also endlessly available. At no point did it cease. Never did the medical establishment simply scratch its head and say, "That's it, we've done everything we can." And, for her part, my mother never said, "I feel better now." Like exhausted but co-dependent lovers, my mother and medicine fell into each other's arms again and again, one never quite being able to refuse the other. But what about "doctors make you sick"—my mother's family credo? What had happened to that? It hadn't gone anywhere, is the answer. My mother needed to be made sick. It provided an answer to the riddle of her life's pointlessness.

At the same time, while convinced that he would outlive her, I had always worried constantly about my father. I worried that he would be taken from me suddenly, unexpectedly—an accident, say. It never occurred to me that he would get sick—or, rather, I vaguely assumed for some reason that illness would descend gently upon him at the proper time and remove him from life in a decorous way. Either way, he was the one who was well. My mother was the sick one, he was the healthy one. This was an article of faith for all of us. If my father made one of his rare excursions—when, for example, he traveled to Washington, D.C., after *Little Casino* was named a finalist for the PEN/ Faulkner award in 2003—he didn't bother asking my mother if she wanted to go, he asked me to call her every day to make sure that she was all right (she was). But we all accepted the necessity of this false duty. Now things were reversed. They were unignorably reversed. Compared to the grand clockworks of my mother's care, my father got sick in an almost simplistic way, with invasive cells sprouting in his chest and sporulating throughout his body with a mission not to put him *under the weather* but to ruthlessly exterminate him. And my mother's vaunted illnesses, the ailments that had defined for everyone what could be expected of her, vanished. The alleged handicaps could be completely overcome in the moment of crisis.

It was always disorienting, and a little thrilling, to see my mother take on the ordinary tasks of living—as it had, for instance, disoriented and thrilled me when I was in the sixth grade and she'd gone to work. The effort of being ordinary, even drearily so, seemed heroic while at the same time it underlined the stark uneventfulness of the way she usually lived. I always wondered what stopped her from building on the triumph of successfully doing what everyone else seemed to do so effortlessly. Was it someone else's fault? I couldn't blame my father for anything apart from failing to take note of what gradually had happened to his wife, for accepting far too easily the handy justification of chronic illness. He was attentive, but to the wrong things. Dora may have thoroughly screwed up my mother's ability to temper her reactions to others; trained her to identify disagreement as betrayal, disobedience as belligerence, willfulness as something to be broken, difference as incurable flaw, and to respond with vilification, violence, and ridicule—but my mother had escaped from her at the age of seventeen, and Dora herself was an adventurous soul, finding new friends and enthusiasms until her mind abandoned her. Poor old George Bradt had simply been the vehicle by which my mother had come to believe that people were not to be trusted, that happiness was suspect, and, above all, that no situation could be relied upon to be permanent, so sentiment was something best avoided.

But my mother refused the challenge posed by these three crucial relationships, which would have needed to be dealt with even if she hadn't been chronically depressed. The problem was that she *was* chronically depressed, which made it difficult for her to deal with anything. Like the rest of us, my mother could at times be courageous. But even courage can't coexist with depression and prevail over anything more than depression's most extreme demands. The stillness, the stagnant despair, that depression insists is the entirety of existence is the delusion that courage must counteract by daring to hope while living within it. A motivated person may seek psychotherapy (and drugs) in the midst of such moments of hope; a truly motivated person will actually do the work psychotherapy requires—an impossible thing to expect of someone like my mother, who refused to be *told* anything. So my mother's bouts of high-functioning behavior were more acts of pure will, driven by the perception of necessity, than they were expressions of a healthy personality peeking out from under the battered carapace.

Suffice it to say that this wasn't how my thinking went while all this was going on. What I thought at the time was something like, *she's been fucking faking all these years.* Granted, I already believed that—nuanced thinking about my mother's continuing avoidance of all but the counterpart privacies of the examination room and her bedroom was beyond me while I was in the midst of timorously attempting to coax her to "engage." I believed that she was depressed, but I also was able to dismiss it as handily as she'd dismissed my incapacitation when I'd returned to Palo Alto at twenty-two after my failure in New York.

But my father was the one who was dying. She was going to live. She was supposed to die, to go grumbling into that good night. But now I was going to be stuck with her. He would die, and she would live. Did I know how angry I was?

This wasn't how it had been supposed to go in 2005. The story of 2005 was supposed to be the publication of *Trance* and my elevation to the plane of "significance." Well before I was aware of my father's illness, my anticipation of the payoff I had coming for my years of work had begun to erode something that had been holding me together, keeping me normal. After I'd finished writing, in 2004, I'd looked up for the first time since the turn of the century and seen clearly the small and tightly controlled existence I'd developed. The book had justified the existence; the existence couldn't justify itself. With time on my hands, I could already feel restlessness taking hold. What I'd been doing, really, was the same thing I'd done in Palo Alto more than twenty years earlier, when I'd gone to work each day and saved 90 percent of my money: the discipline I'd displayed had only been an exquisitely drawn-out build-up of tension leading to a vastly decadent and vastly disappointing release. When the book was published in July 2005, and the reviews began to appear, my self-admiration was such that I already had begun making the mistake of planning ahead based on the specious and inflated currency of prestige. Things would get bigger: they had to.

It might have worked out. There are lots of ways of releasing tension, some stupid, some not so. Nelle already had voiced her alarm about my drinking. It's likely that, if my father hadn't gotten sick, I would have gotten hold of myself a lot sooner. But "getting hold of myself" already seemed like the enemy of fulfillment even before I'd learned about my father. I was high as a king. Hadn't whatshisname from the *Podunk Gazette* called *Trance* the greatest novel since a couple of months ago? This feeling of manic elation collided at high speed with the news of my father's illness. I stumbled, regained some control—and then I was named a finalist for the National Book Award. On the meaningfulness of literary honors I have very little opinion. It would have been nice to win, but I did not. What did happen was that a subjective and chancy selection process pushed me back into a state of mania. I was delusional generally throughout this time, kept afloat by a fantasy that placed *what I wanted* at the center of everything. Maybe I'd always had it there, but for the last decade I'd deferred and deferred, first taking care of my kid for four years and then taking care of a book for another four. Now my venal desires (to be a big-time writer, to live more expansively, to have money to spend) were joined by the desperate desire for my father to get better. The conclusion I drew was that the two were related.

✦

Here's a good moment to talk briefly about intentionality and magical thinking and their role in my parents' lives and mine. They were, and I remain, superstitious and prone to rituals, incantations, and compulsive gestures. My parents spoke of gods and furies, of the Evil Eye; of the power of looks, thoughts, and especially words to bring things into being. In the privacy of their minds, I think things were even darker and more idiosyncratic. My parents' pathological adherence to routine reduced—stylized, really—their lives to the condition of pageantry, but soothed something in each of them. The panic I continually fight against gives me, I think, an accurate idea of what their emphatic rejection of spontaneity or impulsiveness was put in place to ward off.

In exploiting what I shared of these tendencies to facilitate the writing of *Trance*, I'd done serious damage to my life and my marriage. To have come out at the other end of the process to find out that my father was sick didn't help me recognize how completely off the air I'd been for four years, but it did help me declare the neat regularity of my life to be the enemy. The whole point of the routine hadn't been about writing a book efficiently, it turned out, but about protecting and insulating everything in the world from change—and it hadn't worked. It hadn't worked for me and it hadn't worked for my parents, either. Otherwise, why would my father be dying? I'd been *good—I'd sat in a broken chair!*—yet he was dying. *He'd* been good. My *mother* had been good. Their whole lives had been a kind of broken chair in which they dutifully sat. But God was killing him anyway.

Did I really think in terms of God? I believe I did. I believe

I bargained and wheedled with the merciful, gracious, long-suffering One, the bright morning star, filling both roles in the dialogue. Of course the National Book Award was a test. A great temptation. I was supposed to want the right thing.

What do you want? God asked. The prize or your father?

Oh, my father, my response must have gone. Well, the prize is tempting, of course.

But?

But I want my father more. Yes, absolutely.

You're saying you'll *sacrifice* the prize if I let your father live.

Yes, absolutely, that's what I'm saying.

So it's a matter of giving one thing up in order to keep the one you prefer.

That's not exactly—

Very presumptuous. And what if this is it for your career? You hit a wall here and now, but keep your father?

Like forever?

Your father's not going to last forever either way.

Exactly. I think it's fair if the deal just covers this one time, this one book.

Oh, this *particular* book, this *particular* prize, is that it? You're anticipating other books, other chances, are you?

I'm assuming.

You *are* presumptuous, aren't you?

Listen, do I get a choice or not?

Ha ha, you never had one.

Trapped in phraseology, syntax, grammar, precise qualification and quantification—well, what else had my life been about? Our lives, my father's and mine. Writers want to get it right,

believe that the perfected arrangement of language will super-
sede the universe it pretends to map. But God is no writer and
God is no lawyer. The universe couldn't care less.

All of this is in attempt to explain why I decided to wreck everything that might have given me comfort—that might, for that
matter, have given my parents comfort. The steady, faintly un-
satisfying life, the sudden success, the dying father—I couldn't
resist the conviction that seized me and said, *it doesn't matter,
nothing matters, no one's feelings matter, no one's expectations, everything is temporary, good behavior gets you shit-all, see this as an
opportunity, use the opportunity to gratify yourself, your desires, your
forbidden fantasies*. Nothing explains it. Nothing, precisely nothing, is what was awakened in me; a great, invigorating application of nihilism to a life that I suddenly decided I'd been living
badly, in an utterly false expectation of safety and constancy.
Just like my parents. It was a nothing that spoke, finally, with
full-throatedness from out of the preemptive mourning of that
terrible, exhilarating autumn. Nothing was my guiding spirit; in
becoming nothing, I allowed myself everything. To be *something*
would have limited me, it would have required my involvement in
the most basic and essential parts of my life—my marriage, my
children, my parents, my work. As my father surrendered with
exquisite fatalism to the disease that was killing him, I descended
with him, surrendering to the impulse to murder my life. *Something* was what I had been—and for what?

Radiation, five days per week, for three weeks. It addles my father.
He goes to the storefront clinic on Third Avenue recommended

by Dr. Gouvias, over my strenuous objections. I confront Gouvias again.

"You know, he's an important man."

"Of course he is," says Gouvias, soothingly.

"No, you don't understand," I say. "I mean he's actually an important person."

What does Gouvias say? He says, "We're doing everything we can." He says, "He's in good hands." What else can he say?

To Gouvias, I must sound insane, not least because I don't have the chutzpah actually to articulate the substance of my concern: that this shabby, dusty little establishment where my father waits in a stained plastic chair for his turn to get zapped is for *a different class of person.* I am convinced that there is a hidden threshold that most of Gouvias's patients are not given the opportunity to cross, beyond which better, more effective treatment awaits. But even if there is better treatment available, Gouvias himself has no access to it; otherwise he wouldn't shuttle back and forth between his two small-time practices in Brooklyn's boondocks. The final piece of my utterly elitist argument against the neighborhood falls effortlessly into place: Bay Ridge itself is killing my father. When I visit, I corral my mother when my father goes into the bedroom to nap.

"We should go to Sloan Kettering."

"He doesn't want to, Chris."

"Make him."

"I can't make him do anything."

Have I noticed that she's finally begun to go gray? Have I noticed that she's losing weight?

"Let me talk to him."

"Don't bother him, he's made up his mind."

"Made up his mind. Can he even think straight anymore?"

"He gets agitated, Chris, if I bring anything up with him."

"So he gets agitated."

"You're not here when that happens."

"That's why I'm saying let me talk to him."

"Mother of God, help me to go through. *Do not* talk to him, Christopher. Just leave it be."

Minna and I began having our affair in November. It immediately pushed everything else aside and became my chief preoccupation. At last my restlessness had a nonevasive object to focus on, at last my anxiety and grief had something to anesthetize them. It was the affair's seriousness that was its flaw: everything in our lives might have recovered if it had only been a lark. It could legitimize itself only on the ruins of what it would displace, but in ruining those things it extinguished any possibility that it could be legitimized, at least in the eyes of the people, some of them friends, who professed outrage at its existence. We're still together, so the intense need animating the affair at its beginnings, and the petty scandal that resulted, have been ironically and nearly completely overwritten by a domesticity that looks strikingly similar to the one it replaced. I'm reminded of the so-called Flitcraft parable, told by Sam Spade in *The Maltese Falcon*: Spade is hired by a woman to confirm that a man sighted in the area is her missing husband, Flitcraft, who had abruptly vanished one afternoon years beforehand. It turns out that it is indeed Flitcraft, who tells Spade that on the afternoon when he disappeared he had been walking down the street when a beam falling from a building under construction struck the sidewalk right beside him. "He felt like somebody had taken the lid off life and let him look at the works," Spade says. He immediately deserted his life, leaving behind his wife and children. After several years of wandering he returned to the region, married a woman very similar to his abandoned wife and started a new family, and "settled back naturally into the same groove he had jumped out of." Spade concludes: "But that's the part of it I always liked. He adjusted himself to beams falling, and then no more of them fell, and he adjusted himself to them not falling."

I don't know if for me it's beams not falling as much as it's a desire to put the lid back on life and its works. Everything about my upbringing urged that—even suggested that a lid be manufactured and installed if circumstances hadn't provided one. What else was it all about, the endless organization and regimentation of things and actions that made no difference? Some people install alarms, some people buy guns, some people refuse to fly, some people kiss the mezuzah, and some people do the same thing at the same time in the same way every day for their entire lives. The noble end of this behavior had always, if subliminally, seemed to me to be *doing it right*—long after I consciously thought I'd rejected my parents' ways—but my father's illness put me in touch with the darkness of ritual, the staving off of disaster that submitting to ceremony was supposed to bring about. The adjustment I've made now is to avoid enslavement to the things that make me comfortable. No more broken chairs.

Throughout the course of the affair, I remember thinking *I deserve to be happy*, but what I really wanted was not to be unhappy. To feel perfect self-justification, I had only to look at my mother, who was as unmoored as I was. Her jailer was dying and afterward the only place left to live would be in the jail. There are few parallels between my parents' marriage and my marriage to Nelle, but I'm pretty sure I was thinking that I needed to take this opportunity to be free unless I wanted to end up like my mother. It was to her that I finally confessed one day, when my father was napping in the bedroom.

She didn't let me finish my sentence, raising her hand to stop me. "*Don't* say it, I know what you're going to tell me. I know all about men. I know what men do." She never elaborated—I never learned to what men she was referring. My father? Poor George Bradt? Whatever the injury she'd suffered, it was not something she ended up sharing with me during one of our conversations after my father's death. In any case, my mother was unsympathetic to any view that I was attempting an escape. Maybe she knew that I was just rearranging the furniture.

"It just happened," I said stupidly.

"No it didn't," she said.

"I mean, I didn't mean for it to happen. I didn't go looking for it. I'm not the kind of person who has affairs."

She looked at me across the dining table. "You are now."

To her credit, my mother did not allow this to cause a rupture between us, and she did not tell my father until I told her it was OK. It was difficult for me to disappoint my father under any circumstances, especially these. I usually managed to meet his expectations—in fact, I willingly deformed myself in order to make them mine, as well. Our bond was based on my being his creature. But I had no idea how it would go when his expectations had a moral dimension to them. My half sister had died with a syringe in her arm two years earlier following a brief and tumultuous life, and my half brother's estrangement from our father was in its fourth decade. They weren't guilty of anything more than being people whose unruly route through life had so alienated my father that he refused to accommodate it in any way. I needed to figure out a way to persist as something he could recognize specifically as his son.

It was my mother's moral expectations I chose to face. She was forbearing—for a time. By this I mean that she didn't kick me out of her life, not that she supported me in what I wanted. Her disapproval didn't, and doesn't, strike me as unreasonable, although obviously I didn't find it persuasive. I took fragmentary notes of conversations we had over the following months:

Conversation 1:

"I just don't approve of adultery. I don't think it's right under any circumstances."

"You have to understand that this wasn't a catalytic event. It was a climactic event."

"I don't even understand what you're trying to say."

"I mean that Nelle and I were already heading in that direction."

"Oh, what else are you going to say. It doesn't matter, anyway. If you'd left your wife before you had an affair, that would have been one thing. But you went and had the affair."

Conversation 3:

"How good of a person can she be if she cheats on her husband?"

"You said the same thing about Nelle."

"That was Nelle. And you're a married man. A father."

Conversation 7:

"You never ask me about all these things going on in my life. You know that they're happening and you never ask."

"What do you mean? I ask you every time I see you, how are you. And you say fine. And that's that."

"Of course I say fine. Everyone says fine. That's what you say. Everyone knows that."

"I don't know that."

"But you ask for specific details about other things. How are the girls. How's Nelle. Am I doing any work."

"You want me to ask you specifics about this woman?"

"Why not? You can't pretend she doesn't exist."

Conversation 11:

"You've abandoned your children."

Ultimately, she *would* pretend that Minna didn't exist, and for the rest of my mother's life the two of them never met or spoke. But neither of us was willing to permit my extramarital affair, and eventual separation from my wife, to interfere with the hard job of preparing for my father's death.

Things conspired against an easy death—strange and banal inconveniences that would seem to have no role in the crisis of my parents' life. They both needed dental work done. The dishwasher broke. One night, while they were sleeping, the kitchen cabinets somehow tore free of the walls, sending the cabinets and their contents—dishes, glassware, food—crashing to the kitchen floor. The co-op board voted to have necessary work done to the building's facade, scheduling the work to begin after the weather started to grow warm and leaving my parents unable to open the windows or operate their air conditioners because of the noise and dust.

Not that this bothered my father: nothing kept him warm anymore. He was in a state of perpetual cold. There were space heaters all over the apartment: heaters that blew warm air, heaters filled with oil, dangerous-looking heaters with long elements that glowed orange. These were left on even when the steam heat was already blasting, even when the temperature outside climbed above seventy degrees. My mother and I were in the living room while my father napped; I sat sweating on one of the leather armchairs that now sit in my own living room, my mother on the couch that, when he was present, belonged only to my father.

"He was avoiding bathing. I finally got out of him why. The poor man is so freezing cold when he gets out of the tub that he just can't stand it. So. What I did was, I found him a really thick terrycloth robe. He just puts that on as soon as he gets out and no more drying off."

I left Nelle. I crashed on couches and then moved into a sublet a few blocks from the apartment on Smith Street. A month later, I told my parents that I'd moved out.

I took my father to the radiation oncologist's for a follow-up appointment and the doctor took me aside.

"His condition has deteriorated considerably since the last

time I examined him," he said. He wasn't breaking the bad news to me. He was telling me my duty as a son. "You are the only child? You must prepare your mother for the worst."

My mother was bustling, though. For the first time in years, I did not consider her status as a sick person. She cleaned the house. She ran the errands. She did the cooking. She paid the bills. She dealt with Blue Shield, Medicare, the doctors, the nurses, the labs, the pharmacist. She dealt with the doormen, the superintendent, the porters, the neighbors. She also kept everyone at arm's length. People would call, sometimes people they hadn't heard from in decades. Some of them called—often unsuccessfully—to talk to him, but a surprising number, surprising to me at least, called to speak to her, to offer support or sympathy. These calls often frustrated and even angered my mother, who would criticize the callers' choice of words—they spoke as people in such circumstances often speak: with the aid of clichés. My mother found their lack of originality to be appalling. Sometimes my father would be present and afterward the two of them would mock the callers. It was like watching a battered old act take the stage for one last turn. At least now the anger, right there on the surface, had an obvious source. There was no need to wonder why they were so angry at so-and-so: they weren't angry at so-and-so. The only thing I wondered was whether this kind of derision, the staple of my upbringing, had always been so misplaced; if the true source of their fury had always been something as undefeatable and distant and yet as close to the bone as the cancer was now.

My mother called one day when I was sitting at my desk in the apartment I now lived in with Minna. It was May 2006.

"What's wrong?"

"Your father fell down on his way to the bathroom and I can't get him up."

This was inevitable. My father's legs had been reduced to stalks barely capable of supporting him; the apartment, with its furniture arranged for the convenience of able-bodied people, had become an obstacle course.

"Have you called anybody?"

"The only one he'll let me call is you."

I arrived at the apartment to find my father flat on his back on the floor in the narrow passage between the dining alcove and the entryway. My mother had placed a pillow beneath his head and covered him with a thick blanket.

"Are you OK, Pop?"

"I'm OK. I just can't get up." By this time his voice was just a rasp.

I found the wheelchair by the door to my father's study and brought it close. There was a moment when my mother and I jockeyed over the correct placement of the chair, with a hostility almost trivial in its familiarity. I felt that I was entitled to determine where the chair would go since I was the one who was going to haul my father into it. My mother had her own ideas. This ballet played out silently. When I finally squatted to lift him, I had the faintest impression behind my left shoulder of my mother quietly moving the chair into her preferred position.

"Put your arms around my neck, Pop. Hold as tight as you can." I put my own arms around my father's torso and drew him toward me. He was so thin. He groaned involuntarily.

"What hurts? Did I hurt you?"

"It's my back." It had to have been more than his back. It had to have been everything. The last report I'd extracted from my mother was that the cancer had spread into the bones. The only thing to be done was to do it quickly. Holding my father tightly with my right arm, I gripped the corner of the wall with my left hand to brace myself and then raised myself and the old man. He weighed almost nothing, came up with me as if I'd bent to pick up a bag of aluminum baseball bats. I put him in the chair. He went into the hospital that day and never left.

He spent the last week or so of his life in Victory Memorial's Rehabilitation Unit—why they'd stuck him there is something I've forgotten, or never learned. The unit had a day room that my mother and I would retreat to if, during our daily visits, we felt that we were going to quarrel.

"Hospice? Hospice care?" This was the suggestion of the hematologist who seemed to have taken over my father's case, and my latest opportunity to rant about Victory Memorial's countless shortcomings. Whenever I moved outside the envelope of bliss in which I was living with Minna, I felt nothing but rage. My mother's long effort throughout all this had been without respite, but I was furious at her for letting him go so easily.

"Your father seems open to the idea."

"He wouldn't need to be if they hadn't done everything ass-backwards from the day he was diagnosed."

"He's open to the idea and I can't get him to do *anything*."

"They fucked up everything. And now he's going to die."

"Oh, Chris."

"You understand, right?"

"You're always *on* me."

"He's going to *die*."

"Chris, did you just figure that out?"

Yes is the answer. Whatever hopes and beliefs I'd maintained, shored up over months, finally eroded completely. My father had declined steadily from the moment of diagnosis to the moment of death, with no remissions, breaks, bright spots. Somehow he'd finished a novel the previous month and had sat me down to explain what I would need to do to prepare for publication what he flatly described as "my last book." I'd seen him lose weight, lose his hair, lose his hearing, lose his voice, lose his concentration, lose his ability to enjoy the simplest pleasures. He'd been sawn open, blasted with radiation, flushed with poisons, poked until he was black and blue. But, greedily, I wanted him to stay, and I wanted my mother to want the same thing, to be willing to embrace the impossible with me. Had she suggested on the spot that we check him out of the hospital and fly him across the world to receive some experimental treatment, I would have dropped everything to go, and partly that was because this very conversation made me panicky at the thought of losing the barrier he posed between me and my mother. I had already devoted thought to what I was going to do without him, but now, sitting with my mother in the day room, I wondered what I was going to do with her.

Well, no, I didn't, actually. Not at that moment. I didn't identify the feeling I was having until much later, when everything inevitable had happened and everything avoidable seemed to have happened also. When my mother died eleven years later, grief seemed more tangibly categorizable. When my father died, something swung closed without my realizing that it had been propped open, or for how long. Recently, I recalled one of the few times I was able to be alone with him, sitting with him in his hospital room a week or two before he died. He was sick, he was dying—but it was a good day, and he was there, as much as he'd ever been, joking and laughing with me. From him, I could feel the web of connections spanning my life. He was alive and there was no pressing reason, at that moment, to consider that soon he wouldn't be. He was just a man in a hospital, twenty minutes from his apartment, my mother waiting there in a place to which he'd ostensibly return; waiting, living, connected to him and through him to me, and to my children, who were with my wife, separated from me but living in an apartment to which it was by no means established that I never would return; I might have been out anywhere, for any reason, say with friends among whom I would have been just another person with parents, a family, a consistent history. Minna was at the center, yes, but also at the edges because the normal had not yet been completely displaced by her, or by my father's death. Something had started it, this displacement; his illness had accelerated it, Minna's arrival had sent things out of control, but his death was the absolute end of the life I'd lived for forty-three years, since his presence in it was the one continuity that felt indivisible from that life. After that I was just the shell out of which something had burst. If there's a soul, mine was so tied to his that when he departed he took it with him and over the next years I had to acquire a new one. It's a better one, at least in the sense that it's fully mine, but that doesn't mean it's a good thing that he died.

He died on May 18, while I was en route to the hospital. One of the nurses on duty reported that when she'd entered his room that morning to give him his ration of Ensure, he'd said, "Keep it for someone who needs it; I'm dying today."

18

My father hadn't wanted any kind of funeral service, and so he was cremated in a cardboard box without ceremony, his ashes interred at Green-Wood Cemetery beneath a small footstone. A few people suggested a memorial service, but my mother made it clear that she would have nothing to do with planning it and would not attend if it took place, which was enough to shut down the effort.* My mother grieved absolutely privately. Apart from her obvious relief at having been released from the duty of caring for him, she shared none of her emotions. Of course her reticence was a form of grief, prefigured by the letter she'd written me thirty years earlier, after my grandfather's death: "Of course, we were all expecting it, and the whole family has reacted very calmly."

---

* A small service eventually was organized (by others), timed to coincide with the publication of *The Abyss of Human Illusion*, my father's last novel. The evening's highlight perhaps justified my mother's antipathy toward this kind of event: one of the scheduled speakers, Walter Abish, stood up to deliver his remarks and, in his wonderfully blunt way, explained to those assembled that he and my father hadn't *really* been close; in fact, hadn't really been friends at all.

We reacted very calmly. Days of unruffled industry immediately followed my father's death. So many people to call, so many arrangements to make, so many emails to write and respond to, and all of it a breeze compared to my harrowing trips to the hospital. I phoned my mother daily and went to see her when she permitted it. Since my father, worried that his condition would be upsetting to them, had refused to allow my daughters to visit while he was sick, my mother hadn't been able to see them either, so now Nelle or I were free to bring them to the apartment. Gradually, the daily calls became semiweekly calls and then dwindled to weekly calls.

Everything was done very calmly. It wasn't my father's death that finally intruded, but the complications it had interrupted temporarily. Four months earlier, at around the time that she and I had turned things upside down by informing the world of our affair, Minna had become pregnant. We proceeded through all the ordinary prenatal business as if the baby were mine, but Minna's husband, perhaps wary of facing a potential legal obligation to support the child, pressed for a paternity test. Minna was definitively convinced that it was not his baby, which I took to mean one thing and one thing only, but her conviction apparently was based on something else: the DNA results indicated that I was not the father.

I visited my mother to tell her about this gigantic anticlimax. It was unfair of me. Minna had been a problem of mine that she had managed successfully to avoid making hers. I knew how she felt about the whole thing. I had no words to explain why the affair had happened or why, even now, it continued to happen. That conversation would come years later, sitting across from each other at the small dining table; would come after Minna and I had endured the worst in each other more than once and after my mother and I had, in our turn, refused the same burden and become estranged more than once. Only then was I able to talk to her about what had happened to my life, providing an account my mother reflected back at me, more or less accurately, in one line: "You weren't in your right mind while your father was dying."

At the time, I expected her to be trenchant, cutting, recriminatory over my news. She wasn't. "Oh, Chris," she said. "Were you surprised?" This reads differently than it sounded when she said it. She didn't mean that I should have known better, which more than likely I should have. She was asking whether I'd been caught off guard. If there's an implicit criticism in there, it wasn't audible in her tone. Notwithstanding what I perceive as my mother's shortcomings, she did possess knowledge and experience, and, looking back on what I know of her life and its disappointments, I think what she knew from that experience was that disappointment takes many forms, and anyone can be innocent of its approach no matter how obvious it may seem to others. Nothing like this had happened to her, but other things had. Something like this might not have surprised her, but surely something else had. The evidence that her cumulative response to such disappointments had been deficient—her isolation, her bitterness, her voluntary surrender of her life—neither made a difference nor presented itself to me as some kind of crude object lesson. In that moment, she was just a mother.

Minna and I went to Italy that summer, the first time we'd traveled as a couple. The trip was tense and difficult, mainly for the reason I mention above, but also because now it was Minna's turn to anxiously await a parent's death: the front in her mother's fifteen-year battle with cancer had shifted, inoperably, to her brain. Shortly after we returned to New York, Minna left for her mother's house in Massachusetts, where she remained while I waited in Brooklyn. She gave birth to Isaac in Cambridge in early November; her mother died on Thanksgiving Day.

Throughout the fall, Nelle and I entered the phase of our separation during which if we weren't negotiating in earnest over custody, support, and other material issues, we were having anguished conversations about our marriage, whether and in what form it would continue. I would pick Penelope up from school each day and wait with both girls at the apartment on Smith Street for Nelle to come home. Then the two of us would huddle in the half bath off the kitchen to smoke and talk, Nelle making demands, suggestions, pleas, or rebukes and me responding with craven equivocation. No longer armored by expectant fatherhood (what a burden I'd placed on that unborn kid!), I had no way of defending any of the decisions I was making. Nelle was not as temperate as my mother and, as the scorned wife, was perfectly justified in being scathing. Usually I would drink so much of the whiskey that sat on the kitchen counter that eventually I would agree to nearly anything just to escape and run home, where my response to the empty apartment was to drink some more.

During this uncertain period, my mother and I were having speculative conversations that essentially fell under the rubric of What Would It Take to Get You to Return to Your Marriage?, or at least that's how I understood them. If my mother was campaigning, she was doing it with a light touch. It was pretty ingenious: she didn't ask any of the obvious questions that the situation raised, such as what I thought Minna's decision to carry someone else's child to term at the outset of our relationship might signify, or whether I believed that Minna and her husband were, under the circumstances, likely to attempt to repair their marriage, or what role I expected to play in the upbringing of that child, or whether I would be expected to contribute financial support, or how my own daughters would react to the arrival of this ersatz sibling, or whether I felt that, because she had left for Massachusetts and remained essentially unavailable for two months, Minna's absence was motivated by something more complicated than a desire to spend time with her dying mother. Nor did my mother ever mention how much happier she would be if things went back to the way they'd been before. She focused instead on the still-working parts of the existing marriage, the familiarity of it, the persistence of our common interests, emphasizing Nelle's trustworthiness, loyalty, helpfulness, friendliness, courteousness, cheerfulness, and thrift; the totality of what we'd built. Through this lens, the affair with Minna inevitably looked like a lavish self-indulgence, born of a crisis that had now passed. My mother of course knew perfectly well that Minna was two hundred miles away, and that I would consider our conversations in solitude, in an apartment where I felt so uneasy that, months after moving in, I still hadn't unpacked all my things. It was a good campaign, if it was a campaign. It didn't work, though, because the marriage to Nelle had weaknesses and flaws that were invisible to the outside observer, while the affair with Minna had strengths and virtues that I sometimes felt I was the only one interested in considering. One evening, while my mother and I were talking on the phone, I decided to mention this. "You know, Mom," I said, when she'd paused after her latest envoy to my marriage, "there are a lot of things about my relationship with Nelle that you don't know." It seemed reasonable to me. My parents were the ones who had taught me that marriages were secret organisms, closed to all but the relevant two.

"God damn it," my mother said. "Don't talk to me like that."

"Like what?" I asked, genuinely surprised.

"Don't be disingenuous with me. You know what I'm talking about."

"I don't."

"You tell me I don't know what I'm talking about."

"That's not what I said."

"You talk to me like I'm an idiot. I'm telling you something and you have the nerve to tell me I don't know what I'm talking about."

"About this—"

"You called me, I didn't call you. You wanted to talk, I didn't want to talk. Listen to my problems, Ma. I don't want to hear about your problems. I just lost my husband. You want to fuck up your life, go ahead."

"I'm sorry—"

"I'm sick and tired of your *bullshit*. Don't call me with your god damn *bullshit*."

I hung up. It was a purely reflexive reaction, part indignation, part panic. Mostly panic. This was the part I could never really reckon with; the instinctive and irrational terror I felt at any sign of my mother's temper, even now when she hauled her bad humor out like a faded and grimy banner that, on display, should have intimidated no one. I reflexively saluted it by hanging up. I could defy my mother, but because I'd never learned to confront her, to demand that she acknowledge my adult prerogatives, it never moved beyond defiance. Hanging up on her was the same as walking out of the house at midnight when I was seventeen, except that I didn't have to return to her, and she didn't have to accept me back. We didn't speak again for nearly a year and a half, and then only briefly, and after we'd repaired this rift, subsequent ones became effortless, even natural.

DEAREST MOTHER

Fragments, 2006–2012

NOVEMBER 2006

. . . I'm going to lift the covers for a moment to expose the issues. Just for one moment: what I expect of other people is that they take into account my status as an adult. I didn't insult you, betray you, or injure you. I hung up on you, because I don't like getting cursed at, and I don't like getting yelled at, and I don't like getting talked over . . . It seems you have other bones to pick with me, going back decades. I'd be more than willing to discuss with you all of the ways that you feel I've failed as a son or as a human being. I won't try to address any of them here because I don't want to bother you and because I don't really know or understand what it is about me that you find objectionable . . .

MARCH 2007

. . . I think to respond in haste to the rest of your note is to court intemperance, even if inadvertent, but I'll try because I want to before the conversation grows cold, if this even counts as a conversation. I would be pleased to have a "civil and cordial" relationship with you, though it seems to me that what you're saying is that you'd prefer to have no relationship beyond the one to which we're legally bound.* As I've mentioned, it isn't that I find the things you say to be "intolerable." I believe it's the other way around. I think you're a little quick to anger at other people's behavior, opinions, phrasing. Whether the precipitating act is sufficiently incendiary by itself or there's tons of flammable stuff accumulated just beneath, waiting to go up, I'm not sure. When we spoke, you seemed to have issues with me dating back decades. I don't know how to square grievances that go back to my adolescence. I had thought that what I've managed to accomplish as a man had ameliorated what were essentially a boy's transgressions, but maybe not.

I'm not so pessimistic as to think of the relationship (or myself) as being beyond redemption, and I think that to maintain the current situation is to enshrine a really pedestrian argument and raise it to levels of epic significance. That is to say, I'm not sure what's there that can't be seen beyond, at least given the argument's surface. You say you don't want to go below that surface, and while I'm perfectly agreeable to the idea of dropping it entirely, the Catch-22 the situation then presents is that if things don't get talked about, then we aren't able to fix them, and I'm constrained from raising the issues because you don't want to talk about them. To raise the issues, in your formulation, is in itself argumentative. Even if this were the case, which I don't think it is,

---

* I was referring to certain aspects of my father's estate, of which I'd been named literary executor.

what you seem to be saying is that it isn't worth the bother, which seems like a hell of a way to dismiss nearly forty-five years. I don't think you need me telling you that emotional adjustment is part of being in the world, it just seems to me that the richer and more enriching adjustment is toward conciliation, not estrangement.

Concerning what's best for the girls, I think what's best is that they continue to have a relationship with their grandmother. It's important to me and it's important to Nelle as well. What I'm not so sure of is if it's entirely cricket for either you or me to place it on Nelle's shoulders to determine whether that happens or not. I think it's really up to you to decide whether or not you want to see my children under whatever reasonable circumstances proffer themselves. As I said, I have no desire to interfere with your relationship with Nelle, but your granddaughters are my flesh and blood, directly connected to you through me—as will be any children I have in the future . . .

FEBRUARY 2008

. . . I'd like to suggest again that we try to make up. At the very least it's awkward to deal with my responsibilities to Pop's estate this way. I think you can see that. I need, for example, copies of all existing contracts, American and foreign. I am probably going to need access to Pop's manuscripts, correspondence, notes, and other papers generally.

There are also the other reasons I mentioned, which are at least as important, but I think each aspect flows one into the other. Everything wouldn't just work better, it would *be* better.

Even if an argument could be made that the current situation works, why would anyone want it to?

MAY 2008

... By the way, Nelle mentioned that the last time she went down to Bay Ridge you had offered her some of Pop's things—I guess watches and other personal stuff?—prior to disposing of them. I suppose you've donated or otherwise dealt with them by now, but I hope you'll bear in mind that many of these things, even trivial ones, have a lot of meaning for me and I would be happy to take them off your hands in the next round of winnowing ...

AUGUST 2008

... Otherwise, I hope you're OK. I've been thinking a lot about you, and about the way things have stood for almost two years now. I don't know what we can do to make it right, but I am very sorry, about the amount of time itself and also about having brought it on, though I don't suppose I saw it that way at the time ... [T]hat was a weird time, and I suppose on some level I took it out on you and I apologize.

... I think we ought to try to patch this up. The practical reason I can think of has to do with Nelle, her burgeoning new life, etc. I know that she's been taking the kids down to Bay Ridge every couple of months or so and it just seems odd or awkward if she's

going to actually make a go of things with [a man Nelle was seeing at the time]. For him, at the very least. I'm not saying Nelle
shouldn't feel free to go down, or that you shouldn't invite her or
stay in touch with her, but rather that primarily it should be me.
I'm their father, I'm your son.

But it's more than practical reasons, this is just stupid. There's
no point in it. I'm willing to take the stupidity on my own shoulders.
You did say some things that I found hurtful, but I'm assuming
that you were feeling neglected and angry because I was derelict in
my duty to you as a son in the late summer and fall of 2006, and
I apologize for that, too. I couldn't handle everything. I still can't
handle everything, but at least now it's only a matter of having an
ulcer-inducing schedule, not an ulcer-inducing emotional life too.
The point is, I miss seeing you because you're my mother, and
you're a link to my father, and this seems absurd. The point is, we
can either talk about everything at great length, if that's what you
want; or we don't have to talk about, "work out," a thing. We never
have to mention it again if you don't want.

*This particular period of estrangement ended in the summer of 2009.
We stopped speaking again in 2010, started again in 2011, then stopped
again.*

SEPTEMBER 2011

I'd be grateful if you'd let me know, as concisely as you want,
why you've been ignoring my messages over the past couple of

months. I'll spare you a speculative response to your silence, although I've done a lot of speculating about it. I've told you many times that I'm right here if you need me or if you want to talk to me about something. If you don't, that's perfectly all right with me. But I don't quite understand what I've done to merit a snub, if it is a snub, when I get in touch with you. I find it upsetting, distracting, inconsiderate, and strange. There are a lot of things I could add, but I'll leave it here for now.

In any case, it's also difficult, for reasons that range across logistical, emotional, and other boundaries. At the very least I would ask that you respond to specific queries I put to you regarding Pop's estate, particularly considering that you got very upset with me the last time you believed that I was not keeping you informed . . .

MARCH 2012

. . . Sounds kind of like a Yogi Berraism: "I'm so mad at him for not calling that I don't answer the phone when he calls." Gee, Mom, do you really want to live inside of a Jewish Mother joke? Even if I were to accept (which I respectfully don't) the deterministic view that my function is to initiate communication with you and that if I fail to do so then communication will not occur, I would feel justified in begging your pardon, at least on this occasion. As I've pointed out from time to time, I have work, I have school, I have the usual clerical stuff, I have housework and laundry and grocery shopping, and I have FOUR KIDS.* [*A pe-dantic list of child-raising responsibilities follows.*]

. . . I will happily acknowledge, because I know that it has mean-ing and importance to you, that it is primarily my duty to call you, and I will admit that even after taking all of the above into account that I can be and sometimes am remiss in that duty, de-spite my best intentions. What I would ask of you in return is that you not transform this into an ABSOLUTE duty. It would be truly great if, rather than saying to yourself, "I haven't heard from Chris; I'm pissed off that he's ignoring me," you were to say, "I haven't heard from Chris; he must be too busy to pick up the phone." It doesn't even have to be that charitable a thought. You can think I'm a jackass, if you like. But the point would be for you to pick up the phone yourself maybe once in a while, rather than for you to stew. It seems like a better solution than standing on a principle that seems, I don't know, slightly tautological ("The son calls the mother because that's what the son does.") and which doesn't seem to do anything much aside from making you mad.

All of this phone call business is quite apart from other related stuff stemming from that conversation you refer to. You'd said, for example, that I should just invite myself over if I wanted to come down to see you, but the couple of times I did turned out to be not such good times for you, and you didn't suggest any al-ternatives, so that was just sort of left hanging. I asked you about

* Minna and I had a daughter of our own, Anna, in the fall of 2008.

bringing the girls down to see you during Christmas break and you preferred not to see them before you'd had your teeth fixed. So that hasn't happened. You are naturally always welcome over here, but there is of course the question of Minna, who is someone you can choose to meet or not, as you wish, but who is a standing reality in my life in either case. As I've said to you before, in a different context, it's really hard for me to negotiate life when life is often deliberately and forcibly compartmentalized: so many people who can't or won't see each other, so many events to manage so that certain encounters don't occur, so much behavior whose perceived impropriety just sets some people off, so many events that can't be mentioned to one or more people, and somehow it all falls on my shoulders—probably because it's my "fault." This all hit its happy height years ago, but it's still there, has been for six long years now, six years during which I've often felt as if whatever pleasure my immediate family gives me is, or should be, illicit and furtive.

I am not mentioning this to implicate you in any way but to suggest strongly that it is far more complicated—at least for me—than simply inviting you over for dinner, say, or packing everybody into the car and driving down to Bay Ridge on a Saturday afternoon. Which maybe in the end would be a happier and more substantive measure than whatever phone calls:month ratio is supposed to equal filial devotion . . .

Anyway, I don't know where you intended to leave things with your email. I'm sure you can see that by telling me that you're angry enough at me to refuse to answer the phone when I call you,

you're transforming something that I *want* to do (whether I'm doing it "right" or not) into something difficult I *have* to do. And to what end? Are you saying don't call, or are you saying keep calling? Are you familiar with the Parable of the Importunate Neighbor? Should I keep knocking?

My mother responded to this email with one word, No, prompting this response:

MARCH 2012

I'm going to do it anyway.

I told you—promised you—that I'd call you regularly. And I have tried to do that. I can accept that I may fail in your eyes to live up to this promise. But—setting aside the question of your obstinate refusal to mitigate this by any means—I really don't understand why you insist that the only available response is to be vindictive toward me. You're baffled, upset, confused, angry when I don't call for a couple of weeks, yet I'm supposed to take it in my stride that you don't want to see the girls, you don't want to meet Isaac, you don't want to meet Minna, you're not interested in visiting my home. I'm supposed to take it in my stride that you prefer my ex-wife's company to mine. Those are your implicit terms, and I try to accommodate them. Honestly, I can't think of anything more devoted.

I think that there are parts of my life that make you profoundly uncomfortable. That is, as I have said before, OK with me, though I wish it weren't so, and that you could find a way to come to terms with those things. I'm grievously sorry if you can't. I fail you because your terms make it difficult for me to succeed. There's some point in the past when I was acceptable to you. I don't know when it was and I don't know how to get back there for you. I don't think I can. I don't think it was before Minna, I think it was before Nelle. I think you approved of me most when I was isolated, when I was alone and groping and completely receptive to your particular weltanschauung. But you know what? Like everybody else's kid, I evolved my own ways of thinking about things, of living. And I think that sometimes you have really, really resisted the changes that you believed took me out of sync with your way of thinking.

It's strange to put it that way because I don't really think the apple fell all that far from the tree, at least the tree that you and Pop formed together. Of all the things that have happened to me, my upbringing remains really formative. It hasn't been displaced. Whatever the two of you infused me with, it remains there, unless I have deliberately undertaken to squeeze it out, drop by drop, as Chekhov claimed to have squeezed the serf out of himself. And I have not all that often undertaken to do so, which is why I often find myself wondering why I am so often so objectionable to you. If you see my father in me, and you hate my father, well that's not my fault, is it? If you don't see you in me, then you're not looking. And I still don't really know what's wrong with me, anyway. There are schmucks all over the place, and while I can be a schmuck, that is not the quality that defines me. If you think it is, then you must have a really super-low schmuck threshold that simultaneously filters out every other human quality.

I don't even know why I'm cycling back into the I'm-not-such-a-bad-guy self-justification rap that I always find myself delivering to you. I don't think it has any effect on what you think of me, because if it did you might be inclined to think more charitably of me when you haven't heard from me. But you don't. You transform me into a monster of negligence. Well, I don't know how to talk you out of that one. I never have. I remember playing that game when I was kid—you waiting for me to demonstrate how "good" I was, and me failing, and then getting rebuffed in my apologies because they weren't sincere or heartfelt enough. I remember that a word I found to be mysterious and powerful when I was growing up was "disingenuous," because that's what you always accused me of being. And here I am forty years later, still trying to get you to like me—either quailing before your displays of temper, or scrambling to get you to respond to me.

Well, that's that for now. I guess I'll keep trying, and I guess you'll either answer or not as the spirit moves you. I hope you're feeling well, and that all of this isn't upsetting you as much as it's upsetting me.

20

On a gray and windy day in March 2013, I took a car service from my apartment in Kensington to Lutheran Hospital. Lutheran is located on Second Avenue, the ass-end of Brooklyn, or one of its many ass-ends. No matter how stupidly false New York seems to become under the siege of gentrification, there are always places like this to remind us just how ugly, just how degrading, urban life can be at the core of its authenticity. To the south is the Brooklyn Army Terminal. To the north is the Metropolitan Detention Center. In between lie warehouses, garages, one-story industrial buildings, truck lots, abandoned construction sites, the occasional forlorn cluster of tenements. It's impossible to spend a moment here without feeling as if you, too, are being swept out of the world's sight. A dismally perfect spot for a hospital. In keeping with its surroundings, Lutheran's main building looks like it could be a cold storage facility, a hulking container painted battleship gray.

My family's history with Lutheran goes back at least as far as my paternal great-grandmother Agnes, who succumbed there to what apparently was professionally diagnosed, in the 1930s, as "tired blood." My mother has ended up here, her local hospital now that Victory Memorial has closed, by default, absent any ideas of her own about where she might like to be admitted and evidently unwilling to ask for advice.

The previous afternoon, I'd received a call from Nelle.

"Have you spoken to your mother lately?" she said. This was a familiar opening remark from her. She knew how things often stood between my mother and me. At that point, my mother and I hadn't spoken in a year.

"No," I said.

"I just got a call from her. She's in the hospital." She paused. "She's been there a *week*."

"A week. And she just called you?"

"Yep."

"What's wrong with her?"

In the last few years, my mother gradually had begun to suffer from multiple ailments, the most serious of which was chronic obstructive pulmonary disease. Some of these ailments I'd heard about directly from her, when we happened to be speaking, and others I had not.

"Her sciatica got so bad she couldn't walk. She told me she finally had to call an ambulance."

"Sciatica?"

They had carried her out. No doubt whatever the pain, my mother had continued, stubbornly, to vacuum her floors and scrub her kitchen and bath. Typical. How long had it gone on? I had no way of knowing. I could imagine them putting the usual questions to her: Is there anyone you want us to call? No. Then

she lay in her hospital bed for a week, eating the food, enduring the daytime TV, watching her roommates' visitors come
and go, probably watching the roommates themselves come and
go. When she had decided to make a call, it had been to her ex-
daughter-in-law. Typical.

"What hospital?"

"Lutheran."

Typical. My mother gets sick; she picks the one hospital that
makes you want to commit suicide. Probably she didn't even pick
it. Probably she left it to the EMS techs to decide. Maimonides is
friendlier. Methodist is an earthly paradise by comparison. Even
the massive Kings County/Downstate campus, traditional desti-
nation of the downtrodden, has a more human aspect: Flatbush
is at least a real neighborhood, with real street life. She goes to
Lutheran, profound as a cinder block in a vacant lot. You expect
to see tumbleweeds rolling lazily down Second Avenue. Typical. Characteristic. Pathological. Even my father, dying in the
shittiest place imaginable, Victory Memorial—whose signal accomplishment concerning my father's care as he declined was to
promise serially and with increasing earnestness that its broken
CT scanner would be repaired "soon"—had had a view, from the
last room he occupied in this world, of the Dyker Beach Golf
Course. Too bad he could no longer sit up to see it.

Nelle gave me the number at my mother's bedside. It took me
three hours to work up the courage to call her. Calls to my mother
always have this specific ritual associated with them. Wherever
I happen to be—preferably at home—I sequester myself in a
quiet room (a scarce commodity in our house). Perhaps I want

to insulate my mother from the sounds of my life, of which she does not approve. Her disapproval is tacit, but completely legible nonetheless, and she has forbidden me to confront her about it. This is the larger part of the tension between us. My mother consents to deal with me as long as I don't insist that she also deal with Minna, with whom I've been living for seven years at this point. The problem is that sometimes I become, if not insistent, balky. The problem is that I become resentful if I allow myself to sit and brood over the fact that my mother has never visited my apartment, or met my stepson, or invited us to join her for a holiday or birthday celebration, and that to propose such things to her would be completely pointless, as they are not possibilities in her world. The problem is that, understandably, Minna finds the status quo insulting. The problem is that I dislike calling my mother to deliver carefully censored bits of news about my doings—censored to avoid contradicting her view of me (despite the fact that this is a ship that sailed long ago) and to avoid appearing to rebuke her static and solitary life.

So the obligatory call to my mother—granted, a genre of phone call familiar to millions of adult children of elderly parents—often seems to augur the worst. Whenever my mother and I have stopped speaking to each other it's almost always been, as it was the very first time, the consequence of a phone call that's gone haywire, somehow. I don't like the phone, generally; it's not a medium through which I communicate well, generally. It cuts me off from the cues I need to interpret her accurately. In person, I can tell when she is in a good humor and when she is irritated. I can tell when she is tired, when she doesn't feel well, when she is angry at me and when she is angry about something that happened fifty years ago. I can tell when she is impatient and when she is melancholy. I can tell when she is in the mood to reminisce and when she is done reminiscing. Above all, I can tell when the subject is closed—whether the subject concerns a personal matter, such as the location of her will and other personal documents ("Around here someplace," accompanied by a vague gesture that takes in the whole of the apartment, which happens to be filled with papers), or something idly conversational, such as Bill Murray's performance in *Broken Flowers* ("I do not like that man," she says; as a conversational gambit my maneuver is risky but not necessarily stupid, since my mother *does* like Jim Jarmusch). So I don't find out where the will is, or ask how she felt about Murray in *Coffee and Cigarettes*. But, in person, it's possible to preserve, or quickly restore, the mood: the will always will be around there, someplace. Bill Murray may never earn a reprieve, but I can bring up one of the TV shows we both like.

I also prefer writing to speaking to her on the phone. When we're not talking, I make a point of writing her long and detailed letters, some of which are excerpted in earlier pages of this book. In them, I tell her about my life with a candor that I usually can't manage when I speak to her. I'm not being spiteful. I'm simply uninhibited by the fear of observing her reaction, of having it inflicted upon me. I send photos—places I've been, the kids, Minna. I receive no reply to these letters. After she dies I will find them, opened and read.

It takes me three hours to work up the courage to call because this has been a long silence, one specifically ordained by my mother in the email where she responded to my asking her whether she wanted me to keep trying with a single word: No. So, always the obedient son, I'd stopped. It wasn't difficult, as decisions go. I have a life that's complicated enough, rich enough, daunting enough, frustrating enough, interesting enough, busy enough, to not miss paying court to someone who not only is not interested in it, in that life, but who sometimes can't help but give the impression of being actively against it.

And yet. I picture her alone in the hospital, *that* hospital. I see the nurses in their silly patterned scrubs, friendly or unfriendly, always efficient; I see the doctors in their glazed uninterest. There was a time when my mother was a prize patient—in Palo Alto, her rheumatologist made her case the subject of grand rounds on several occasions, residents and students gaping at her as she answered questions about her lupus and other afflictions. Now she simply suffers the commonplaces of aging, like anyone else among the elderly here at this working-class hospital. In the hospital, as I picture her, she is more alone than she is at home. And this I can't bear. I am literally fifteen minutes from her by car; for the entire week that she has been there I have been fifteen minutes from her.

Suffice it to say that my insouciance concerning the rift between me and my mother is just a thin and sloppily applied coat over a number of more anxious emotions: pain over not being loved; embarrassment over being one of *those people* who end up estranged from their parents; a feeling of being prematurely adrift in the world without the only person left who can confirm (in her fashion) the earliest and most obscure facts of my own history;

concern that my mother will disinherit me; and the prescient worry that my mother will end up dying, unexpectedly and alone, in her apartment, to be found God knows when by God knows who (I never quite could acknowledge to myself that most likely it would be me). But also compassion—never enough, it occurs to me now: never enough compassion to insist on changing things, insist on her increasing her tolerance for the unknown; never enough to overcome a fear of her displeasure that prevents me from being insistent—but also compassion, for a lonely old woman who, having been dealt a shitty hand, has done nothing more egregious than to play it badly. I cannot bear her being alone in the hospital. There is not even the hint of an inner voice saying "Fuck *her*"—although that voice certainly has found its way out into the world to express similar sentiments many times over the preceding months, when my mother was simply and forbiddingly there, six and a quarter miles away in Bay Ridge, immovable, immutable, a mountain I did not need to see to believe in, to feel the chill when I let it block the sun. At any rate, reluctant though I may be to make the call, I do not hesitate to do my duty to her.

(That sense of duty—how familiar. It's almost as if our estrangement has existed to test the durability of a mythical family pathology: the fortitude to see through what needs to be done no matter how unhappy we are about it. In leaving Nelle for Minna seven years ago, I have, according to my mother, committed the most serious breach of this sense of duty in family memory. This is most emphatically not true; my family history on both sides is filled with abandonments, affairs, betrayals, disappearances, disinheritances, disownings, divorces, estrangements, fallings-out, rifts. Some things people got over. Some things people didn't get over. But only people like my mother cling—against all the evidence—to the idea that such events are anomalous and unnatural. A half century of divorce and deracination had its way with us all—and was it all that bad? Was it really better for those child brides and boy husbands of the past to stick it out until the bitter end? For no one to pitch their ambitions beyond the borders of the Neighborhood and the Family, as if after the Bronx came the edge of the world and an endless drop into the abyss? My mother couldn't possibly *really* believe that. The greatest effort of her young adulthood was expended in furious opposition to such ideas, in leaving home, in leaving her first marriage. But I—I had *left my wife*. I had *abandoned my children*. I regret everything about the way this was done—or, to abjure the passive voice at this crucial juncture, the way I did this—but the fact remained that it needed doing, for reasons somewhat more complicated than that I had found someone else I liked better, which is my mother's lasting interpretation. My mother thinks that I am incapable of doing my duty, that I don't even acknowledge that I have a duty to anyone, to anything.

The point is that when we are speaking, things between us are fraught, that the only thing that has relieved the tension is not to speak, and that to call her—which, I am perfectly aware, she has not requested that I do—is to begin again the process of tautening the filament that connects us until it reaches the breaking point. But duty will permit nothing else.)

Yet she seems pleased to hear from me, when I call. It's a short chat, mostly to establish that I will be coming to see her and to bring some things that she needs—she left the house without her cell phone charger, her glasses, any warm clothing, or anything to read. I do not scold her: I decide well before dialing that I will not scold her for not calling me earlier, or for having allowed herself to deteriorate. Scolding doesn't work, even scolding disguised as affectionate scolding. My mother does not feel cared for when someone suggests that she could treat herself better, that she deserves more—whether it's better groceries, better investments for her savings, having her air conditioner installed, receiving a doctor's care before she cripples herself. And what's the point? She's already in the hospital.

"What happened?"

"Oh," my mother begins, "this damn sciatica."

"I didn't know you had sciatica."

"I told you, Chris. Why do you think my back is always bothering me?"

"OK. Anyway, what happened?"

"It got so bad I couldn't walk."

"At all?"

"I couldn't get out of bed one day."

"So you called an ambulance."

"I called the doctor. *He* called the ambulance."

"OK. So what's been going on at Lutheran?"

"What do you mean? I'm just sitting here. I'm hospitalized."

"But they're treating you."

"They have me on antibiotics."

"For sciatica?"

"No, Chris. They say I have cellulitis."

"Oh! OK. All right."

"My stomach is in turmoil."

"So the diagnosis is cellulitis and sciatica."

"And something with my heart."

"Your *heart?*"

"Chris, you remember when I had heart failure that time."

"No," I say. "No, I don't remember when you had heart failure that time. When? Recently?"

"Oh, years ago. I told you, Chris."

"So," I say, unsure what I'm asking, "are they *fixing* it?"

Apart from the characteristically resentful and suspicious tone concerning those responsible for her treatment—despite being under the continuous care of doctors for more than thirty-five years, my mother never swerved from her belief that *doctors make you sick*—what's worth noting here is the way that my mother's secretive attitude toward her ailments and their treatment had created a confusing alternate reality within which neither of us could tell the difference between what she'd told me that I'd forgotten, what she'd deliberately concealed from me, and what was a misremembered conflation of details drawn from among the hundreds of diagnoses and treatments she'd received over the years. The earlier heart failure episode, as it happened, was genuine—after she died I found a medical document in her files referring specifically to it in those terms—and there is no way that I would have forgotten that.

It turned out that "fixing it" wasn't exactly what they were doing. They had her on formidable doses of antibiotics, to kill the cellulitis, and on ACE inhibitors for the inflammation they'd discovered in her heart. But primarily they were hydrating and feeding my mother, who, when I walked into the room she shared with two other women, was unrecognizable. She was emaciated, the bare skin of her arms shrunken and wrinkled, as well as black and blue from the intravenous drips she was on. She'd lost a lot of flesh on her face, revealing her high cheekbones and the fine contour of her jaw, although any flattering effect this might have had was offset by the fact that she was now missing so many teeth that the lower half of her face had a sunken look. Her hair had thinned considerably and finally had become more gray than not. She had a slight tremor. She looked ready for the grave. It was, I thought, like looking at her corpse.* That was my second thought. My first thought was, She's had it. She was seventy-five, but I had become accustomed to the twenty-first-century seventy-five, the seventy-five of vigorous exercise, of intrepid world travel, of vocational productivity, of sexual insatiation, of new beginnings. My mother's seventy-five was a throwback to the mid-twentieth-century dark ages, when threescore and ten was what you could expect, preceded by a steep decline into senescence. My third thought was: This is my fault.

The beds in the small room were wedged in every which way, and she was sitting up in hers. I was surprised to see that she was talking on the phone. It was to Alba, her cousin, my "titi." She interrupted the call to allow me to press my lips against her cheek.

"Chris just got here," she said into the phone. Then she held it out to me. "Here," she said, "talk to your aunt."

---

* It wasn't at all like looking at her corpse.

Titi Alba, who had recently been diagnosed with cancer and would die at the end of the year, spoke with the staccato, syllable-timed New York accent distinctive to people of Puerto Rican descent, the accent my mother would have had, had she not decided not to have it. "So, you're gonna take care of your mother, right?" she said. Titi was always no bullshit. She knew perfectly well that my mother and I hadn't been talking. But she was happy I was there: clearly my mother had called to tell her that I was coming, that I wasn't going to let her down.

"It's good you're there," she said. "It's good."

"I know," I said. "I'm glad she called." Was this a mistake, or was it just that I knew that my mother's calling Nelle was her way of calling me? Could my mother have been as frightened of me as I was of her?

We talked for a few minutes more. Alba was five months younger than my mother and growing up they had been as close as sisters. She was now legally blind, living in Connecticut with my cousin Amanda, and about to face the final ordeal. But these facts were unimportant. She had intuited exactly what I had, the same emotional barrenness, about my mother's being alone in a Brooklyn hospital. *Alone, hospital, Brooklyn*—the combination of any two of those three words was enough to pierce the heart. Alba had buried a husband, she'd buried a mother, she'd buried a father. She'd raised daughters, she'd been a daughter. The rightness of my being there was a given; what she managed to impress on me during our brief (and final) conversation, eloquently but without really mentioning it at all, was that a thing's rightness gave no one the privilege to expect it. It was good that I was there because it was just as likely that I might not have been. When we were done talking I asked if she wanted me to put my mother back on: no. She'd saved the end of the call for me.

My mother and I were then on our own, albeit in the presence of her roommates and the hospital staff busying in and out. We handled it the way we had generally handled the mending of our relations: understatedly. As I said, my mother had been fairly explicit that clearing the air was not something she was interested in doing. I'm still surprised to consider the possibility that for my mother, the most ferocious, tenacious arguer I have ever encountered, the prospect of confrontation was too painful or daunting. I wonder what she imagined I had to say to her?

This is of course the era of latent accusation. It's possible that she thought I had found her liable for some act, error, or omission committed in the distant past, a historical outrage of which I had decided to declare myself a justice-seeking survivor. That was never my thing. I don't think of myself as a victim, or of my mother as an abuser. She crossed the line sometimes—but who doesn't cross a line from time to time? We are a depraved species and only the spiritually bourgeois believe in their own moral perfection. My mother's behavior toward me was not systematically cruel, nor was it sadistic. She took no pleasure in it. It did not give her relief, although I think she was always seeking relief. She sought relief in outbursts and she sought it in silence. My mother was trying to quiet the static in her brain, the angry dissatisfaction that never went all the way away. And now my childhood was decades in the past. So she really had nothing to fear from me in terms of recriminations. What I would have had to say to her, had it been imaginable to say it, would have had to do with the way she and I lived in relation to the world and to each other: my mother remote from everything and passively and impatiently waiting for me to join her in her remoteness, and me resisting her pull but refusing to pull back. I thought she was unhappy, and it made me unhappy. I thought she would be happier if she tried some of the things that she was convinced she was incapable of, all of which involved encounters with the most pedestrian unknowns. I thought that if she tried such things, it might encourage her to try others. That's what I would have talked to her about. That is, in fact, pretty much what I did talk about in the email that had earned her one-word negative reply.

Now, though, I could see that it was much too late. My mother was obviously dying. What would have been the point? I thought of the people who had once been important to her, dozens of people, daily parts of her life, of our lives. And they were dead, they were gone, they were missing, nothing would bring them back and no one could substitute for them. "The living people we've lost in the crypts of time sleep so soundly side by side with the dead that the same darkness envelops them all," wrote Céline. And now its shadows had begun to creep closer.

Enough, I said. Enough, already. On her behalf and in her best interests I am deciding that she never has to deal with the inconvenient complication of my life, with my importunate reminders of it, with my threatening invitations to immerse her in an impossible reality. My mother has become who she has become. How much time could she have left to change into something that suits me and no one else? Enough, already.

Within a day of that first visit, the hospital had determined that my mother was out of danger and that, therefore, there was nothing for which she needed to be hospitalized. What she needed was nursing care, and intensive physical therapy. They had provided her with a list of more than thirty facilities and told her to select five and rank them in order of preference. They would be discharging her in twenty-four hours.

Do you have any idea how to select a nursing home for someone? I hadn't. My mother left the decision entirely in my hands. "I know you'll choose the best one, Chris," she said. It was moving. A day earlier, we'd been estranged. Of course, neither of us had any other choice. It was a milestone: my mother was forced to recall that I was fundamentally competent at being an adult. And so was I. At that point I'd been letting a lot of things slide, first because of an inability to deal with them and then because disarray of all kinds seemed to govern my life at that moment. To attempt to be disciplined about matters I'd already decided it was beyond my capacity to handle struck me as moron's work, when it struck me at all. So this marked the end of what, in retrospect, looks remarkably like a multiyear depression. The details of this depression have little place here, except to give me the opportunity to note that life is the difference between what you let slide and what you don't. I might have let this slide, too. But I couldn't. So I made phone calls and did research on the internet and scheduled appointments and schlepped from one part of the borough to another and made copious notes and checked financial and insurance documents and spoke with the social worker at Lutheran. I had to be polite, persuasive, interrogative, and insistent, sometimes at once. The consequences of adulthood came into focus clearly and, for once, rewardingly. No one was going to do this for me. I either did it or my mother was rolled out onto Second Avenue and left there; either I did it or I had to live with that. I had to will myself into what initially felt like a pose of maturity—despite the fact that nothing had changed, i.e., that all the conditions that had combined to make it otherwise remained the same. I was suddenly ashamed at the way I'd decided that helplessness was the most comfortable way to justify my own inertia. Today I was no less broke, no less unsuccessful, no less disappointed, no less lacking in attractive options, than I had been a week before. But helplessness—real helplessness— was waiting in that hospital bed already earmarked for someone else, waiting for me to report the good news.

The good news was a place I shall call the Perkins Rehabilitation and Healthcare Center. It was a clean place, modern and cheerfully decorated, with a good reputation that had survived its operations being taken over from the Diocese of Brooklyn by a private corporation. It was in Boerum Hill, adjacent to my old neighborhood, and three blocks from the subway, friendly territory, familiar to both of us. I made the arrangements with Lutheran's social worker and, around dinner time the next day, an ambulance delivered my mother there. We went through the admissions procedure together, my mother was given a brisk tour of the local landmarks—the dining room, the lounge, the common areas, the terrace, the gymnasium where she would receive physical therapy—and finally she was wheeled to her room upstairs. Her roommate, a Mrs. Jackson according to the handwritten nameplate on the door, was out but had unmistakably marked her territory: mounted on the wall opposite each bed was a television, and hers was blaring. Uh-oh, I thought. But my mother took it all in blandly. I found the remote control on Mrs. Jackson's bedside table and turned down the TV.

"What do you think?"

"It's very nice."

There was no disguising the fact that it was a room in a nursing home, but I'd seen worse places—I'd seen some of them within the prior twenty-four hours, in fact—and after Lutheran's fortress of despond it was quite cheery. My mother's window looked out on Dean Street's brick rowhouses and plane trees. The functional furniture was reminiscent of a college dorm room. The place also was lacking the peculiar aura of illness that a hospital radiates. The people here were old, and they were damaged, but they were not sick.

I'd wanted to sit with my mother until Mrs. Jackson returned because I wanted to make sure the intimate presence of a stranger didn't precipitate a crisis of some kind. She'd been in the hospital for more than a week, but her neighbors there had been begowned ciphers, spoken of by my mother as "that one" and "this one." I could see why, in that crammed and chaotic room, obscured behind IV stands, batteries of equipment, and curtains, they might have been difficult to distinguish from each other, and I could see why, with each of them engrossed in the exigent disaster that had brought her there, none of them had wanted to get friendly. But this was different. Mrs. Jackson's bed was turned down and she'd left a pair of eyeglasses on her pillow, as if she'd simply left her bedroom to get a snack from the kitchen. The room did not buzz, click, whir, cheep, beep, hum, or throb. Staff did not barge in and out. It would be my mother with someone else for the first time since my father had died, and with a stranger for the first time in more than fifty years.

But my mother dismissed me. "I'm tired," she said. "I'll be fine."

"I'll come see you tomorrow afternoon."

"You don't have to."

"Of course I do. I'll bring you something to eat."

"I'm sure they'll feed me."

I gave her a look that must have telegraphed my extreme skepticism over the quality of the food, because she burst out laughing. "All right, then," she said. "Bring me something to eat. Now off with you. Go home. Your children are waiting."

We established a routine. It evolved rapidly, both of us being creatures of habit. Every day, I would work until the afternoon and then I would take the subway to Bergen Street, where I'd pick up something on Smith Street for my mother to eat. Sometimes when I arrived at her room she wasn't in, and after saying hello to Mrs. Jackson and whichever of her relatives might be there, I'd go to the common area and sit on a sofa reading my book until she returned. It didn't escape me that I was seeing more of my mother than I had since I'd moved out of the house nearly thirty years earlier. The circumstances we found ourselves in restored us to the essential two: the mother, the son. One provided care, one needed care. One left, the other awaited a promised return. One worried about the other in a new situation, the other adapted quickly. The roles had simply been reversed.

Although I was seeing her every day, we spoke to each other with ease. We invented new jokes: about certain residents, about certain staffers, about the routines, about the food. This also was when my mother began for the first time in years to talk freely to me, about her life, her upbringing, her first marriage, her marriage to my father.

I came home one evening and said to Minna, "That fucking place is good for her. You know what she did? I was wheeling her around the floor, doing a circuit. She said hi to about five people."

"She *did?*"

"Yeah, and then you know what? We're going by this room just past the nurses' station and she says, 'Push me in here, will you, just inside the doorway.' So we go in and she starts jawing with the guy in the bed in there."

"No way."

"Yeah. She took so long I had to excuse myself to go and pee."

So there it was. My hopeful hypothesis was: this will fix her. Every day she talks fluently and easily to Mrs. Jackson, Mrs. Jackson's daughters, Mrs. Jackson's granddaughter, the nurses, the nurse's aides, the orderlies, the other patients, the physical therapist, the nutritionist, the social worker, the occasional doctor. This is life again. This is reality reflecting itself back at her; this is her figuring out how to perform being herself, day to day, in front of people whose propinquity little by little exhausts their strangeness—no, more than that: what's exhausted is the attitude that strangeness necessarily is hostile to the human spirit. And meanwhile her strength is returning, her weight, her color, the sheen of her hair. And meanwhile I would visit. Nelle would visit. Violet and Penelope would visit. Sometimes all four of us would wind up there with her at the same time and we would push her onto the elevator and, if the weather was good, sit with her on the first-floor terrace overlooking Dean and Hoyt Streets. And I would think, This is nice.

But of course that was the problem. That was the rub. My mother enjoyed the illusion of togetherness. Me and Nelle, or me and Nelle and our children, restored to my mother the dream of an intact family—we were intact, there. She didn't see us go our separate ways, Nelle and the girls down Smith Street to the apartment I'd left seven years earlier, me down into the subway to ride out to Kensington. She knew it happened, once we'd left, but it was an easy thing not to think about. And who would force her to think about the other thing: the other family—new, fraught, shaped by the pressure and weight of the old? By now Anna, my youngest, was in prekindergarten; Isaac, my stepson, in first grade. I had introduced Anna to my mother, but the silences between us had destroyed much of the time in which they might have gotten to know each other. The tricky partition separating the two parts of my life was the thing I found it easy not to think about. And forcing my mother to deal with such things was against the rules of the new Enough Already policy I'd instituted.

So it was partly with the aid of a slightly galling fiction that my mother knitted herself back into shape. Nelle and I play-acted at being, if not married, together. Which of course we were: we both wanted my mother to recover. We both wanted our daughters to spend time with her. To that extent, it wasn't a charade, but what my mother wanted to be real, wasn't. It was, not childish, but childlike in a way I could recognize. *Don't ruin the story:* this is the protest defending doomed things from Santa Claus to first infatuations. Don't spoil it; we both know how it ends but let's not mention it. But the exclusion of the other family was the salt sown in the furrows of this garden we were planting.

For a long time I'd been wondering about the trove of family photographs my mother had kept but which I hadn't seen in years. She spoke of them, when I asked, as if they were as inaccessible as the past they documented, but insisted that they were safely "put away somewhere." I had begun to suspect that she'd tossed them in some momentary fit of rage, because the embargo she'd imposed was otherwise inexplicable. Apart from the very few I had on hand at home, neither my children, nor Minna, nor Nelle for that matter, had ever seen photos of my childhood. So on one of my occasional visits to my mother's apartment to check that things were OK and to get something she'd requested, I decided to satisfy my curiosity. First I entered my father's study, the door to which my mother had kept closed since he'd died. Everything was pretty much exactly as he'd left it, I discovered, but my mother now used the tiny room to store papers, boxes of clothes intended for donation, and other things that she wanted out of sight. But no photos. With trepidation—as if at any moment my mother might walk in and discover me in the act of prying into her business—I poked through the apartment, looking through closets and in drawers and under large pieces of furniture until finally I found, on a high shelf in the utility closet, a cardboard carton that looked as if it might actually have remained sealed since my parents had packed it more than a decade earlier. Dare I? I dared. There they were: two albums as well as several shoeboxes full of the outtakes and negatives, still in the envelopes in which they'd been packaged when my mother had picked them up from the drugstore.

I brought them home and sat down with them. Everything was there: the dead and the missing, my half brother and half sister dressed for Sunday visits, my grandparents and aunts and uncles and cousins in the Bronx, the family friends, the playmates, the put-to-sleep pets, the forgotten toys, the discarded furniture, the outmoded packaging, the erased neighborhood, the fads and fashions that pin people to a moment in time and announce their perishability. Someone brings you into this world, but who's going to help you out of it? Not these people. They were gone. Everyone and everything in these photos was gone, except me. Why would my mother have wanted to look at them, a record of loss? But it was a past centered, I quickly realized, on me. Sprawling on my back, unable even to raise my head. Sitting on my father's lap. Standing in my crib. Walking uncertainly in Stuyvesant Square. Running through the spray of the wading pool in Tompkins Square Park. Blowing out the candles on a cake. Lying on the couch in our Westbeth living room, reading, signs of the preparations for the move to California all around me.

One day, the social worker popped in to talk. She sat down and told us that my mother needed to sign an order concerning life-sustaining treatment.

"Sure," my mother said, immediately. "I don't want anyone keeping me alive."

This was the obvious answer: we'd both watched enough TV to know the dignity-destroying effects of extraordinary measures. In the abstract, I agreed: when it's time to go, it's time to go, etc. I imagined what you might imagine: the hopeless case, the ventilator, the liquid nutrition administered drop by drop, the bags filling with waste, for months and years on end.

"I'll leave this with you, then," the social worker said, removing a form from a leatherette portfolio she was carrying. "Read it over and I can answer any questions you have before you make a decision."

"I don't need to read it over," said my mother.

"Mom," I said. "Let me read it. What's the rush?" I don't know what moved me to say this. Maybe it was something about the daunting amount of fine print. The health care proxy I had at home was at most a few short paragraphs in clear language.

"All right, Chris," said my mother. "Whatever you say."

"Sure," said the social worker. She was a tall, good-natured redhead. "Take your time."

She left and I folded the form up and put it in my jacket pocket. When I got home that evening I took it out and read it.

The next day I found the social worker in her office.

"Tell me if I'm reading this right," I said. "If my mother opts for the DNR order, that means that if she chokes on her oatmeal tomorrow morning or something and can't breathe, that's it. You do nothing."

"Technically, yes," she said. "Generally, respiratory or cardiac arrest arises from other causes, though."

"But that's not the case with my mother though, is it? She's here to learn to walk again."

"Well, that's something the doctor can address when you talk to him."

Doctors make you sick. I silently considered the likelihood of deriving satisfaction from a talk with a doctor in which he justified the ethics of standing by while an otherwise sound patient strangled to death on a grape from her fruit salad, thanked the social worker, and went to my mother's room.

"Mom," I said, showing her the form, "I'm not so sure about this. It's pretty general."

"What do you mean?"

"I mean, it's not like just if you have a coronary or something. It means that if you stop breathing for any reason, they won't try to resuscitate you."

"Really?"

"I'm pretty sure. And I just asked the social worker to confirm it."

"I don't know why you had to go talk to her about me without asking me first," she started to complain. But abruptly she changed tack. "I never knew that."

"Neither did I. But why would we?"

"Your poor father. I signed one for him." She appeared to be on the verge of tears.

"Mom, Pop was dying. You're not dying."

"Yes, he was, wasn't he?"

"He was ready to go."

"Yes." She was silent for a moment. "So you're saying I shouldn't sign?"

"That's what I'm saying."

"Whatever you think is best."

"That's what I think. Besides, I have your health care proxy. Now that I think of it, I'm not sure we have to deal with this at all."

"You know what I want, though, right? You know my wishes?"

"Of course. I won't let them do anything you don't want them to do."

"I really don't want to be kept alive artificially."

"Oh, don't worry. I'll unplug you first chance."

She broke up. "Oh, Jesus, Chris, they'll throw you in jail."

"They'll probably give me a fucking medal."

"Oh, Jesus." She kept on laughing. "You are *bad*. All right. I'll do what you say. You know best."

In this case, maybe. My mother's wishes, what were they?

She got better. About six weeks after she'd been admitted, she was informed that she was going to be discharged. A visiting nurse would be assigned to her, as well as a physical therapist who would work with her in her apartment. She was happy to be going home, of course—for one thing, it was a measure of the strength and mobility she had been so focused on restoring. But I'm not sure that my mother recognized what else had begun to be restored to her at Perkins. What she'd taken were baby steps; I don't want to leave the impression that over a month and a half my mother had transformed into an outgoing, sociable, bingo-playing dynamo. To begin with, this would have been the equivalent of a personality transplant, and anyway the atmosphere at Perkins hardly constituted that of an extended episode of *The Golden Girls*. The elderly there clearly were shaken by their infirmity: to not walk, to be unable to peel an orange, to *need*—these were matters to be dealt with (or not) through concentration and inward focus, not through mah-jongg and wisecracks. The environment determined a baseline of sociability toward which some people regressed, but toward which others advanced. My mother advanced. The change was remarkable. She grew used to dealing with people again, grew undaunted by it. This one poking, this one prodding, this one asking questions, this one patronizing, this one brusque, this one friendly, this one funny, this one nuts, this one sweet, this one boring—there was a world of people out there, and you could get along with most of them. All I could do was hope. Her isolation had been a taboo subject, so I couldn't raise it. I didn't know what would happen when my mother was alone again in her apartment, door closed against the outside world.

21

She settled back into her secluded life, of course. She would not visit, she would not call. After a while, she stopped picking up the phone when I called, and then stopped returning the calls, and then stopped answering and/or returning the calls I made following up on the calls I'd made to begin with.

The only thing that had permanently changed, really, was that I was willing now to accept her terms without reluctance. Going through my old datebooks from 2013 on, I discover regular reminders—*Call Mom*, they say, or, in the case of a few days' delinquency, something like *CALL MOM!!*. No sooner would I have spoken to her than I would make another notation reminding myself to call her within the next week. Losing touch with her again was definitely out. In a way, it was a triumph of her vision of herself. She had wanted to be seen as an invalid, and after she recovered from actual invalidism, I consented to treat her like one. My diary from this time forward is full of entries that chronicle her decline. I record her miscellaneous physical complaints, and my anxious observations about what seemed to be her lapses of memory, "beginning to lose feathers from the spaces between the seams," as I put it in January 2015, after she told me that she been referred to an oncologist to be tested for multiple myeloma. I'd recalled aloud that my grandfather had been diagnosed with multiple myeloma and she had said, "Grandpa who?" It wasn't that she'd forgotten her father, but she had forgotten the diagnosis, which surprised me because I could recall vividly how upset she'd been whenever they painfully drew the marrow from his bones, which happened when he was already weak from leukemia.

Not that my mother wanted to be taken care of. About a year before she died, I had trouble getting in touch with her and, over the course of a week or so, became increasingly worried. Finally, I got hold of her and she told me that she'd been laid up again with cellulitis.

"Why didn't you call me?" I asked.

"What could you do?"

She made it plain that she was waiting to die. Her apartment began to take on a neglected look. When her living room air conditioner broke, she refused to let me install the new one, a massive unit intended to fit through the wall, which then sat uselessly on the floor through some of the hottest days of August. Her refrigerator seemed to have less and less food in it each time I checked. She was sick with a dozen things, but I don't think physical illness influenced her thinking about life and death. Her social isolation was a progressive disease, and the impulse to remove herself from the normal transactions of living evolved naturally into the impulse to remove herself entirely from life itself. I don't think anything I might have done could have altered that evolution. While I've sometimes concluded that I should have *pushed harder*, it's difficult to come to rest on that conclusion since our entire relationship, my mother's and mine, turned on her having conditioned me from an early age to know when to stop pushing; to fear the consequences of pushing.

In any case, I genuinely took her for granted—her durability, at least. I fully expected her longevity to rival that of Dora (88) and my great-aunt Rosalina (87), if not that of Doña Ana (96). When I would say as much, she would respond, "God, I hope not." One day she said to me, "I don't want to die, but I'm ready for it," which struck me as a first cousin to desiring death, or a nearer relation. Yet the machine kept kicking into gear every day.

When we spoke, she was happy to hear from me. I made sure that there was no friction between us. Some time after the multiple myeloma testing (negative), she casually mentioned for the first time a CAT scan she'd had a few months later, ordered by the same doctor. "He may have found something," she said, but added that if he wanted her to undergo more tests, she might decline.

"Why?"

"I don't want to tempt fate," she said. "The gods may say, OK, this time we're going to give you cancer." She said this in complete seriousness.

"Ha, well," I said—lightly, lightly—"I can understand how you feel, but I hope you're not going to let that kind of thinking guide your medical decisions."

Immediately, I could tell I'd blown it. "Christopher," she said. The use of my entire first name never boded entirely well. It's an amazingly easy name to pronounce through gritted teeth. How dare I call her superstitious. Very offended. I've known her my entire life, I know perfectly well that she's not a superstitious person. What do I think she is. Who do I think I am. Etc. I let her anger wash over me without either bolting or contradicting her. Then I apologized up and down and managed to avoid a rupture. Now that I had finally figured out how to deal with her, I would sometimes start laughing once I'd hung up after one of our conversations, wondering exactly who it was who had been speaking to her, I sounded so unlike myself to myself.

I would go to see her. Every now and then I would bring one or more of the girls, but mostly we were alone. We established a routine. I would bring lunch and any groceries she said she needed. Sometimes I would surprise her by picking up some kind of treat I thought she'd like, although the gesture was diminished somewhat because my mother always insisted on writing me a check for whatever I'd spent at the supermarket. I held these in my wallet, checks for fifteen or twenty-five or forty dollars, eventually depositing them in clusters of three and four when she would kvetch at me for making her carry them forward when she balanced her checkbook. We would sit across from each other at the small dining table and run through various topics—whatever was happening in the world, what TV shows we were watching, how things were going with the kids, what I'd heard from or about old friends I knew she'd remember from my adolescence, literary gossip, and then, these preliminaries taken care of, we would settle in to discuss the great topics of her life—her childhood, her adventures as a young woman, her marriage to poor George Bradt, our life on the Lower East Side and at Westbeth, and, always, her marriage to my father.

It was a chance for her to make a record, and I was very receptive. My father hadn't merely talked about his life again and again but had written it, reworking the smallest details of a story that had never failed to fascinate him. Not incidentally, he had completely drowned out my mother. Her own storytelling was oblique, patchy, suggestive, occasionally contradictory. Past events floated out of memory wholly formed, isolated, perfect stories. Others stubbornly remained fragments—"So-and-so was this, you know," or "This was after, you know, such-and-such had happened." I didn't know. There are things I never learned and gaps I never filled. It was sometimes as if I were listening to John Dowell narrate the story of *The Good Soldier*. There were things she'd mentioned to me just once, when I was a child, and never discussed again; and there were of course the parts of her life which I'd witnessed as a child and discovered I needed to reinterpret from an adult's point of view. "So 'my mother' is both who she is and a monster of my own creation, roiling beneath all my anxieties and partly the author of them," I wrote in my diary. Turgid, but accurate. Despite the fact that the past became a regular topic of discussion between us, I never felt as if my mother wanted to return there or was preoccupied with it the way that my father had been. It was really a matter of making a statement. Sometimes, I think, she wanted a witness, other times I think my presence was just the pretext for rehearsing these matters as she readied herself for the end.

One day, she got annoyed at me for some flippant comment I made about a local politician, a Puerto Rican, who was in the news for some misbehavior.

"What's this problem you have with being Puerto Rican?" she said, taking me by surprise.

"I don't have a problem with it," I said. "But wait, you always told me that I wasn't a Puerto Rican."

"You know perfectly well that I'd never say such a thing."

"You were making a point, I think."

"What could that have been, I wonder."

"Well, I'm pretty sure I understood what you meant."

"Which was?"

"I think you were just talking about the difference between me and, like, the more, ah, typical way a Puerto Rican might grow up."

"Mijo," she said, "there's no such thing as a typical Puerto Rican."

"Of course not, right. I misspoke."

"Some of them are white, some of them are brown, some of them are black."

"I know."

"Some are poor, ignorant people and some are perfectly elegant. Your grandfather's family were very cosmopolitan people, professionals and scholars."

"'Pure Castilian blood.'" This was a running joke between us, a line Rita Moreno had spoken in a movie we'd both enjoyed, *I Like It Like That*. I delivered it in my Ricardo Montalban voice. She laughed.

Changing direction suddenly, she said, "It wasn't your fault the way you were brought up."

"I never thought it was anybody's fault."

"I could have done a better job."

"Everyone could do a better job at raising their kids, Ma."

"I'm just talking about *this*, Christopher."

"Right."

"We really could have spent more time with my family."

"I always thought of them as my family, too. I liked visiting them. I missed it when we stopped."

"That god damned Dora."

"Water under the bridge, Mom. She's been dead almost fifteen years."

"But you need to understand that you were brought up the way you were because that's the way I wanted things."

"I figured."

"Not for you. I mean, yes, of course for you—but originally for me."

"Of course. You wanted a bigger life."

"Bigger. Ha."

Around here the conversation ordinarily might have been shunted down a lengthy siding having to do with my tyrannical father's failings. But her mind traveled somewhere else, instead. She said, "Have I ever told you about my friend Marcia Alleyne?"

"I think you've mentioned her. From high school, right?"

"I knew her at Rhodes, yes. A West Indian girl. Her family was from Barbados. She was a beautiful girl. Just a heartbreaker. She stopped traffic. I loved her dearly. We had so much fun together."

"What made you think of her?"

"I don't really know, I just did." She sipped her coffee. "She was very light-skinned. And so she passed. Not at school. Everyone there knew she was West Indian. But outside, in the world."

"Sounds like *Imitation of Life*."

"Oh, Chris. It was nothing like that. She wasn't *ashamed*."

"OK."

"It just made some things easier sometimes."

"Did it make that big a difference? In New York? Did people really care that much?"

"You mean because her skin was *light*, Christopher? Because she wasn't *dark?*" She looked at me. "Of course they did. It was 1954, '55. Anyway, we graduated and went our separate ways. Lost touch completely. Years later, oh, after you were born, I bumped into her one day in the Village."

"Did she know you?"

"Well, I hadn't changed that much. But her!"

"What was she up to?"

"I'm getting to that. I ran into her and I almost didn't recognize her. She was wearing her hair natural, and a dress made out of kente cloth. Still beautiful."

"She found her pride."

"I guess she did. And I was always a little envious, that she could go back and forth like that."

22

The pile of newspapers. The sound of the oxygen machine. The smell. The light from the bathroom. The medicine chest open. An empty box of tissues on the floor. Tissues, balled up, forming a trail into the bedroom. A towel, folded but mussed, placed on the floor before the toilet. Rust and brown stains on the bathroom floor. Stains on the bedroom rug. The light from the bedside lamp.

Sound of the machine. The smell. The light from the bathroom, falling into the short hallway. The gaping medicine chest. The empty box, dropped to the floor. The trail of tissues. The mussed towel, the blood and feces on the bathroom floor, the bedroom rug. The bedside lamp.

The smell. The pools of light, in the hall and in the bedroom. The open chest. The empty box, lying on its side. The trail of tissues, wadded up, leading to the bedroom. The mussed towel, blood and shit on the floor. A blackened hand.

The light, falling into the short hallway, pooling on the floor. The chest. The trail of blood, shit, tissues. Bedside lamp casting light on the blackened hand, the limp and splayed legs, the bloated belly.

Open chest. Empty box. Trail of blood and shit. Shrunken,

blackened hand, clutching a length of plastic tubing. The bloated belly, the limp and splayed legs, the lividity in the visible calf, pant leg riding up.

The box of tissues. The trail of tissues leading into the bedroom. The folded towel. The balled-up tissues. The empty box, its contents balled up, forming a trail. The mussed and bloody towel, the blood and feces on the bathroom floor, the bedroom rug.

The trail of blood and shit. The smell. The sound of the oxygen machine.

The legs, the hand, the plastic tubing snaking up the torso. The head thrown back.

The head thrown back, skin here drawn tight against the skull, there falling from it like drapery, mouth agape, something moving inside it. Custard-colored in the dim light.

Blackened hand, the limp and splayed legs. Crumpled tissues littering the floor.

Blood and feces, spotting the bedroom carpet. The empty box. Light falling into the hallway. The open medicine chest. The smell. The sound of the machine, the trail, the stains.

What could have been in that medicine chest?

The blackened hand, gripping the tubing. The lividity of the ankle, between the pant leg and the sock. The head thrown back, mouth agape, something working inside of it. The hair lustrous. The smell. The windows: one, two, three, four, five, six, seven, eight windows.

I spoke to my mother for the last time on Saturday, May 27, 2017. It was a week after my birthday, which my mother never acknowledged with a phone call. She would always, however, send a check (at least when we were speaking), so my practice was to wait for the check to arrive and then, before calling to thank her, allow just enough time to pass so that I didn't put her in an awkward position by appearing to remind her of the event, but not so much time that it looked like I was ignoring the check. This was my annual birthday balancing act (at least when we were speaking): I would strategize about the best way to ignore the fact that my mother ignored me without appearing to ignore her.

We spoke for fifty-seven minutes, during which I reminded her that I would be spending much of the next couple of weeks out of town, traveling first to Iceland for nearly a week and then, after a couple of days back in Brooklyn, to the midwest, where the entire family would be attending Violet's graduation from the University of Chicago. I took a few notes during this conversation:

— Broken finger (healed itself—Easter—set this week.)
— Nebulizer broke. New one? They can deliver by middle of upcoming week.
— EKG—results??

I hadn't heard about the finger. (How had my mother broken a finger? How had she managed with it broken? How had it gone untreated so long when she always seemed to have doctors' appointments?) I can't remember whether the EKG was routine or in response to a specific concern. My mother had been complaining about trouble with her nebulizer for a few months, and I was relieved that she would be receiving a replacement.

My mother asked me to send her a postcard from Iceland.

Instead, I emailed her pictures and videos I took there: falls, geysers, a panorama taken from the side of the highway. She still hadn't acknowledged them by the time we returned to Brooklyn.

I thought little of it when I didn't reach her while I was back in Brooklyn and when I didn't hear from her while I was in Chicago. Still, I'd emailed her those pictures.

While we sat in unrelenting heat on the Midway Plaisance, watching our daughter receive her diploma, Nelle leaned toward me and asked whether I'd spoken recently to my mother, saying that she'd tried her unsuccessfully the previous week. We laughed it off—we both knew that she couldn't be relied on to answer or return calls. But this set off an uneasy sense that all was not right. The first thing I'd thought, reflexively, when I hadn't heard from her was that I must have done something wrong. But my mother adored my ex-wife and had no reason to ignore her. She adored her and had no reason to be angry at her, but she could easily have taken offense at something I'd done or not done, said or not said, written or not written. I imagined her disappointment at the photos and videos I'd sent. She'd asked for a postcard. They weren't the same thing.

Nelle had no such issues; where my mother was concerned, she had nothing at stake. If my mother snarled at one of her wayward opinions, she could afford to take it in stride—it was just this batty old lady she was fond of. Nelle invited herself to my mother's apartment and felt none of my fear of rejection. Nelle bought her gifts without agonizing over whether they were appropriate, whether they would be liked, whether they would end up in a drawer, unused. She wouldn't have second-guessed emailing my mother photos and videos.

Back in our hotel room, I said to Minna, "Shit, Nelle hasn't heard from my mother either."

"You should call her."

"I can't."

"Why not?"

"I think she's mad at me."

"Don't be ridiculous. Just call her."

"Maybe Nelle should call her."

"You're being ridiculous."

"Since they're such good friends."

"Oh my God. And childish. Besides, you said that Nelle hadn't heard from her either."

"Yeah, but not because my mother's angry at her."

"You're out of your mind."

When we returned to Brooklyn on June 12, I forced myself to call my mother on three successive days, leaving increasingly agitated messages, before finally conceding to myself that my mother's quirks and/or my own offensiveness to her could not possibly account for her silence; that she was likely incapacitated and unable to get to the phone.

On Thursday afternoon, June 15, my therapist urged me: "Go down there! Just tell her you were worried about her because you hadn't heard from her!" I complained, "Why does it have to be like this? Why can't she be normal?"

That afternoon, Anna had a classmate over to play. At about
four thirty, I walked the girl to her house on East Third Street.
Minna was going to take Anna to a gymnastics class in Benson-
hurst. I told her that I needed a lift to Bay Ridge. I called my
mother's number and spoke to her voice mail. "I'm coming down,
Ma," I said. "I'm sorry."

Minna dropped me off at the corner of Eighty-sixth and
Fourth, and I walked quickly from there to my mother's apartment. As I walked, Anna's classmate's mother texted me. "Thanks
so much for watching my girl," she said. "It was fun," I responded.
When I arrived at the building the first thing I did was head for
the doorman's post.

"Help you?"

"My mother's apartment."

The doorman leaned back and looked at me, as if mildly
amused, left forearm draped over the arm of his task chair.

"Mrs. Sorrentino. A605. I'm her son."

"Oh, Mr. Sorrentino, hey. How's it going."

"Can you buzz? She's not expecting me. I don't want to barge
in on her."

"Sure thing." He picked up the intercom and called her
apartment. "I didn't see her leave or anything." He waited, hung
up. "She's not answering," he said.

"OK."

I knew as soon as I rounded the corner after getting off the elevator: her apartment was at the end of the hallway, and I could see
the copies of the *Times* that had piled up outside her door. There
were at least a dozen. What about the neighbors? The porters?

Hadn't they wondered? The newspapers told the entire story; I knew, but I banged and I called. Then I pressed my nose to the crack where the door met the doorframe and I *knew*. The smell was an insult to hope.

I found her on the bed, on her back. The stench was overpowering. Her extremities were withered, the hands blackened, with lividity visible wherever flesh was exposed. One hand gripped a plastic tube that ran from the oxygen machine to a nasal cannula that had slipped from what was left of her face. The oxygen machine hummed noisily, and I turned it off. It was large, and sat directly on the wooden floor. The incessant noise, why hadn't the downstairs neighbors complained? Her torso appeared to have sunk into itself. Her head was thrown back, her face the color of caramel custard. The skin had slipped and seemed to hang loosely from her skull, her cheeks, her jaw. Her nose had collapsed. Her mouth was agape, and full of larvae. I didn't look closely to see what was where her eyes had been. Her body was surrounded by a foul, wet-looking stain from its leaking itself through its various orifices. A rotting body tends to ooze out from the nose, the mouth, the eyes, the anus, the vagina.

It seemed very important to bring the newspapers inside. They now radiated out from the central place, the doormat I suppose, whatever notional target the deliveryman aimed for when he flipped the paper each morning, delivering it; radiated out, blocking the corridor, because I had stood among the pile, slipping on the plastic bags that held the papers, banging on the door and yelling, whenever that had been, minutes ago perhaps. I had some idea that privacy would be preserved if I could just get the papers inside the house where no one could see them. Anymore. I scooped them up, two or three armfuls, dropped them inside the entryway. In the moment it felt like an accomplishment.

Some kind of crisis appeared to have occurred. Despite the fact that she had died in bed, I couldn't tell if death had been peaceful. The apartment seemed to testify otherwise: there was an empty box of tissues on the floor in the hall outside her bedroom, and stained tissues littered the floor, trailing from the hall into the bedroom and around the bed to where the oxygen machine was. The bedroom carpet was stained as well, as was the bathroom floor, on which a folded towel, also stained, had been placed before the toilet, as if she'd been kneeling there. The stains were part blood and part feces, I determined. The smell was overwhelming. No one had noticed it, apparently; no one in this building that had banned smoking and pets and window air conditioners had noticed it. The medicine chest was thrown open as if she'd been searching for something, and I stood staring at its remaining contents, trying to figure out what she'd been looking for. The rest of the house was in perfect order, as always. A lamp was lit in the living room, and one of the leather easy chairs was turned toward the television, as it would have been had she been watching. So this had happened at night, possibly late. She had turned off the television. She had gotten up. Her medical alert pendant was next to her bed. Did she press it? Did it fail? Did she try to dial 911? I never found out.

Did she know she was dying? Was she terrified? Panicky? Calm? Resigned? In pain? Did she die slowly, over hours, even days? Or did she die suddenly, her body abruptly and unexpectedly shutting down? They really shouldn't allow the newspapers to pile up like that, what kind of building was this. I went around the apartment opening the windows as wide as they would go. I took one last look at her and shut the bedroom door.

Close the door.
Close that door.
Close it.

After several hours, and visits from paramedics, police officers, and technicians from the medical examiner's office, her body was removed. No investigation of the circumstances of her death was deemed necessary; no autopsy was performed. The immediate cause of death was listed on her death certificate as chronic obstructive pulmonary disease, with systemic lupus erythematosus as a contributing cause. The technician from the medical examiner's office had refused to let me identify my mother's body, despite my protests that I'd already seen it, and so before they would release her to the undertakers I had to wait until they were able to compare postmortem X-rays to ones they'd obtained from a radiology lab she'd been to. Like my father, she'd wanted no service. Like him, she was cremated in a cardboard box, her remains interred in the same plot as his.

23

Before I discovered that my mother was dead, perhaps on the very day that she died, I dreamed about her while sleeping in a hotel room in Reykjavík. In the dream, I met some old friends and we made plans to go to my mother's house, where I was living, to drink whiskey. In the not-uncommon way of dreams, the house where we went was not my mother's apartment or any other place where she'd lived, but was unquestionably hers. I realized that I didn't have enough food or booze for everyone, so I went out to buy more, and when I returned my friends were leaving: my mother had appeared suddenly and thrown them out. I was embarrassed, even humiliated, and I began to tell her off, explaining to her that I was an adult, that I could do what I wanted within reason, that this fell within reason, that just because she didn't want to see or involve herself with others she had no right to prohibit me from doing so, etc. As I reached the pitch of my argument, I realized that I was no longer asleep—I had awakened in the four a.m. daylight of Iceland, thinking, "I did it! I stood up to her!"

I have been at her house with old friends since then, even

if those "friends" sometimes are nothing more than the familiar objects, tucked away in boxes, in drawers, and on closet shelves, that my mother hid from view for years and years. A beautiful cloisonné copper matchbox holder that she bought for nothing in a secondhand store on Avenue B. Photos of my parents as children, their apartments, their dogs, their trips to the beach. My father's autograph book from his elementary school graduation. (Favorite Author: Percy Crosby. Favorite Book: *Skippy*. Favorite Song: "You Made Me Love You.") A ridiculous pair of hanging earrings that I insisted on buying for my mother's birthday when I was eight or nine years old. A small sculpture that my father acquired from John Chamberlain in exchange for a bottle of scotch to give to my mother on her twenty-fifth birthday. An earthenware cookie jar that my mother bought from a pottery shop on St. Marks Place. Some bawdy prints by Thomas Rowlandson. Notes and letters and drawings from me. As I excavate—slowly, slowly—I feel a specific pain in my gut, unique to this experience of sustained exposure to what's left of my parents, this mass of material, as orphaned as I am, that I find myself able to handle, bring home, sell, store, give away, toss, ridicule as I see fit.

I find, too, in my mother's apartment all the signs of the loneliness that I deliberately refused to confront while she lived. The ways she passed the time marked the passage of time. Lists of movies she'd seen, written on quadrille paper in small, meticulous capital letters. Lists of movies she wanted to see. Lists of books she had read. Lists of books she wanted to read. Lists of her medications, their dosages, the dates they were prescribed, the dates she stopped taking them. Slips of paper tucked into videocasette boxes noting the television programs recorded on them, the dates they were recorded, one-sentence summaries of the episodes' plots. A pad listing, year by year, her Christmas tips to the staff of her apartment building. Stacks of catalogs, circulars, and other junk mail on which she had painstakingly blackened out anything identifying her as the recipient. File folders containing evenly scissored clippings of recipes she never cooked. Cardboard boxes filled with neatly folded plastic bags, with packing materials, with other cardboard boxes like matryoshka dolls, the filled boxes filling my father's study. Heartbreaking to consider her occupying her days this way, year after year; heartbreaking to violate all her careful, meaningless work by undoing it, by throwing out what she'd saved, breaking down what she'd preserved intact.

Another old friend to whose presence my mother might have objected was Minna, who came to the apartment with me when I returned the day after discovering the body. It was her first visit there. She sat across from me at the small dining table—my mother's spot, which reflexively struck me as a small imposture—and picked up a little red datebook from the corner of the table. It was another of my mother's scrupulous documents, in which she recorded, as a method of organization or as an aid to memory, the times of her life:

Mailed check to Violet

Chris called, left message

Fresh Direct

Appt. Dr. Abott 11:15

Talked to Jim

Nelle called, left message

UPS package: Amazon

Appt. Dr. Caruana 3:30 (CANCELLED)
Talked to Chris
E-Mail from Violet
UPS package: QVC, Wen Hair
Sal repaired bathroom ceiling
Fresh Direct
Nelle called, left message
Talked to Nelle
UPS package: Amazon
Chris called
Denise called, left message
Talked to Jim
Fresh Direct
Chris for lunch
Appt. Dr. Abott 11:30,

all of this taking place over a span of weeks. Minna read from it aloud in a neutral voice, the one you'd use to read the names of war dead at the unveiling of a monument, and finally I said, "Please stop." We sat for a moment in silence, and then I said, spontaneously and without any guile, "I want my mommy." I can't remember the last time I referred to my mother as "my mommy." Was it 1969? And yet the sentiment was genuine, not quite cathartic, self-revealing.

I found out things about my mother that were familiar, that were unknown, and that were forgotten. The extent of the listmaking surprised me, but it seemed like her. This was, after all, the woman who had once posted on my closet door a daily schedule for me broken down into fifteen-minute segments of time. It was the extreme side of a methodically organized nature that made it easy now, despite our never having discussed it, for me to find the documents and other information I needed to bury her and administer her estate.

The hoarder, however—the QVC and HSN enthusiast, the woman who could not resist costume jewelry, cosmetics, kitchen gadgets, subscriptions to hair-care treatments, miracle cleaners, electronic gizmos, cashmere sweaters, casual shoes, umbrellas, special soaps, sheet sets, microfiber blankets, travel irons, skeins of yarn—startled me. She bought thousands of dollars' worth of such things, storing them unused and often unopened, and often, even more surprisingly, among rosaries, crucifixes, miraculous medals, and other Catholic artifacts recently acquired.

The forgotten woman was the young one, buried in the bureau drawers. Here, in these old possessions, as much as in the photographs and the old letters, was the almost-obliterated record of connection. That hat, that scarf, that watch—in them, in my memory of their useful life as everyday articles, frugally saved for, discriminatingly chosen, meticulously cared for, I could recall my mother as a force in the world, a woman for whom life hadn't yet become a broken clock, a desultory list of small events scattered across the pages of a giveaway diary.

I am a person who suffers from depression, and so sadness always comes as a surprise to me. Like most other people, I tend to confuse the two. When my father died, I hadn't experienced sadness. I'd been angry—always, for me (if not for others in my life), a much more tolerable emotion; probably a matrilineal gift, engraved on my genes. I had persuaded myself that I would be relatively unaffected by my mother's death, but I was amazed by the size of the absence her death created. I knew that I had wanted her to live; had felt, finally, that her presence in my life was an asset. But what I discovered, to my astonishment, was that I really had loved her.

After my father died, I felt him. He took form in various ways, had a "presence" that transcended the physical. And of course it would have been stubbornly like him to avoid departing. I've spoken to various people about this phenomenon, and while there's no way, of course, to substantiate the *feeling* of a loved one's lingering aura, it appears to be a common-enough experience that my attitude toward doubters is simple: Prove me wrong. Strangely, and admittedly sentimentally, my mother's oppositely stubborn *absence* seems equally to demonstrate the persistence of will—as if when her body, that tenacious machine, had finally, grudgingly, accepted its failure and the life had rushed from it, her essence, coolly welcoming the radical opportunity her life had denied her, unhesitatingly rushed along with it, recognizing freedom in the serene remove of death. She left without looking back.

"As for me, I will behold thy face in righteousness: I shall be satisfied, when I awake, with thy likeness."

Selah.

CHRISTOPHER SORRENTINO
is the author of six books, including *Trance*, a
National Book Award finalist, and was awarded
a Guggenheim Fellowship in 2022. His work has
appeared in *Esquire*, *Harper's Magazine*, *The New
York Times*, *The Paris Review*, *Playboy*, and many
other publications. He has taught at Columbia
University, New York University, The New School,
and Fairleigh Dickinson University. He lives with
his family in New York City.